Abortion Rights

This book features opening arguments followed by two rounds of reply between two moral philosophers on opposing sides of the abortion debate. In the opening essays, Kate Greasley and Christopher Kaczor lay out what they take to be the best case for and against abortion rights. In the ensuing dialogue, they engage with each other's arguments and each responds to criticisms fielded by the other. Their conversational argument explores such fundamental questions as: What gives a person the right to life? Is abortion bad for women? What is the difference between abortion and infanticide? Underpinned by philosophical reasoning and methodology, this book provides opposing and clearly structured perspectives on a highly emotive and controversial issue. The result gives readers a window into how moral philosophers argue about the contentious issue of abortion rights, and an in-depth analysis of the compelling arguments on both sides.

KATE GREASLEY is a Lecturer in Law at University College London. She is the author of *Arguments about Abortion: Personhood, Morality, and Law* (2017).

CHRISTOPHER KACZOR is Professor of Philosophy at Loyola Marymount University. His publications include *A Defense of Dignity* (2013) and *The Ethics of Abortion* (2nd ed., 2015).

Abortion Rights

For and Against

Kate Greasley
University College London

Christopher Kaczor
Loyola Marymount University, California

CAMBRIDGE
UNIVERSITY PRESS

CAMBRIDGE
UNIVERSITY PRESS

University Printing House, Cambridge CB2 8BS, United Kingdom

One Liberty Plaza, 20th Floor, New York, NY 10006, USA

477 Williamstown Road, Port Melbourne, VIC 3207, Australia

314–321, 3rd Floor, Plot 3, Splendor Forum, Jasola District Centre, New Delhi – 110025, India

79 Anson Road, #06–04/06, Singapore 079906

Cambridge University Press is part of the University of Cambridge.

It furthers the University's mission by disseminating knowledge in the pursuit of education, learning, and research at the highest international levels of excellence.

www.cambridge.org
Information on this title: www.cambridge.org/9781107170933
DOI: 10.1017/9781316758441

First published 2018

Printed in the United Kingdom by Clays, St Ives plc.

A catalogue record for this publication is available from the British Library.

Library of Congress Cataloging-in-Publication Data
Names: Greasley, Kate, author. | Kaczor, Christopher Robert, 1969- author.
Title: Abortion rights : for and against / Kate Greasley, University College London; Christopher Kaczor, Loyola Marymount University, California.
Description: Cambridge [UK] ; New York : Cambridge University Press, 2017. | Includes bibliographical references and index.
Identifiers: LCCN 2017027447 | ISBN 9781107170933 (hardback : alk. paper) | ISBN 9781316621851 (pbk. : alk. paper)
Subjects: LCSH: Abortion–Law and legislation. | Fetus–Legal status, laws, etc. | Human rights.
Classification: LCC K5181 .G725 2017 | DDC 342.08/78–dc23 LC record available at https://lccn.loc.gov/2017027447

ISBN 978-1-107-17093-3 Hardback
ISBN 978-1-316-62185-1 Paperback

Contents

Contents

Preface and Acknowledgments

The authors of this work passionately, vehemently, and stead-fastly disagree about the moral and the legal permissibility of abortion. One of us, Kate Greasley, describes herself as strongly pro-choice. The other author, Christopher Kaczor, would call himself strongly pro-life.

But we do agree that the legal and ethical question of abortion is of signal importance. We agree that political, cultural, and social debate about this topic is enhanced by civil disagreement in which opposing views are openly aired and subject to intense criticism and rational scrutiny.

Most importantly, we value the freedom of speech that makes possible the rational pursuit of deeper insights into political, ethical, and legal issues such as abortion. We are also alike in appreciating the possibility of moral error in our own conclusions. Thus, even while we remain resolute in those conclusions, we recognize that it is worthwhile to engage in thoughtful and respectful exchanges with others and to listen and learn from one another.

Veterans of philosophical abortion argument will no doubt notice that we do not disagree with one another about every element of the traditional debate. While this may sacrifice something in the breadth of the argument, it is, we believe, more than compensated for by the ability to reach greater depth on the matters about which we do disagree. It also means that the book better emulates a real conversation between two people who are engaging with one another not in their capacity as representatives of a cause but as individual thinkers who find some arguments on both sides more intriguing and potentially convincing than others. What we find to be the most compelling arguments weighing down on our own or our interlocutor's side, other people may not. Again, this makes the book more of a unique dialogue than a textbook of arguments for and against abortion rights. But it is in this respect in particular that we hope it will contribute something of value to the existing discussion. The hope is that readers whose sympathies lie on either side of the debate (or indeed, are as yet undecided), will find within this one conversation some arguments and objections upon which it is worth reflecting, and will perhaps at least deepen their understanding of the other side's point of view.

Christopher Kaczor would like to thank the James Madison Program at Princeton University for providing the initial support for this project. He would also like to thank *First Things, The Public Discourse.com,* and the *NCBQ* for permission to reprint materials that appear in this book.

Kate Greasley would like to thank the many friends and colleagues whose wisdom has influenced her thinking about abortion and related issues over the past few years, and Chris Kaczor for his kind patience with her many delays.

1   In Defense of Abortion Rights

Kate Greasley

1.1   Clearing the Cobwebs

Attitudes on abortion rarely exist in a vacuum. Most often, they are tied up with a wider set of beliefs or worldview. As the philosopher Michael Tooley has noted, many people come to adopt their personal stance on abortion as part of a "package deal" (Tooley 2009). That "package" may be identification with a religion or it may be subscription to a set of cultural or political values. The prevalence of "package deal" thinking can mean that convincing people of anything in the realm of abortion ethics is an uphill struggle from the get-go.

Getting people to think clearly about abortion as an independent question in morality can be especially difficult in the case of those whose attitudes are inextricably linked to their views about legitimate sexual relations, traditional notions of the family, or the belief that all humans are made in the image of God. Perhaps more so than anything else, the fact that the abortion issue is so deeply intertwined with ideas about ethical sexual behavior is especially liable to muddy the waters with those who have strong views about such things, the drive toward enforcing perceived sexual morality and punishing deviance being so universal and, apparently, irresistible.

Because of all this, the first, and possibly most important, stage in any defense of abortion rights is to encourage people to see how they might have embraced a position on abortion as part of a "package deal" and to exhort them to interrogate their predispositions, as well as to ask whether the anti-abortion stance is a nonseverable component of their wider commitments. It is often assumed, without much reflection, that a hostile attitude to abortion goes hand in hand with a particular religious affiliation or belief, such as the belief in the existence of an enduring human soul, making the abortion question closed for discussion. In the face of such assumptions, there is a certain amount of "cobweb clearing" to do before we can properly begin. (The cobwebs I am referring to here are not the religious precepts themselves, but the strands running between them and the anti-abortion moral stance.) If a person is convinced that to be Christian he must be opposed to abortion, and he is not about to give up being Christian, then there is little practical point saying much else before we can get him to question whether this is really true.

We may take, as one example, the belief in what is termed the "sanctity" of all human life. For many, the commitment to the sanctity of human life quite naturally and obviously entails the immorality of all, or almost all, abortion. But is this quite so obvious? For one, we will still have to ask when the human life that is supposedly sacred actually begins, or what *counts* as a "human life." Is a single-celled zygote a human life in the relevant sense? Is a sex cell, or a single, living human skin cell? Sex cells and skin cells are, after all, both human and alive. But they do not seem to be what the "sanctity of life" value marks out as sacred. A basic commitment to the sanctity of human life does not by itself answer the crucial question about what counts as a human life in the morally relevant sense. One can certainly imagine someone who believes that human life is sacred but does not consider "human life" to begin in earnest until enough of a human form has developed. Such a claim would not be logically incoherent.

A second question, and one with which the philosopher Ronald Dworkin was concerned, is exactly what it looks like to demonstrate respect for the sanctity of human life when it comes to abortion (Dworkin 1994). Does respect for the sanctity of human life require the preservation of all biological human life, no matter how radically immature or radically degenerated?

Could respect for the sanctity of human life not also be compatible with the sacrifice of some very nascent forms of human life so as to prevent a much more mature life, with far more investment, from being squandered? Dworkin believed that discussants equally committed to the sanctity of human life could understandably differ on these questions. In particular, they may differ on the question about which is the more intrinsically valuable, or "sacred," *part* of human life: nature's pure biological creation or all of the human creative investment that goes into human beings throughout their lifetime? Perhaps, then, the sanctity of life does not straightforwardly entail the immorality of all abortion.

A similar point can be made with respect to specific scriptural passages that are often taken to be religious authority for the proposition that abortion is morally prohibited. The writer of Psalms proclaims to God that "you knit me together in my mother's womb," that he is "fearfully and wonderfully made," and that God had ordained all of his days before any of them were lived (Ps. 139:13–16). In Jeremiah, the prophet, speaking as God, says: "Before I formed you in the womb I knew you, before you were born I set you apart" (Jer. 1:5). These verses seem to suggest that "we" begin to exist in the womb – that is to say, we are already, before birth, in existence as the beings that we most basically are, and worthy of strong moral protection. However, "we" may be identical with the being God formed in the womb in a number of different ways, not all implying the moral equality of embryos and fetuses with more mature human beings. It might have been "me" that God formed in the womb only in the sense that the early human creature is the same biological entity as am I – that we are physically one and the same thing. But not everyone thinks that this kind of identity means that if I have strong moral rights now, I also possessed them as a fetus. Perhaps we do not possess strong moral rights at all times in our existence. Whether or not we do is a philosophical question the answer to which does not follow from what is contained in the Bible verses. Thus, someone who believes that she was created and identified by God in the womb may still doubt that *while* in the womb she already had a strong right to life.

Equally, in Genesis, the first book of the Bible, it is written that mankind was made in the image of God (Gen. 1:27). This is taken by some to entail that all human life, no matter how radically immature, is a reflection of God's image and, as such, is inviolable. But again, the inviolability of all early human life does not follow inexorably from the belief that mankind is made in God's image. It is not clear, for instance, that when this passage refers to mankind it means to include all of the early precursors to developed human beings. Are these organisms also a reflection of God's image, or merely biologically continuous with creatures that bear a resemblance to God? Whatever "God-like" features one believes are reflected in human beings are presumably those that are present only in developed humans, and not in zygotes and embryos. It is hard to think of ways in which embryos reflect God's image; not, surely, in virtue of being human and mortal, since God is neither of those things.

On the other side of the coin, Christian opponents of abortion rights are also prone to overlook scriptural passages which indicate that human beings in utero do *not* possess the same moral standing as born ones. In the book of Exodus, for example, the punishment meted out to a man who strikes a woman and causes her to miscarry is to pay compensation to the woman's husband (Exod. 21:22–25). But any harm suffered by the *woman* as a result of the attack is to be repaid equally, "an eye for an eye, a tooth for a tooth," as the well-known passage proceeds. The implication here is that the fetus does not have the same inherent value as an adult human being. While causing injury or death to a woman must be punished severely, killing a fetus is akin to a property offense – the value of the fetus is a monetary value.

Some discussants may be mistaken, then, to think that the spiritual beliefs they hold leave no room for maneuver on abortion. This is extremely important because I suspect that "package deal" thinking motivates much abortion opposition, even if it does not form the content of anti-abortion arguments. In many cases, the philosophical questions at issue in abortion simply transcend the propositions for which there is scriptural authority, or do not seem to be determined either way by them. And to compound things, scriptural authority pointing in the opposite direction tends to be ignored.

Before I am accused of one-sidedness, I concede that "package deal" thinking is prevalent on the other side of the debate as well. Many of those who identify as feminists, liberals, or progressives may find it difficult to separate their defense of abortion rights from a whole roster of other political and moral commitments. The abortion issue is bound up with values and ideologies of all kinds, not all religiously grounded, and many of which rouse just as strong passions. Perhaps it is especially difficult for someone staunchly committed to women's equality to consider the possibility that abortion is seriously immoral, given just how much sex equality suffers when reproductive rights are denied.

Of course, to a considerable extent, our thinking about abortion is bound to be directed by the other principles and commitments that we embrace, and quite rightly so. Nevertheless, there are certain kinds of commitments in particular, often tied up with group affiliations and political identity, which seem to exert an irresistible pressure to endorse one or other conclusion in advance of much careful thinking. These are the kinds of package-deal arrangements that can be the enemy of clear-headed deliberation about abortion and to which it is worth calling people's attention, most especially to the potential that they are wrong in supposing that only one view of abortion morality is consistent with all of their beliefs.

Plenty more can and probably should be said by way of introduction to my argument. But I would rather make a start.

1.2   The Silver Bullet

I want to begin by conceding a very important proposition to the anti-abortion side. This is that, if the fetus is a person, equivalent in value to a born human being, then abortion is almost always morally wrong and legal abortion permissions almost entirely unjustified. The truth of this claim is a huge question in its own right in abortion discussion. The issue here is about which further philosophical questions need to be answered before we can say whether abortion rights are morally or legally defensible. Some proponents of abortion rights do not believe we need even get on to considering whether or not a fetus is what we would call a "person," morally on a par with all born human beings, to know that abortion is defensible. On their view, other philosophical considerations show that we can get to a permissive answer on abortion without having to make up our minds about that question – in other words, the question about when morally important human life begins. Others, quite differently, find it an obvious and inescapable truth that whether or not the fetus is a person in the philosophical sense is the central question for abortion ethics.

Before expanding on this debate, it will help to clarify the terms a little. What do I mean here when I use the term "person"? Aren't human beings and persons just the same thing? Well, not in some important ways. When philosophers use the classification "person" they generally mean to capture a category of beings with strong moral rights, in particular, the almost inviolable right to life. "Human being," on the other hand, is used to denote individual members of the human species. All embryos and fetuses are certainly human beings, in that they are all individual human organisms. But this does not mean that they are all necessarily persons.

First of all, we can see that human beings and persons are not conceptually the same thing by performing a simple thought experiment. Suppose that, many years from now, we discover a highly intelligent species of alien on another planet, the members of which can reason, learn, communicate, and construct advanced technology. It is beyond doubt, I think, that the members of that species fit our concept of a person. Like us, we would surely want to recognize their strong moral status and right to life. But they are certainly not human beings. So "human being" and "person" do not *mean* the same thing. It is possible to be a person without being human.

But is it possible to be a human being without being a person? Someone may try to argue that even if "person" and "human being" do not mean the same thing, all human beings are, by virtue of their human biology and nature, also persons. This would be the case if every human being also met the correct conditions for personhood. While it is conceivable that they do, an argument will need to be made as to why that is. The fact that the two categories are conceptually distinct just shows that it is an open question whether all human beings are persons. The need to make an argument connecting the two cannot be circumvented by insisting over and over (as some opponents of abortion are wont to do) that embryos and fetuses are *human lives* or *human beings*. This much is not usually in contention. The relevant moral question is whether, *just* by being human, they are also persons. Maybe there is more to personhood than bare humanity.

But *is* that the relevant moral question? As I have already said, not everyone agrees that it is. The prima facie case for thinking that the question about prenatal personhood is the central issue for abortion law and ethics is, I believe, fairly intuitive. If the fetus is a person, then abortion is homicide, tantamount to the killing of a human child. And if this is true, then it will hardly ever, if ever, be permissible. Indeed, if one regards the fetus as a person, in possession of the same fundamental right to life as you and me, abortion will be difficult to justify even in the most extreme cases such as pregnancy caused by rape, severe fetal disability, or serious physical risk to the health or life of the pregnant woman. We do not ordinarily think that homicide is justified to avoid huge emotional distress, the burden of disability, or even to avoid physical trauma, unless carried out in self-defense. And this is to say nothing of the many lesser hardships that abortion might be chosen so as to evade.

According to this line of thinking, then, the conclusion that embryos and fetuses are properly considered persons and the moral equivalent of all born human beings is a silver bullet for abortion rights. This is the view I want to concede is correct. I want to concede it despite the fact that there is a huge wealth of argument, some fairly persuasive, against it. In different ways, some philosophical defenders of abortion rights have sought to argue that whether or not the human fetus is properly considered a person is in fact irrelevant for the moral or legal status of abortion. That is, they have sought to establish that abortion is morally and, or, legally defensible *regardless* of how we answer that question.

One argument of this kind, famously made by the philosopher Judith Jarvis Thomson, claims most abortion does not really amount to killing the fetus, but only, rather, the refusal to save it with the use of bodily support (Thomson 1971). Moreover, she argued, what it takes to sustain the fetus's life – continued gestation – is not something any pregnant woman can be morally obligated to provide. In other words, continuing to gestate an unwanted fetus is a supererogatory act, or a form of Good Samaritanism. And since no one is morally required to be a Good Samaritan, and certainly should not be so required by law, abortion rights are defensible. Consequently, abortion is permissible *whether or not* the fetus is a person because no one is morally required to offer the use of her body in order to keep another person alive.

A different sort of argument claims that even if abortion does amount to killing the fetus rather than failing to save it, almost all abortion could be subsumed into a recognized category of justified homicide. This argument points out that it is sometimes permissible to kill other persons, for example, in situations of self-defense or, perhaps, in exceptional circumstances where killing one person is the only way to avoid the deaths of a greater number. If it can be shown that all or most abortion mirrors these justified homicide scenarios, then the relevance of fetal personhood will be greatly diminished. There will be another way of showing that abortion is permissible whether or not the fetus is properly considered a person.

I am going to assume that both of these arguments ultimately fail. There is insufficient space here to explain why I reject them,[1] but opponents of abortion do not, in any case, need to be convinced of their falsity. I will therefore assume in the following that abortion does indeed involve the deliberate killing of the

---

1 Although for a full account, see Greasley 2017, chapters 2 and 3.

fetus and that, were the fetus a person, hardly any abortion scenarios would meet the moral and legal conditions for justified homicide.

Further attempts to displace the relevance of fetal personhood in the abortion debate might take a different tack. It may be claimed that even if abortion is *morally* impermissible, the *legal* right to abort is still defensible for reasons to do with counterproductiveness or justified toleration. Claims about counterproductiveness of regulation point to the hugely harmful consequences of banning abortion practice, given the realities of imperfect compliance. Abortion practice does not disappear because it is banned. Rather, the argument goes, prohibiting or restricting abortion in law only drives women intent on procuring abortion to unregulated and unsafe practitioners – the "backstreet" abortionist – resulting in worse overall outcomes. This is what I term the "back-street abortion argument."

Somewhat differently again, it could be argued that even if abortion is morally impermissible, there exists, to some degree, a "right to do wrong" (Waldron 1981). Not all kinds of immoral conduct ought to be proscribed by law, or so we tend to think. There are many kinds of immoral conduct that are not the appropriate targets of legal sanction or regulation. Lying in one's personal life and infidelity are two clear examples of conduct that most would regard as immoral but as not suitable for legal regulation. Law does not, and should not, enforce all forms of morality. There are immoral behaviors that we have good reason to tolerate, although we might wish to discourage them. Perhaps abortion falls into this category of activities – that which there is reason to tolerate in our laws even if (or when) we think them morally wrong.

Both the "back-street abortion argument" and the "right to do wrong" argument underscore the distinctness of the legal and the moral realms and the fact that there is more to think about when it comes to the appropriateness of legal prohibition than what is or is not immoral. Still, I do not believe either of these considerations can show that abortion rights ought to exist *even if the fetus is rightly considered a person*. This is because neither consideration can justify toleration of abortion if it amounts to homicide. Concerns about counterproductivity and endangering the participants would never be accepted as arguments against the prohibition of infanticide. This is the apt control test for whether the "backstreet abortion argument" displaces the relevance of fetal personhood. Moreover, norms of justified toleration can never extend to conduct that seriously harms others, especially to homicide. The law cannot consign abortion to the realm of private immoral conduct *if* it entails the unjustified killing of rights-holding persons. Since the right to engage in infanticide could never be defended with arguments about justified toleration of immoral conduct, neither can abortion rights if we are assuming the fetus has equal moral status. Neither of these arguments, then, is capable of bypassing the question about the fetus's personhood status in discussion about abortion rights.

To reiterate, then, I am going to grant in everything that follows that if human beings really are full persons from conception, morally equivalent to born human beings, this would indeed be a silver bullet for the defense of abortion rights. Those who believe abortion rights are unsupportable will likely be in full agreement with me thus far. They too will believe that the question about when and how persons begin is central to the moral and legal status of abortion. Here, though, is where our likemindedness is probably going to end.

1.3   What Is at Stake for Women in Abortion

To recap, I have argued so far that if the fetus is indeed a person, morally on a par with all born human beings, abortion will hardly ever be morally permissible. This seems to follow even if it is true that prohibiting abortion will result in the proliferation of illegal and unsafe abortion practice, resulting in significant harm to women. But what follows about the morality of abortion, and the case for abortion rights, if the fetus is instead very far from being a moral, rights-holding person? I think it clear that if the fetus has little or no moral considerability, then not only is abortion morally permissible, but denying women the abortion right is a serious injustice. This is because of what is at stake for pregnant women in securing abortion access.

The potential interests that women have in obtaining abortion are threefold: the interest in procreative control, the interest in being free from the bodily burdens of pregnancy, and the interest in sex equality. The strength of these interests is undoubtedly enough to justify abortion morally if the human embryo or fetus lacks the status of a person.

We can begin with the interest in procreative control. Everyone has a significant and very personal interest in determining if and when he or she will become a parent. Undeniably, procreation is one of the most profound and meaningful (and, of course, irreversible) aspects of human life. Becoming a parent, with everything that entails, goes right to the heart of one's personal identity and life story – it changes *who* one is in potentially transformative ways. Owing to this, if the termination of pregnancy does not entail ending the life of a person in full possession of the right to life, it seems that we ought to allow people control over this intimate and hugely meaningful dimension of their lives – their own role as procreators – by enabling them to choose against parenthood and terminate their pregnancies when contraception fails or is not used.

The recognition of a right to procreative liberty was an important pillar of the US Supreme Court's decision to recognize the fundamental constitutional right to terminate pregnancy in *Roe v. Wade* (1973). The majority of Justices on the Court found that the right to procreative liberty had already been given recognition by the Court in cases involving state restrictions on the use of contraception (*Griswold v. Connecticut* (1965) and *Eisenstadt v. Baird* (1972)). In those cases, the Court had struck down state prohibitions on contraception as unconstitutional on the ground that they interfered with the fundamental right, under the Constitution, to control one's own reproductive destiny. In *Roe*, the Court reasoned that this broader right to procreative liberty also underwrote the right to terminate one's pregnancy. The upshot of recognizing this right was that there were considerable restrictions on constitutionally valid state legislation that regulated abortion practice.

Writing the majority judgment, Justice Blackmun summarized the potentially detrimental consequences of unwanted motherhood, which can include, he said, the medical harms of pregnancy and the "distressful life and future" brought about by becoming a mother, or bearing yet more children, against one's will (*Roe v. Wade* (1973), 152–153). As he acknowledged, unwanted parenthood can have extremely destructive implications for a person's life, implications that can, moreover, extend out to those around them. But even where the consequences of unwanted childbearing are not severe – where the child can be adequately cared for and the effect on the woman's life is not ruinous – the interest in procreative liberty should still have considerable weighting in our moral accounting. However things happen to turn out, the decision whether or not to become a parent (or to become a parent again) is important and intimate enough that it cannot justifiably be obliterated for anything but the strongest counter-considerations.

One possible objection is that the interest in avoiding unwanted parenthood can be adequately protected so long as adoption is available as an alternative to abortion. Where this is so, it might be argued, it is possible to protect what is important in reproductive liberty, that is, control over whether or not one becomes a parent, without resorting to abortion. But such an argument would have to claim that it is only *social* parenthood and not biological parenthood that constitutes the important interest in procreative liberty, and I am not convinced this is correct. Becoming the biological parent to a child from whom one is then separated, even through choice, is not without its emotional costs and, indeed, its ramifications for one's personal identity and self-conception.

It could be retorted that this is only so because of the unsupportable value we place on purely biological relations. I am not altogether sure that attaching special value to biological relations *is* unsupportable (see Velleman 2005). But that does not have to be decided here. Even if not rationally defensible, the value we do ascribe to biological parenthood, and the meaning that is thereby attached to becoming a biological parent, means that the interest in procreative control cannot be protected simply by providing adoption as an option. Carrying a fetus to term and surrendering the subsequent child to adoptive parents is not the equivalent of avoiding parenthood, as far as the interest in procreative control is concerned. It is clear that through choosing abortion what women seek to avoid is either of two seriously burdensome eventualities: becoming a social parent against her wishes or being estranged from a biological child whom she knows to exist. As I see it, both of these burdens are implicated by the interest in reproductive control, which surely trumps the fetus's interest in continued life if it is not a morally considerable person and has no greater moral status than that of a lower mammal.

Second, in the passage above Justice Blackmun also underscored the direct physical harm that women can suffer during and as a result of pregnancy. The bodily burdens of pregnancy, even where nothing goes wrong, are without doubt fairly imposing. Susan Estrich and Kathleen Sullivan summarized those burdens as follows:

> Even the healthiest pregnancy can entail nausea, vomiting, more frequent urination, fatigue, back pain, laboured breathing, or water retention. There are also numerous medical risks involved in carrying pregnancy to term: of every ten women who experience pregnancy and childbirth, six need treatment for some medical complication, and three need treatment for major complications. In addition, labour and delivery impose extraordinary physical demands, whether over the six to twelve hour or longer course of vaginal delivery, or during the highly invasive surgery involved in a Caesarean section, which accounts for one out of four deliveries.
>
> (Estrich and Sullivan 1989, 126)

As the authors also state, normal pregnancy increases a woman's uterine size 500–1000 times, her pulse rate by 10–15 beats per minute, and her body weight by 25 pounds or more (ibid.). And this is by no means an exhaustive list of the bodily burdens that accompany pregnancy. In short, pregnancy involves serious physical changes and nonnegligible medical risks. As with the interest in procreative liberty, the value in being free of these burdens and risks when they attend unwanted pregnancy is enough to render abortion permissible if the fetus lacks a strong right to life.

More than this, though, assuming the fetus lacks the status of a person, preventing women from being able to exercise control over their bodies through abortion is a serious injustice. By passing abortion restrictions, states indirectly impose on women the considerable physical burdens and risks of pregnancy. Indeed, it is hard to imagine state-mandated prohibitions on a healthcare practice that aimed to relieve people of comparable bodily burdens could be justified in any context other than pregnancy. If there is no serious moral objection to abortion, such restrictions unjustly withhold from individuals the means by which they can avoid serious health problems and yet more serious health risks. Consequently, if the fetus has little or no moral standing, abortion prohibitions and restrictions cannot be defended except insofar as they are themselves necessary to safeguard the health of pregnant women.

Third, abortion prohibitions harm women as a class. As feminist scholars have argued at length, the unavoidability of pregnancy and childbirth has particularly detrimental consequences for the status of women and their equality with men. From this perspective, any analysis of the harmful implications of abortion prohibitions cannot leave out of the equation that only *women* experience unwanted pregnancy and childbirth, and what this can mean in light of their existing condition as a disadvantaged class.

Denying women the abortion option can impede their equal standing with men in a great number of ways. Women forced to continue unwanted pregnancies can find themselves unable to work or to progress in their career, precluded from getting an education, kept financially dependent on men, and, perhaps, stuck in a situation of domestic abuse. These potentially life-altering consequences of unwanted pregnancy, as well as the bodily burdens that attend it, are not equally experienced by men who reproduce. As Catharine MacKinnon writes:

Although reproduction has a major impact on both sexes, men are not generally fired from their jobs, excluded from public life, beaten, patronized, confined, or made into pornography for making babies. This point is not the biological one that only women experience pregnancy and childbirth in their bodies, but the social one: women, because of their sex, are subjected to social inequality at each step in the process of procreation . . .

A narrow view of women's "biological destiny" has confined many women to childbearing and childrearing and defined all women in terms of it, limiting their participation in other pursuits, especially remunerative positions with social stature. Women who bear children are constrained by a society that does not allocate resources to assist combining family needs with work outside the home. In the case of men, the two are traditionally tailored to a complementary fit, provided that a woman is available to perform the traditional role that makes that fit possible.

(MacKinnon 1991, 1311–1312)

On MacKinnon's view, only by being afforded abortion access can women engage in sexual intercourse on the same terms as men: without the threat of unwanted pregnancy and childbirth and its further potentially damaging consequences. The significance of the abortion right for women's equality as a whole is only magnified by the background context of sex inequality that persists regardless of abortion access. As Susan Sherwin claims, "virtually all feminists seem to agree that women must gain full control of their own reproductive lives if they are to free themselves from male dominance" (1991, 327). The prevailing conditions of sex inequality and the social subordination of women by men contribute greatly to the unequal burdens of childbirth. Structures of male dominance ensure that women rather than men are traditionally the primary caregivers, that this role is incompatible with lucrative jobs and important social positions, and that reproductive labor and child-rearing is not remunerative work but merely the expectation that comes with being female.

The basic feminist contention that women's in equality is greatly exacerbated by restrictive or prohibitive abortion laws is,

I think, beyond serious doubt. Nevertheless, the class-based interest in sex equality will still not be enough to justify abortion
morally if it is true that abortion is tantamount to homicide,
because the enhancement of sex equality is not ordinarily
accepted as a justification for homicide. This, I believe, is something that we would all accept on reflection. One can construct all
manner of imaginary scenarios in which killing one or more
innocent persons will have a tangible positive impact for the
empowerment of women, but which we would not, for that
reason, deem permissible. This goes to show that the sex equality
defense of abortion rights cannot withstand a finding that the
fetus is the moral equivalent of a born human child.

But if the fetus *lacks* strong moral status, denying the abortion
right does not just inflict injustice on individual women; it helps
to sustain the conditions in which women are socially disadvantaged relative to men and are vulnerable to male oppression. In a
patriarchal context, denying women the option to end their
pregnancies forces on them consequences of sexual intercourse
that are not equally shouldered by men. Consequently, if the
fetus lacks the status of a person, the value of sex equality is a
solid, and in itself sufficient, basis for the abortion right.

Someone may reply here that the sex equality interest is not
deeply implicated in abortion prohibitions since women do have
the means to liberate themselves from the unequal burdens of
pregnancy and childbirth either by abstaining from sex or by
using contraception. But this is a wholly inadequate answer to
the sex equality problem. Part of the reason for this is that
women's control of sexuality itself, including the use of contraception, is compromised in conditions of patriarchy. Indeed, feminist scholars have argued that part of what makes reproductive
control so vital for women's liberation is its intertwinement with
control over sexual access (MacKinnon 1991; Sherwin 1991).
Where women and men are not equally empowered, pregnancy
can often be difficult to avoid, whatever a woman's wishes.
Sexual autonomy is constrained when exercised in a context of
vulnerability or subjugation. Acquiescing to the demand for
sexual intercourse can be the price of financial support, domestic

peace, or maintaining the unity of a family. As MacKinnon says, "women often do not control the conditions in which they become pregnant ... Sexual access is regularly forced or pressured or routinized beyond denial" (MacKinnon 1991, 1312).

Furthermore, and especially in this context, contraceptives cannot be fully relied on to provide women with reproductive control. The most effective contraceptives can come with undesirable health risks or side-effects; women may find their partners unwilling to use barrier methods, or contraceptives may be stigmatic or socially awkward. In short, as MacKinnon puts it, "Contraception is inadequate or unsafe or inaccessible or sadistic or stigmatized" (ibid.).

To summarize, the very considerable interests that women have, both individually and as a disadvantaged class, in being free to terminate their pregnancies leads, I think, inescapably to the provisional conclusion that *unless* the fetus possesses considerable moral status, the abortion right is an integral feature of social justice. To prevent women from exercising reproductive control through abortion can force on them serious and unequal costs to their well-being (as well as forcing on them a new parental identity), such that it cannot be justified if abortion is not seriously immoral.

1.4   Does Abortion Harm Women?

Someone might yet object to this provisional conclusion. That is, he might object to the suggestion that the abortion right promotes women's well-being and insist that notwithstanding the burdens of unwanted pregnancy and childbirth, abortion does not tend to secure the prudential good of women that choose it. These so-called women-protective arguments against abortion[2] have gained considerable traction in recent decades, with the suggestion that abortion is positively harmful for women running alongside, or in some cases, substituted for, the traditional moral objection to abortion on the ground of the fetus's right to life.

---

2 I take this terminology from Reva Siegel, 2008.

"Women-protective" anti-abortion arguments range from the claim that abortion is physically dangerous to women to claims that abortion is typically attended by negative psychological and emotional sequelae, and that women are particularly prone to experiencing post-abortion regret.

The distinct advantage of opposing abortion rights under the aegis of women's well-being is that it deemphasizes or even renders moot the traditional moral problem about the status of the fetus. If abortion does not, in any case, serve the real interests of women, there is nothing that needs to be counterbalanced by a robust theory about the moral personhood of the fetus. The heavy burden of having to persuade people of the moral human-ity of the fetus, on pain of doing women an enormous injustice through abortion prohibitions, lessens considerably as soon as one can convincingly make the case that women's interests do not lie with procuring abortion, whatever the answer to that question. Through its systematic invocation by the anti-abortion lobby, the "abortion hurts women" doctrine has even found its way into US Supreme Court jurisprudence.[3]

Needless to say, I find these "women-protective" arguments deeply suspect both in terms of their claims and in terms of their authenticity. I do not think it profitable to use up too much space rebutting the highly spurious claim that abortion rights do not benefit women in general. Still, it is worth saying something about the now prevalent women-protective strain of abortion opposition.

First, dismissing such arguments does not require anyone to maintain that it is inconceivable that women could ever be harmed by abortion, physically or emotionally. Naturally, it is not. But almost anything can be potentially harmful in the right circumstances. This is particularly true of medical procedures and

---

3 See *Gonzales v. Carhart*, 127 S. Ct. 1610 (2007) at 1633 (cited by Siegel 2008) where the Court states: "While we find no reliable data to measure the phenomenon, it seems unexceptionable to conclude some women come to regret their choice to abort the infant life they once created and sustained. (See Brief for Sandra Cano et al. as Amici Curiae in No. 05-380, pp. 22–24.) Severe depression and loss of esteem can follow. (See ibid.)"

important life decisions, and abortion is both of these things. Consequently, setting abortion apart from other medical proced- ures and important life decisions in terms of its detrimental results – enough to show that the right to abortion has little to recommend it – requires believing more than that abortion could sometimes be harmful. It requires believing that abortion is especially or generally harmful, and does not typically secure women's well-being, but quite the contrary.

When held to this standard, the women-protective claims have to be exaggerated beyond reasonable belief to speak against abor- tion rights. One such counterfeit claim is that abortion is physic- ally harmful to women undergoing it, or subjects them to serious health risks. In this vein, much weight was historically thrown behind the now entirely discredited claim that abortion increases the risk of breast cancer.[4] Legally provided abortion in countries with good standards of medical practice is, in fact, an extremely safe and straightforward medical procedure, and is particularly safe when performed earlier on in pregnancy, when the vast majority of abortions are carried out.[5] The UK Department of Health found that for 2014, complications were reported to arise in abortion at a rate of one in about every 550 cases, with no reported deaths (2015). The rate of complications in abortion increases when it is undertaken later in pregnancy, but remains nevertheless extremely low.[6]

4 The Royal College of Gynaecologists, having reviewed four scientific studies, concluded: "From the literature we reviewed there is no established link between induced abortion or miscarriage and development of breast cancer." RCOG, Briefing Note: Scientific Information on Abortion (www.rcog.org.uk/ en/news/campaigns-and-opinions/human-fertilisation-and-embryology-bill/ briefing-note-scientific-information-on-abortion/).

5 In 2015, the British Pregnancy Advisory Service (one of the biggest abortion providers in the United Kingdom) recorded that 92 percent of abortions were performed in pregnancies of less than 13 weeks (see www.bpas.org/about- our-charity/press-office/press-releases/england-and-wales-abortion-rate-is- stable-more-than-half-of-women-ending-pregnancies-are-already-mothers/).

6 The Royal College of Gynaecologists "Best Practice in Comprehensive Abor- tion Care" document (www.rcog.org.uk/globalassets/documents/guidelines/

More to the point, however, abortion, especially in early pregnancy, is *safer* than childbirth, the only other alternative once a
woman becomes pregnant. Indeed, in *Roe v. Wade* itself, Justice
Blackmun took it to be well established that mortality rates in
abortion at the end of the first trimester were much lower than
mortality rates in normal childbirth (*Roe v. Wade* (1973), 163).
Thus it was that state prohibitions on abortion in the first trimester could not be rationalized under the auspices of maternal
health, and were thereby unconstitutional. This is in line with
current, accepted medical opinion. In its guidance document on
"Best Practice in Comprehensive Abortion Care," the Royal College of Gynaecologists states, "If performed in line with best
practice, abortion is safer than childbirth" and that the earlier it
is undertaken, the safer it is likely to be.[7]

The relative safeness of abortion as compared with childbirth
more or less puts paid to the argument that abortion is bad for
women because it endangers their physical health. Furthermore, where abortion rights are opposed on the ground that
they put women's physical health at risk, the back-street abortion concern considered in the previous section becomes

best-practice-papers/best-practice-paper-2.pdf) notes that the following complications can occur at the following rates:

- Severe bleeding requiring transfusion (less than 1 in 1000 for first-trimester
  abortions and 4 in 1000 for gestations beyond 20 weeks)
- Uterine rupture with second-trimester medical abortion (less than 1
  in 1000)
- Uterine perforation (1–4 in 1000 but lower for first-trimester)

Marie Stopes International (an abortion provider) reports that death occurs in
fewer than 1 in 100,000 medical abortions; 3 in 100,000 for surgical abortions
performed at 13–15 weeks, and 12 in 100,000 after 21 weeks (www
.mariestopes.org.uk/women/abortion/surgical-abortion-explained/what-are-
failure-rates-and-risks-abortion).

7 Above (n 27). See also Raymond, E. G., and Grimes, D. A. (2012), The
Comparative Safety of Legal Induced Abortion and Childbirth in the United
States, *Obstetrics and Gynecology* Feb *199*(2 Pt. 1), 215–219, where the authors
state: "Legal induced abortion is markedly safer than childbirth. The risk of
death associated with childbirth is approximately 14 times higher than that
with abortion. Similarly, the overall morbidity associated with childbirth
exceeds that with abortion."

especially salient. Safe and legal abortion cannot be said to compromise women's health across the board where the realistic alternative is a great deal of unsafe, illegal abortion. Numerous accounts of the horrors associated with so-called butchers (unconscionable and exploitative abortionists) before the widespread legalization of abortion in the United States and Britain well document the extent to which women's physical health was compromised by lack of access to regulated abortion, all too often with tragic consequences (Joffe 1995). As between abortion prohibitions and abortion rights, the latter will present the greater danger to women's health only if many more women are likely to suffer serious physical damage as a result of safe, legal abortion than are likely to suffer as a result of illegal abortion practice. Any engagement with the evidence concerning both the health risks of legal abortion and the prevalence of illegal and unsafe abortion pre-legalization makes this proposition highly doubtful.

A different kind of "women-protective" argument against abortion is that abortion is not beneficial for women because it damages their mental health or is often accompanied by negative emotional side-effects. Related to this is the widespread contention that women are more likely than not to regret having an abortion and to experience feelings of loss, shame, and guilt in the aftermath. Since the 1990s, this idea has been channeled through the increasing promulgation, by pro-life groups, of so-called post-abortion syndrome (PAS), a supposedly common post-abortion mental health disorder whereby women experience trauma and psychological damage in the wake of undergoing abortion.

The US Supreme Court Justice Ruth Bader Ginsburg was surely right to describe PAS as an "antiabortion shibboleth" (*Gonzales v. Carhart* (2007), 1648). Borne out of the strategic decision by religious anti-abortion groups to shift the focus of their opposition from the protection of the fetus to the protection of women (including from their own choices), PAS was developed in large part by one or two key anti-abortion activists who made it their mission to provide anecdotal and statistical evidence for the claim that women are traumatized by abortion.[8] One such key figure was an anti-abortion activist named Vincent Rue. In a string of cases, Rue recruited women to appear in court testifying to the extreme psychological damage they sustained as a result of abortion, often ghost-writing their testimony (Greenhouse and Siegel 2016). As Reva Siegel and Linda Greenhouse have documented, Rue's conduct has "drawn reproach from judges in Alabama, Texas and Wisconsin" (ibid., 1459). Reva Siegel details specific elements of Rue's own testimony before the South Dakota Senate about the social effects of abortion in which he described abortion as "anti-family," as an act which "emasculates males" and "reescalates the battles between the sexes." Against the widely accepted view by clinical psychologists that the procedure had only limited and temporary emotional sequelae, he also claimed that "guilt and abortion have virtually become synonymous. It is superfluous to ask whether patients experience guilt; it is axiomatic that they will" (quoted in Siegel 2008, 1658).

Another key figure whose "empirical" research is still one of the primary sources of anti-abortion claims about the incidence of PAS is David Reardon, also an avowed moral opponent of abortion who, along with other early adopters of the women-protective abortion argument, exhorted anti-abortion activists to refocus their opposition on the harmfulness of abortion to women as a way to gain ground with the "middle majority" who were not convinced that killing fetuses was an evil.[9] As well as being explicitly adopted as a matter of political expediency, Reardon's arguments, Siegel points out, are not empirical "in the conventional social-scientific sense," being anchored heavily in claims about "sex role morality" and the assertion that the interests of women and fetuses, when understood correctly, do not truly conflict. (As he wrote: "The intimate connection between a

---

8 For a detailed account of the origins of PAS, see Greenhouse and Siegel 2016 and Siegel 2008.

9 Notable works by Reardon include *Making Abortion Rare: A Healing Strategy for a Divided Nation* (1996) and *Aborted Women: Silent No More* (1987). See also Siegel 2008, 1669.

mother and her children is part of our created order. Therefore, protecting the unborn is a natural byproduct of protecting mothers" (Siegel 2008, 1672).) Siegel explains that this "no conflict" claim was not itself substantiated by ordinary empirical methods ("for example, by identifying measures through which one could compare the situation of pregnant and caregiving women with other women not performing the work of motherhood"), but was instead a claim "rooted in divine and natural law" (Siegel 2008, 1675).

In fact, the empirical studies that have been conducted indicate that most women do not regret undergoing first trimester abortions or experience negative emotional reactions in their aftermath.[10] Moreover, while it would be no surprise to find that some emotional ambivalence is commonly experienced by women in respect of their abortions, concerns surrounding "post-abortion regret" are liable to seriously exaggerate the effect on overall well-being of intermittent feelings of regret, which may surface only from time to time in a person's life as passing feelings of sadness or reflectiveness. Regrets of this kind cannot serve as a proxy for how well off an abortion has made a woman in comparison with the alternative, all things considered.

1.5   Three Thought Experiments about Personhood

Let us take stock again. My arguments so far place the issue of fetal personhood squarely at the center of the abortion rights debate. If the fetus possesses only very low moral standing – if it

10 See my 2012 article, Abortion and Regret, *Journal of Medical Ethics*, 38, 705–711. See also Major, B., Cozzarelli, C., Cooper, M. L., et al. (2000), Psychological Responses of Women after First-Trimester Abortion, *Archives of General Psychiatry*, 57, 777–784, and Adler, N. (2000), Abortion and the Null Hypothesis, *Archives of General Psychiatry*, 57, 785–786. The American Psychological Association has concluded that "abortion is generally 'psychologically benign.'" A 2009 *British Journal of Psychology* article found that 90 percent of 500 women sampled believed in retrospect that having an abortion was the right decision (Fergusson, D. M., Horwood, J., and Boden, J. M. (2009), Reactions to Abortion and Subsequent Mental Health, *British Journal of Psychology General Section*, 195, 420–426).

is not, in other words, a "person" in our estimation – then it appears that abortion restrictions or prohibitions will not be justifiable except insofar as they are necessary for the protection of women's health. Moreover, withholding from women the opportunity to relieve themselves of unwanted pregnancy, with all of its possible consequences, involves inflicting profound injustice on them individually and denying them equality with men as a class. On the other hand, if the fetus is rightly regarded as a person in the philosophical sense, morally equivalent to born human beings, few abortions will be morally permissible, and state toleration of abortion practice will appear as indefensible as the toleration of infanticide.

As I have set things out, then, the general legitimacy of abortion rights stands or falls on how one answers the personhood question – the question of whether the human fetus possesses the same moral standing we readily accord to born human beings, including, most importantly, the fundamental (if not absolute) right to life. But how does one go about answering this question? One might worry that the issue of when a human being becomes a person is philosophically intractable: either someone just sees the fetus as a person or does not.

Of course, we should entirely expect discussion about fetal personhood to be complex and, in some measure, intractable, since it implicates our beliefs about what it is that confers personhood universally. What is it that makes *us* morally considerable beings, in possession of the fundamental right to life? In virtue of what do we hold such a status? Is personhood a matter of attaining certain capacities, such as rationality, or agency, or self-conscious thought? Or is it a question of being endowed with a certain kind of nature or essence, expressed in genetic programming or human biology? And is it possible that the same creature might be a morally considerable person at one stage of its existence but not at another?

These are without doubt difficult questions, and they are questions that any sustained discussion about fetal moral status will, I think, inevitably invite. It is little wonder, then, that many discussants view the moral status question as an unattractive line of inquiry in abortion debate. Given the sorts of problems that inquiry invokes, it may be feared that argument about fetal personhood is ultimately profitless in discussion about abortion rights, unable to admit of reasoned argument. As one philosopher put it, vagueness surrounding the very concept of a person could mean that any attempt to solve the abortion problem through argument about personhood is "to clarify *obscurum per obscurius*" (English 1975, 233, 236).

I believe that we should resist this kind of skepticism regarding the possibility of rational argument about the conditions for personhood and the moral status of the fetus. Those questions are indeed intractable in one sense, in that they involve deep-seated moral disagreements that cannot be resolved by appealing to any single fact or revelation. As Ronald Dworkin expressed it: "[T]here is no biological fact waiting to be discovered or crushing moral analogy waiting to be invented that can dispose of the matter" (Dworkin 1994, 10). Put otherwise, there are no undeniable "winning shots" in the personhood debate, facts that, if established beyond question, would force one side to concede victory to the other.

But intractability in this sense is a feature of all moral argument, which cannot be avoided in debate about abortion rights, nor should it be. As I have shown, the status we accord to the fetus is integral to our moral calculations about abortion. Moreover, the fact that this disagreement is in some measure interminable (to the extent that there is no scientific fact, even in theory, which either side must accept as defeating) does not mean that it is unreasoned and resistant to principled argument. On the contrary, it is possible to argue rationally about fetal personhood by thinking about what is generally salient for our assignations of moral status, what those assignations suggest about the properties on which we take personhood to supervene, and what further conclusions we must be committed to when embracing one or other set of personhood-conferring properties. Whether they ultimately persuade or not, appealing to interlocutors using these considerations can form the basis of principled and fruitful argument about fetal personhood.

Accounts of the basic conditions for personhood status are numerous and complex. For simplicity's sake, I here want to juxtapose two kinds of views about the constitutive features of personhood, having radically different implications for when, in its lifespan, a human being becomes a rights-holding person. The first view takes personhood to supervene on human species membership, and possession of human genes as the necessary and sufficient condition for inclusion in the category of persons and the right to life. It follows from this account of personhood's conditions that all human beings are persons from conception; newly formed zygotes as well as embryos and fetuses all qualify.

The second, antithetical view takes personhood or moral status to supervene on developmentally acquired capacities, most notably psychological capacities such as consciousness, reasoning ability, communication, independent agency, and the ability to form conscious desires. One well-known iteration of this kind of view is the philosopher Mary Anne Warren's contention that personhood is constituted by five key characteristics: (1) consciousness (especially the capacity to feel pain), (2) reasoning ability, (3) self-motivated activity (or, we might say, *agency*), (4) the capacity to communicate, and (5) a concept of the self (Warren 1973). While Warren believed that not every person need possess every one of the five key traits, she thought it clear that a creature could not lack *all* of these traits and yet be a person. On an account such as Warren's, which analyzes personhood in terms of sophisticated degrees of sentience and psychological capacities, a human being is not a person merely in virtue of being human. Zygotes, embryos, and fetuses, which presumably lack the requisite cognitive capacities, therefore fall outside of the category of morally protected persons.

It is worth restating that we cannot take it as a foregone conclusion that personhood depends only on biological humanity. As we have seen already, the two categories are conceptually distinct, making this an open question. Supporters of (what we might call) the species membership criterion of personhood cannot make their case just by pointing out that zygotes, embryos, and fetuses are *human beings*. In the plain sense that they are creatures belonging to the human species, this much is trivially true. The far more questionable proposition is that all genetically human beings are *by virtue of their humanity* morally rights-holding persons. This is a normative contention about what matters for our ascriptions of moral status and cannot be established merely by pointing to biological facts.

In the rest of this part, I want to introduce what I take to be a good prima facie case for believing that the core constitutive features of a person are developmentally acquired capacities, such as those enumerated by Warren, and for rejecting the view that pure human species membership, in the form of human genetic coding, is sufficient for the possession of personhood. That case will revolve around three thought experiments (undoubtedly familiar to some) that aim to draw out some of our settled judgments about the nature of moral status, judgments that do not cohere with the belief that all human beings are persons from conception and that the property of being a person supervenes on human species membership.

The Embryo Rescue Case

The first thought experiment is the well-rehearsed and frequently invoked "Embryo Rescue Case" (ERC) scenario. The hypothetical scenario runs along the following lines:

> You are on the ward of a hospital that is quickly burning down. In the ward with you are five frozen human embryos, stored for implantation in fertility treatment, and one fully formed human baby. You have time to grab and rescue either the five embryos or the one baby, but not both. What should you do?

The assumption by discussants who invoke the ERC is that almost everyone confronted with such a scenario will respond that you must rescue the fully formed baby. Surely it would be quite unthinkable to do anything else, despite the fact that the embryos number five and the baby only one. But the common intuition is problematic for the belief that all human beings from conception are morally considerable persons on account of their human species membership. If embryos are equal in moral standing to born human beings, then surely one should save the five of them rather than the one baby. When given a choice as to whom to save, and when all other things are equal (say, when none of the imperiled parties is a close personal relation, in which case we might be permitted some leeway), our moral duty is arguably to save the many over the few – the five over the one. Consequently, if the ERC intuition is correct, this suggests that the moral status of the baby seriously outweighs that of an embryo, such that, even though the embryos are greater in number, saving the baby is the only reasonable course of conduct. And this in turn casts doubt on the human species membership criterion of personhood. The embryos and the baby are all human beings in the sense that they are genetically human organisms. But it still seems that we accord the baby a moral standing we withhold from the embryos.

Defenders of the view that all human beings are persons from conception could just reject the common intuition that, in the ERC, you are morally obligated to rescue the baby rather than the embryos. That intuition, they may say, is simply mistaken. However, given the strength and prevalence of the judgment that you must rescue the baby, the favored response by those holding to a "personhood-from-conception" theory is to attempt to explain the ERC intuition in ways that are consistent with the moral equivalence of embryos and human babies. Those explanations tend to underscore features such as the greater grief and loss that is usually experienced by others when babies rather than embryos die, the relatively greater investment by others in the lives of babies, and the stronger relational bonds that tend to be formed with them as reasons why you ought to rescue the baby over the embryos *even though* they all possess equal moral standing.

For example, in his book *The Ethics of Abortion* Christopher Kaczor considers a slightly modified version of the ERC I presented, in which the choice is between rescuing ten frozen embryos or five adult patients.[11] Kaczor argues that we may be

11 Christopher Kaczor (2015), *The Ethics of Abortion*, 2nd ed. (Routledge), 146. Kaczor borrows this version of the case from Dean Stretton (2008), Critical

justified in saving the patients over the embryos even though they are fewer, because "we have moral justification for treating human beings enjoying basic equal human rights in different ways," and because it may be worse to allow the adult patients to die for the reasons that others have invested in their lives, that they have plans which death would thwart, and because they have formed "strong relationships" with others. In choices about whom to save, Kaczor suggests, factors like this can reasonably influence our decision without calling into question the equal personhood and basic right to life of all human beings.

Robert P. George and Christopher Tollefsen also resist the standard implication from our intuition in ERC, although they do so in a slightly different way (George and Tollefsen 2008). The authors underscore the fact that in the problem case, the decision is about whom to rescue, not whether we are permitted to *kill* the embryos. They believe that this is an important point of disanalogy with abortion. In a decision about whom to *rescue*, they suggest, there may be much weighing in favor of the developed human being – in their version of the case, a five-year-old girl – that does not throw into doubt the embryos' equal personhood status. For one, they suggest, the girl will suffer "great terror and pain" in the encroaching fire, while the embryos will not. Like Kaczor, George and Tollefsen also think it consequential that the girl will have "bonds of attachment" and relationships with others, which would mean that far greater grief accompanies her death. The authors think that while none of these features makes a difference to the morality of killing, they can legitimately influence our choices about whom to rescue. Thus it is, they say, that in choices about whom to rescue, it can be permissible to save one's own child, "even if saving him or her means that we cannot save, say, three of our neighbors' children." But this does not entail that the neighbors' children are less morally valuable (George and Tollefsen 2008, 140).

Notice – Defending Life: A Moral and Legal Case against Abortion Choice by Francis J. Beckwith [review article], *Journal of Medical Ethics*, 34(11), 795.

The driving ambition of arguments such as these is to provide counterexplanations for the pull toward rescuing the fully formed human being(s) over the embryos that are compatible with an account of personhood as beginning from conception. Advancing these sorts of explanations, the idea is to reconcile common attitudes toward embryo death attitudes toward the death of infants and adults with the view that human species membership is sufficient for full personhood status. Now, the claim that embryo personhood is compatible with our intuitions about the ERC is plainly valid in one way. The fact that we prefer to save the one fully formed human over the many embryos does not logically preclude embryos being persons with equal rights; we may just be very mistaken about what we ought to do when faced with the ERC dilemma. But this point does not engage with the real argument from the ERC intuition, which emphasizes the ostensible *force* and *reasonableness* of the decision to save the more developed human over the embryos.

As I said, the thrust of the rebuttals by Kaczor and George and Tollefsen does not seek to challenge that common judgment, but to reexplain it in a way that leaves the "personhood-from-conception" thesis undamaged. The main reason I find such rebuttals unconvincing is that they fail to dislodge the very compelling notion that the reason for our common conclusion that one ought to save the baby (or the girl or adult) rather than the embryos is our belief that the moral status of the baby vastly outweighs that of any embryo. The most obvious explanation for why embryonic death is not treated as seriously as infant death is because people simply do not believe that death is as serious *for the embryo*, or as tragic from an impartial point of view, as infant death or the death of an adult human being. The mere fact that one can hypothesize counterexplanations for the ERC intuition does not make them the preferable. And if the ERC intuition is far more plausibly explained by our conviction that embryos lack equal moral standing with born humans, then, insofar as we find that conviction irresistible, we will have grounds to disbelieve the "personhood-from-conception" thesis.

That the rejection of moral parity between embryos and born humans is what underlies our conviction about ERC can be, I think, clearly brought out by an amended version of the case, where the sorts of features that Kaczor believes explain our reaction are controlled for. Suppose, for instance, that the baby in question had no connections to any living human beings, that no investment had been made by anyone in its life, and that it would not be wanted for adoption. And suppose, also, that the frozen embryos belonged to progenitors who felt deeply invested in and connected to them, and who would grieve their destruction significantly. I do not believe these features would change our intuition about whom to rescue where the choice is between the five embryos and the one baby. Indeed, I think that most people would find the choice to save the embryos not only strange but morally repugnant, even if, in the particular circumstances, vastly more collateral harm will be occasioned by the embryos' deaths. If this is right, then the intuition here can be explained only by the underlying belief that embryos have a lower moral standing than infants and adult human beings.

It might be thought that some of George and Tollefsen's answers to the ERC miss the point of the challenge completely. I am presuming it is true that there is a morally significant difference between killing and not rescuing, as George and Tollefsen point out, and I conceded already that all, or almost all, abortion is an act of killing. However, George and Tollefsen still need to explain why this distinction weakens the force of the judgment in ERC, which is simply that the pull to save the baby (or girl, or patients) rather than the embryos – *even though this would mean saving the one over the many* – tells us something meaningful about our view of the relative moral status of embryos and born human beings. In rescue choices between persons of equal value, at least where all of the imperiled are strangers to the rescuer, the morally obligatory choice is to save as many as possible. Yet in ERC we rebel against that imperative, which can only be because we do not regard all parties as having equal moral status.

If George and Tollefsen insist, we could even amend the case to *make* the choice one about whom to kill rather than whom to rescue, and still draw out the same implication. Suppose that someone, under duress, is instructed to kill *either* five human embryos or one little girl, in circumstances where failing to make any choice will result in the destruction of all. Here too, I think most people would quickly come to the conclusion that killing the embryos is not only one morally permissible option, but the *only* morally permissible course of conduct. Note that it would be no reply to this point for the authors to say that directly intentional killing of another person is morally prohibited in all circumstances, even extreme ones such as these, since this would be to presuppose that the embryos in the case *do* count as persons, the very judgment that our instinctive reactions to this dilemma is meant to pronounce on. Given a different choice between, say, killing one little girl or killing five different ones (and no way out that would not result in the death of everyone), I agree that there would be grounds for moral hesitation about whether it is permissible to kill *anyone*, and that this hesitation would be reflected in most people's attitudes when presented with the dilemma. But this only strengthens the observation that, when confronted with the amended embryo case (what we might call the "Embryo Killing Case"), our attitudes reflect a strongly rooted belief in the lesser moral status of human embryos.

Like Kaczor, George and Tollefsen also argue that our intuitions in the embryo rescue case can be alternatively explained by the bonds of attachment, relationships, and more intensified grief that are all in play when babies and children die but rarely when embryos do. As we have seen, though, these factors can be excised from the thought experiment without affecting our judgment about what to do. Furthermore, the fact that the little girl would suffer more in death than the embryos can also be controlled out of the hypothetical, by supposing that her death would occur in a painless way, perhaps because she is unconscious throughout. Again, I cannot see that this would make any difference to the universal inclination to rescue the girl rather than the embryos.

Next, the authors argue that just as it can be morally acceptable to save one's own child over even greater numbers of children, so could it be legitimate for progenitors to choose to save their own embryos over saving born human beings. The former point is, I think, right. Many philosophers think that personal attachments permit us to rescue those closest to us in "whom to rescue" scenarios, including, possibly, where this means refusing to save the greater number (hence, if a number of children are drowning in a pond, I am permitted to save my own first). But the same conclusion about saving one's own embryos does not follow unless we are already willing to accept that embryos are morally equivalent to born human beings. For one is not permitted to save "one's own X" over saving other persons no matter what the independent moral status of that "X" is. I am not permitted to save my own cat before rescuing other people's children, however attached I am to it. However excusable such a choice may be, it would surely be regarded by others as deeply erroneous. My assumption is that most would feel similarly about the person who chooses to rescue her own embryos rather than another person's child. Even if we could understand such a person's motivation (say, because the embryos were her only chance of having a biological child), it would be hard to view that choice without moral opprobrium.

Rather than strengthening their conclusion, then, the new scenario with which George and Tollefsen present us in fact just underscores how deeply held our beliefs about the lesser moral status of embryos really are. Whether it were understandable or not, almost no one, I believe, would regard the decision to save the life of one's embryo while allowing someone's fully formed child to perish (assuming that the ease of rescuing both is equal) to be a permissible one. If George and Tollefsen's argument is instead that regardless of how we react to it, such a choice *is* permissible, then it will no longer be an argument about how our common intuitions in embryo rescue scenarios are properly explained. Instead, the claim will be that we ought to disregard those intuitions, since they are wrong.

As I acknowledged earlier, it is *possible* that the standard intuition about ERC is a moral error. Perhaps the out-of-sightness of embryos and their estrangement from our common life blinds us to their moral importance despite the fact that they do, in truth, possess an equal right to life. If so, it would by no means be the only time that the lack of affinity one group of human beings feels in respect of another resulted in the unjustified abrogation of the fundamental rights of the latter group. Still, that it is possible we are wrong is not really the point. The point is that insofar as we feel the force of the judgment that in ERC you are positively duty-bound to rescue the baby (or child, or adult), that intuition cuts against the conclusion that all conceived human beings are persons.

The strange result it appears to give in the ERC is not the only problematic implication of the claim that personhood begins at conception. Its upshot for ERC is one apparent reductio ad absurdum of that view, but there are also others, familiar to those immersed in the abortion ethics literature. For example, what does the personhood-from-conception thesis entail about natural embryo loss? If a human organism is a person in the philosophical sense from the moment of conception, then it would seem to follow that spontaneous miscarriage is the greatest natural threat to the human race – the single biggest killer, outrunning cancer, malnutrition, and natural disasters by a huge margin.[12] If zygotes and embryos are persons, therefore, surely more resources should be devoted to preventing natural miscarriage than to anything else. This will strike many as an unacceptable implication, and it is certainly not one that opponents of abortion rights advocate.

Another strange upshot of the conception threshold of personhood is that the majority of persons who have ever existed in fact perished as blastocysts before they ever implanted in the womb. This is because the great majority of pregnancies naturally abort at a very early stage, prior to the point of implantation.[13] The

12 For a developed explanation of this point, see Toby Ord (2008), The Sourge: Moral Implications of Natural Embryo Loss, *American Journal of Bioethics*, 8, 12.

13 In a testimony before the President's Council of Bioethics in 2003, pediatrics professor John M. Opitz estimated that around 60–80 percent of embryos naturally abort after failing to implant in the uterine wall or as a result of chromosomal abnormalities. Dr. John Opitz, presentation to the President's

notion that the vast bulk of persons ever in existence did not emerge from the womb is a strange proposition indeed. Moreover, if it were true that personhood begins at conception, this also suggests that embryo loss ought to be *mourned* every bit as much as the deaths of small children, since a creature with the same basic moral value has perished. Many will, again, have some trouble accepting this, and it is certainly not an attitude that is typically reflected in our grieving practices. To be sure, some people may feel a similar degree of grief over losing an embryo as the grief that others feel over losing a child. But this is both unusual and, more to the point, is a comparison that I think most would regard as quite inappropriate. (While we would not chastise someone who felt a similarly acute amount of grief over embryo loss, a person who likened that loss to someone else's child's death would, I think, be met with some dismay.)

Retorts to these reductios by supporters of the personhood-from-conception view follow a similar structure to the answers given in response to ERC. One kind of answer simply stresses the logical compatibility of the relevant attitude or practice with embryonic personhood. So, for instance, it might be pointed out that a high mortality rate among embryos does not mean that they cannot be persons. In the past (and still in some parts of the world), the mortality rate among small children was also extremely high, but this does not, to our minds, suggest that they were not persons. Again, the logical incompatibility point is sound, as far as it goes. But again, it does not take very seriously the strength of the intuition and the further commitments that it is meant to reveal. Why does the notion that most persons perish in the womb strike us as quite implausible, and what does this suggest about our concept of a person?

The typical answer to the reductio concerning the implications of natural miscarriage, like the answers to the ERC, is to field counterexplanations that separate our responses to natural

Council on Bioethics, Washington, DC, January 16, 2003, at https://bioethicsarchive.georgetown.edu/pcbe/transcripts/jan03/session1.html.

embryo loss from the conviction about the lesser moral status of embryos or fetuses. In response to the question as to why there are no 5K runs to raise money for research into the prevention of miscarriage, it is answered that we do not do more to prevent spontaneous miscarriage only because it is an invisible tragedy (and thus less moving), or because our attempts are likely to be inefficacious, most miscarriages being unforeseeable and unpreventable. Likewise, it is suggested that the reasons we do not mourn embryo death as we do infant death simply have to do with the fact that they do not form the kind of relational attachments with other people that make the death of more developed human beings particularly painful and tragic for others. This, the argument might run, does not undermine their equal moral standing. Just so, the death of an adult human being who has no friends or relations of any kind will be less keenly felt than the death of another adult with numerous personal attachments. But these attachments clearly have no bearing on the moral status of either person.

It is doubtless thinkable that our failure to treat natural miscarriage as a natural disaster, or the typical failure to mourn embryo loss as we do infant mortality, can be explained away by these sorts of considerations. Again, however, the question is whether they really *are* explained thus. In other words, is it really the case that people on the whole fail to treat embryo death and miscarriage more seriously than they do only because it is hidden from sight and hard to prevent, or because they do not form relationships with embryos? The resurfacing problem with debunking explanations such as those just described is that they do not take seriously the more obvious explanation for such phenomena: that we do not ascribe to embryos the same moral status we ascribe to born human beings.

But the strength of the simpler explanation is revealed as soon as the debunking explanations are controlled out of our moral thinking. We saw this in the ERC, and can see it again by reflecting on a different hypothetical scenario that tests what really underlies our failure to treat embryo death as every bit as sobering as infant death. In this hypothetical, both an embryo and a five-year-old child perish. However, while the embryo is valued and loved by its progenitors, the child is an orphan with no attachments of any kind and no one who will be personally bereaved by her death. I believe that most people, when comparing the two deaths, will find the death of the child considerably more lamentable – a far worse thing to happen – than the death of the embryo, completely notwithstanding the fact that, unlike in the embryo's case, no one is personally affected by her death. The relevant point here, then, is not that we just do not *happen* to treat embryo death as on a par with infant death (which may be for any number of reasons) but that we share an intuition about the *inappropriateness* of regarding it as equally sobering, from the impersonal point of view. (This again is not to say that it is inappropriate for a person to grieve more for the loss of *her* embryo than for the death of an unknown child, any more than it is inappropriate for a person to mourn *her* cat in a way that she does not mourn the deaths of many strangers.) For those who find that judgment compelling, the counterexplanations offered by supporters of the personhood-from-conception thesis will not constitute a rebuttal.

Intelligent Aliens

I now want to turn to consider a second thought experiment, reflection on which, I believe, strongly suggests that it is not human species membership per se that is constitutive of personhood, but rather other properties that are not possessed by all human beings from conception. The thought experiment is one that I already introduced in Section 1.2 when demonstrating the conceptual distinctness of humanity and personhood. Imagine that our capabilities of galactic exploration were far more advanced than they in fact are, and that we discovered, on some faraway planet, an intelligent alien species. These aliens, it transpires, are capable of rational thinking (they understand mathematics, for instance, and have developed their own advanced technology); they communicate with each other using their own sophisticated language, are self-conscious and possess a developed concept of the self, and form deep emotional attachments to one another. But they are not human. I think it is not in doubt that if we were to discover an alien species fitting this description we would have to acknowledge, unequivocally, their personhood status. But if the aliens are persons, and owed the strong right to life, this cannot be on the basis of biological humanity, since they are not human.

This tells us that biological humanity is not a necessary condition for personhood. But the thought experiment tells us more than this. For it is obvious, I think, that the basis on which we would confidently ascribe members of the alien species full moral standing is their possession of the sorts of sophisticated cognitive capacities that Mary Anne Warren took to be constitutive of personhood. It is only *because* they are endowed with such capacities that their moral standing is not in doubt. And this in turn suggests that it is attributes of this kind, rather than human species membership, that are core to our concept of a person.

Moral theorists have tried to account in different ways for the importance of capacities such as these in assessments of moral standing. While those accounts all take slightly different forms, most attempt to draw a relation between sophisticated psychological capacities and having morally significant interests, in particular the interest in continued life. Michael Tooley, for example, has argued that personhood or moral status requires self-awareness in the sense of "possessing a concept of oneself as a continuing subject of experiences."[14] Briefly stated, Tooley argues that in order to be capable of having morally relevant interests, including the interest in continued life, an individual must be capable of desiring things. But being able to desire anything, he suggests, and particularly the continuance of one's own existence, requires a certain degree of self-awareness, a concept of oneself as an individual *subject*. The notion "I desire X" necessarily implies a conscious awareness of the "I" who is doing the desiring. On Tooley's account, the kind of *self*-consciousness necessary for desiring one's own continued existence does not obtain until

14 See Tooley, M. (1983), *Abortion and Infanticide* (Clarendon Press), and Tooley, M. (1972), Abortion and Infanticide, *Philosophy and Public Affairs*, 2, 37.

sometime after birth. Consequently, both fetuses *and* very young infants fail to qualify as the kind of beings that possess the fundamental right to life. (For those who think the idea that young infants do not possess the right to life a repugnant conclusion, this implication will be a reductio ad absurdum of a theory such as Tooley's. This problem and others like it will be considered in the next section.)

The capacity to desire things is also extremely pertinent to David Boonin's account of moral status (2003). Boonin contends that fetuses become morally considerable beings when their brains are capable of organized cortical brain activity and, hence, basic conscious desires, somewhere between 25 and 32 weeks of pregnancy (2003, 102–104 and 115–129). On his account, killing another human being is wrong when it frustrates the desires of the victim, most importantly the strong desire to keep living. However, to be capable of desiring continued life, Boonin argues that an individual must first be capable of conscious experience – the kind of experience that facilitates desires of any kind. He argued that the beginning of conscious life should be taken to coincide with the advent of "organised cortical brain activity," the process by which the cerebral cortex of the brain becomes operational around 25–32 weeks of gestation.[15] The cerebral cortex is the part of the human brain responsible for consciousness and higher thought. As Boonin says, although scientists cannot "locate" consciousness exactly, they do know that any active cerebral cortex is necessary for it to obtain. Humans whose cerebral cortexes are completely destroyed may still breathe, circulate blood, and exhibit some reflex responses – all things regulated by the lower parts of the brain. But they will completely lack conscious awareness of themselves or their environment. All mammals possess a cerebral cortex, but the cortex in developed human beings is uniquely large in the animal kingdom, which provides for all of the "higher" mental capacities that characterize

---

15 Ibid. Boonin draws many of his descriptions here from Harold J. Morowitz and James S. Trefil (1992), *The Facts of Life: Science and the Abortion Controversy* (Oxford University Press).

the human species, such as language, rationality, and intelligent learning. Boonin explains that although low-level electrical activity has been recorded to emit from the brain stems (the lower brain) of fetuses as early as six to ten weeks, these are akin only to the random electrical firings of signals in a nonconscious living human body. Only the brain waves recorded in fetuses at 25 weeks or more are those associated with organized cortical activity. This is because it is within the period between 25 and 32 weeks that the synaptic connections in the cortex begin to form at a rapid rate, and the cortex effectively "comes into existence as a functional entity" (Boonin 2003, 109).[16]

Boonin regards the arrival of consciousness as a morally relevant difference between organisms. Being conscious, he explains, simply means that there is something it is like to *be* you, from the inside, so to speak, and it is for this sound reason that we tend to think conscious beings matter in ways that nonconscious ones do not. Since organized cortical activity marks the beginning of conscious experience, it also marks the point at which an early human being has the capacity to consciously desire things, including continued life.

These are just some examples of how theorists defend the importance of certain cognitive capacities – in particular self-awareness and the capacity for conscious desires – in an account about the conditions for personhood and the right to life. These accounts are, to be sure, subject to some challenging counter-arguments (some of which will be considered in the next section). At the very least, however, reflection on the intelligent alien thought experiment gives us a good reason for thinking that the constitutive features of personhood are traits that are severable from human species membership. Our intuition about the alien hypothetical undercuts the notion that humanity per se is the basis for moral status, and leans in favor of the view that moral status and the fundamental right to life supervene on capacities that embryos and fetuses do not possess (or certainly not until a

16 Quoting Morowitz and Trefil (ibid., 116).

fairly developed stage of gestation). These are the capacities –
such as reasoning ability, language, and self-consciousness – in
virtue of which it is clear that the intelligent aliens qualify as
persons notwithstanding their lack of humanity.

The Transgenic Spectrum

Finally, I want to consider one more thought experiment that
points us in the direction of a capacities-based (or "developmental") view of personhood's conditions. This hypothetical, called
the "Transgenic Spectrum," is formulated by the philosopher Jeff
McMahan. McMahan postulates an entire spectrum of creatures
that are hybrid human-chimpanzees, all possessing differing
ratios of human to chimp genes. It runs as follows:

> The Spectrum begins with a chimpanzee zygote that has an
> unaltered genome. In the next case, a single human gene is
> inserted into a chimpanzee zygote and a chimp one swapped
> out. In the third case, two human genes are inserted. In each
> case further along in the spectrum, one more human gene is
> inserted while the corresponding chimpanzee gene is deleted.
> Thus, at the far end of the spectrum is a case in which *all* of
> the chimpanzee genes are replaced by corresponding genes
> from a human source, and the creature is fully human. In all
> cases the genetically altered zygote is implanted in a natural or
> artificial uterus and thereafter allowed to grow to adulthood.
> (2007)

The point of the spectrum is to show that it is not really species
membership but rather something else that matters in our ascriptions of comparative moral status. McMahan takes it that "individuals at one end of the spectrum with only a tiny proportion of
human genes are unambiguously chimpanzees" and that "those
at the other end with only a tiny proportion of chimpanzee genes
are unambiguously human beings" (2007, 146–147). However,
he thinks our reactions to different cases along the spectrum
reveal that we do not think the moral status of any individual
creature on the spectrum depends solely on having a "sufficiently
high proportion of human genes to count as a member of the
human species." For example, it seems wrong to think that an

individual on the spectrum whose genes have given it the brain of a dull chimpanzee should come within strong moral protection only because a sufficient proportion of its *other* genes are human, or that such an individual should be treated any differently from a neighbor on the spectrum whose proportion of human genes fell just short of making it *overall* human even though its brain functions more like that of a human than that of a chimpanzee. If this is correct, it speaks against the notion that human species membership is itself a "source of moral status." The "humanness" of the transgenic creatures varies in accordance with their proportion of human genes, yet this does not appear to be the correct basis to morally differentiate them. Instead, it is apparent that the more morally considerable creatures along the spectrum are so because of their greater cognitive capacities, not their sum total of human versus chimp genes.

If we agree that in the Transgenic Spectrum it is brain functioning rather than percentage of human or chimp genes that really matters for moral standing, then we will have another reason for thinking that cognitive capacities, rather than humanity, is really what matters for moral considerability. It is possession of these capacities, not pure human species membership, that seems to be constitutive of moral status. Yet these capabilities (reasoning ability, self-awareness, and so on) are certainly not possessed by embryos, and it is doubtful that any of them are possessed by late-term fetuses either. This throws into serious doubt the moral status of human beings in utero.

Indeed, some philosophers have derided the assignation of moral status on the basis of biological humanity alone as an example of *speciesism*: the arbitrary preference of one species over another without reliance on features that are morally differentiating.[17] For example, someone who invokes the allegation of speciesism may assert that there is no defensible basis for awarding a human being more basic moral protection and a stronger right to life than a chimpanzee whose sense of self and

17 See Tooley, M., Abortion and Infanticide, and Singer, P. (1975), *Animal Liberation* (HarperCollins).

cognitive capacities are equal to or more sophisticated than the human's. Equally, it might be argued that treating a human fetus as more morally valuable than a cat fetus can be premised on nothing but speciesism if the human fetus is no more developed than the cat fetus in ways that matter for moral status. Of course, the speciesism allegation rests critically on a view of moral status according to which pure species membership is indeed irrelevant. Those who propound it are, therefore, already committed to a "developmental" account of moral status that views species membership as such to be morally empty. However, insofar as the thought experiments considered above endorse such an account of moral status, they will double-up as ammunition for the speciesism complaint.

1.6   Defending the Developmental View

Counterexamples

In the last section, I presented the prima facie case for believing that moral status – or what we might call "personhood" – ultimately depends not on biological or genetic humanity but rather on developmentally acquired capacities, more specifically, higher cognitive capacities such as reasoning ability, consciousness, and a concept of the self. According to this view, although mature human beings are indeed persons, they are not persons *because* they are human but because of the capacities with which they are endowed. Equally, as the intelligent alien hypothetical demonstrates, a creature *need* not be human in order to qualify for personhood, so long as it is in possession of the morally relevant capacities.

With regard to pre-born human beings, the upshot of this view of moral status is that they do not count as persons with the strong right to life if they do not bear out the morally relevant capacities, which, it seems, they do not. Even late-term fetuses are not capable of reasoning and communication, and are not self-conscious in Tooley's sense of possessing a concept of themselves as a continuing subject of experiences.

Moreover, while it is suggested by some that late-term fetuses exhibit some limited forms of sentience and consciousness (responsiveness to stimuli such as touch and light, or basic satisfaction or comfort derived from thumb-sucking), these limited levels of sentience do not go beyond that possessed by any number of nonhuman animals. We might take, for example, the capacity for minimal conscious desires, which, as we saw, David Boonin links to the onset of organized cortical activity at 25–32 weeks of gestation. What does it mean, we might ask, for a late fetus to harbor "conscious desires" in this sense? Boonin acknowledges that the nature of those desires could not go beyond the primitive desire for comfort, a preference for the mother's voice, or aversion to noxious stimuli (2003, 84–85). Yet *these* sorts of conscious desires are equally attributable to any number of nonhuman animals. A mouse has a primitive desire for comfort and warmth, an aversion to noxious stimuli, and so on.[18] And of course many nonhuman mammals possess a conscious life that is far more sophisticated than this. Dogs also harbor basic desires for food, water, warmth etc., but are, at the same time, self-conscious and thoughtful to a degree that late-term fetuses are not (they are able to understand, for instance, when commands are addressed to them, and to follow those commands). If basic conscious desires suffice for full moral status, we would have to ask why equal moral status is not extended to all nonhuman animals possessing the same degree of sentience. If no satisfactory answer can be provided for this, it will seem as though the attribution of personhood to late-gestated human fetuses but not to a vast number of nonhuman animals is merely speciesist and incapable of moral defense.

At first blush, the argument for the so-called developmental view of moral status is quite compelling. However, I have yet to attend to the main objections to the view that moral status depends on the acquisition of certain capacities. The most obvious kind of objection comes in the way of putative counterexamples.

---

18 This point is made by Mary Anne Warren (1989), The Moral Significance of Birth, *Hypatia, 4*, 46.

Opponents of the view that personhood depends on developmental capacities such as consciousness, rationality, or communication ability are quick to point out that these conditions wrongly exclude too many individuals from the category of persons. Neonates and young infants, for instance, are *not* rational or capable of communication. Some accounts suggest that they do not evolve a concept of the self until sometime after birth. On a theory of personhood that makes cognitive capacities central, how are we then to account for the moral status of infants? The natural implication of such a view is that young human infants do not in fact possess any stronger a right to life than that of fetuses, or, indeed, nonhuman animals that are equally sentient. But this suggestion, which entails that infants can be killed in the same circumstances in which fetuses may permissibly be aborted, will be wholly unacceptable to many, and count as evidence against the developmental view. This, in short, is the *infanticide problem*.

The counterexamples do not stop with infants, however. Adult human beings that are in comas are not currently capable of being rational, do not experience conscious desires, communicate, and so forth. Are they thereby lacking in personhood status? What if the coma is reversible and the insentient human being is destined to wake up in a week's time? Are we to conclude that she temporarily lost her personhood status, and strong right to life, while asleep, but regained it on waking up? This seems somewhat counterintuitive. This is known as the *episodic problem*. Adult human beings suffering from severe cognitive disabilities may, like infants, lack the sorts of cognitive capacities that are constitutive of personhood on the developmental account. Again, though, it seems both wrong and alarming to suggest that they lack full personhood status for that reason, although this is indeed where the developmental view I sketched seems to lead us. Any theory that denies cognitively deficient human beings full moral standing will, for that reason alone, strike most people as patently false. We can call this the *problem of radical cognitive deficiency*.

Some people may be tempted to endorse a version of developmentalism that treats independent living ability as the core condition for personhood. On this account, only human beings who are capable of living and breathing without the bodily assistance of another can qualify as persons. Those who defend such a criterion might consequently endorse fetal viability – the point at which a fetus becomes capable of life outside the womb – as the threshold of personhood. But the independent living ability criterion is also subject to counterexamples. Intensive care patients on life support are not capable of breathing independently of assistance, but are surely still persons on our estimation. Moreover, it might be objected that newborns are not capable of independent living either, insofar as they cannot survive without the assistance of mature human beings. Perhaps, then, the rationale underlying the viability threshold would fail to accord personhood status to a whole host of born human beings.

The viability threshold for personhood has also been criticized for its propensity to endorse arbitrary distinctions regarding who is within or outside the class of morally protected persons. Fetal viability can often depend on a host of circumstantial factors including, most obviously, the standards of neonatal care available. A 26-week gestated fetus in a developed country with good standards of neonatal intensive care may be viable, whereas a fetus at the same stage of gestation in a country lacking those medical capabilities is not. It could be suggested that personhood status cannot possibly depend on such arbitrary factors.

Finally, let us return to David Boonin's suggestion that the capacity for conscious desires, and in particular the desire for continued life, is what underlies the moral right to life. In a similar vein to the reasoning employed above, it is easy for an antagonist of this view to throw doubt on the importance of the desire to keep living for our ascriptions of moral status. The suicidal depressed person who no longer desires life is doubtless still a person. So too, surely, is the person who has achieved the Buddhist ideal of nirvana and no longer has any earthly desires, including the desire to keep living.[19] Again here,

19 Kaczor provides a similar counterexample: Kaczor, *The Ethics of Abortion*, 63.

counterexamples can be raised that challenge the proposed basis for moral status. Surely, one might say, whether or not a human being desires to keep living does not go to determine whether or not she is a person. Rather, it might be thought, born human beings are endowed with the fundamental right to life owing to the kinds of creatures that they are, regardless of the strength of their desire to keep living. It does not appear *less* morally wrong to kill someone whose desire for continued life is weak than it is to kill someone whose desire for continued life is strong.

At this point, things look very bad for the developmental view. It seems that counterexamples of the kind considered above can be marshalled against almost any developmental criterion of moral status one might pick, and thus show that criterion of moral status, and whichever threshold of personhood it recommends, to be rationally unsupportable. The counterexamples are, in effect, reductio ad absurdum arguments against the developmental criteria. Their point, for those who invoke them, is to show that developmental criteria for personhood commit us to untenable conclusions regarding who is owed strong moral protection, and should for this reason be rejected.

Now, some discussants will be willing to bite the bullet with regard to some or all of the counterexamples and respond to them by advising that we adjust our moral sensibilities to fall more in line with a rationally persuasive account of moral status. Thus it is that Michael Tooley, for instance, answers the infanticide problem by suggesting that the traditional (complete) moral condemnation of infanticide in fact rests on a mistake and that we ought, perhaps, to open our minds to the possibility that the prohibition of infanticide is only another kind of unsupportable social "taboo" (1972). Perhaps, in other words, we should just think the unthinkable. However, while maintaining that the correct basis for personhood status cannot be reconciled with the moral equality of early human infants, Tooley, along with other philosophers, has suggested that there are nevertheless good moral and pragmatic reasons to value the lives of newborns and to award them a strong right to life at a fairly early stage. A number of important considerations might go in favor of treating infants as morally equal, even if they do not possess the moral rights of persons. These considerations might include the fact that newborn babies are often wanted by adult humans (even if not by their biological parents), and that treating infants as expendable has a potentially morally deadening effect, especially given how close they are to becoming fully realized persons (Tooley 1972; Warren 1989). Perhaps it is practically impossible for a populace to deny the rights of neonates while relating to one-year-olds as full rights-holders. Equally, it might be suggested, there may well exist compelling pragmatic reasons to accord personhood status to human beings with radical cognitive deficiencies even if they are not in fact within the category of persons, particularly given their striking resemblance to fully realized persons, their involvement in common human life, and the bonds of attachment that they form with others.

Like the counterexplanations offered by defenders of the personhood-from-conception theory in response to the Embryo Rescue Case, these sorts of explanations for the impermissibility of infanticide will strike many as deeply unsatisfying. It might be replied that such considerations simply do not reflect the core intuition that neonates are morally equivalent to born human beings and possess the fundamental right to life. The fact that it is this intuition, rather than concern about slippery slopes and collateral harm, that fuels people's revulsion toward infanticide could be drawn out when we stipulate those considerations out of a particular case. We might imagine the case of a newborn infant whom nobody wants, to whom no one is attached, and in circumstances where the act of terminating its life would be undiscoverable, so that there is no potential for breeding desensitization to the real moral interests of older infants. In such circumstances, I think that the common adverse reaction toward terminating the life of the neonate would still hold. And to the extent that this intuition has argumentative force, it suggests that the infanticide issue is still a stumbling block for developmental accounts of personhood status. Without having to perform the exercise, it should be clear how the same rebuttal could be constructed against the view that we ought to recognize the equal moral status of the radically cognitively defective (say, whose cognitive capacities are no more developed than that of a chimpanzee) for contingent moral reasons, not having to do with the intrinsic moral status of such human beings.

The ostensible victory for defenders of the claim that personhood begins at conception, when a new human being is on the scene, comes from the fact that it alone seems able to account for the personhood status of *all* human beings after the point of birth. A theory that ties moral status to human species membership has no trouble including infants, the comatose, or the radically cognitively defective within the remit of full rights-holding individuals. For they are all, at the very least, human beings. The trade-off for this inclusiveness is, of course, that a theory which grounds moral status in human species membership extends equal moral protection to zygotes and embryos as well. And this, as we saw, seems to be a reductio ad absurdum of *that* view. Could it really be correct that the difference between a sperm approaching an ovum and the single-celled human organism made up of 46 human chromosomes that comes into being moments later is the difference between two human cells of no more moral importance than skin cells and a creature that possesses all the moral importance of a fully grown human being, and whose death is as lamentable from the impersonal point of view? This is extremely difficult to accept.

In sum, the two broad views of moral status I have pitted against each other – the human species membership criterion and the developmental view – compare favorably on different counts. The personhood-from-conception theory avoids the problems associated with infanticide, the radically cognitively deficient, and comatose human beings, yet brings with it its own reductios, partly captured in the Embryo Rescue Case. Defenders of that view may retort that the full moral standing of zygotes and embryos is the conclusion that the most plausible theory of moral status requires us to accept, and that those of us who find it hard to believe should simply reconsider our firmly held convictions about the moral status of radically immature human beings. However, as we saw, the defender of a developmental theory can respond the same way to the reductios with which *she* is confronted. She equally might reply that this is just where the argument leads and where we must follow. One cannot demand that an antagonist's theory is thrown out as soon as it meets a counterintuitive implication but that equally counterintuitive upshots of one's own theory should instead just prompt the thinker to reconsider his starting convictions.

On the antiabortion side, however, we have yet to be presented with a developed argument for why it is that all human beings as of conception are full rights-holding persons. What sort of theory could explain the importance of human species membership in our assignations of personhood?

Potentiality Principles

Some defenders of the view that all human beings are full rights-holders from conception seek to explain and justify the moral significance of human species membership by reference to *potential*. Embryos and fetuses may not be persons in the fully realized sense. When we reflect on the sorts of capacities and traits that seem to be distinctive of persons, we see that they lack them. However, they are at least *potential* persons in that they are individual human organisms that will, if they survive and develop, eventually become persons. According to this view, the property of being a potential person qualifies one for the same basic rights as a fully realized person, especially the right to life. We can call this the *potentiality principle*.

Supporters of the potentiality principle might claim that only a potentiality-based theory of moral status is able to account for the full moral standing of infants or of human beings in reversible comas. Such human beings do not currently exemplify the characteristic qualities of personhood. Hence, if we award them equal moral status, this can *only* be on the basis of their potential to exercise those capacities in the future – for the infant, when she matures, and for the comatose person, when she awakes. But if potential personhood is a basis for conferring full moral rights, then it seems that those same rights must be extended to zygotes, embryos, and fetuses, which possess the same potential. Like infants, they too have the *capacity* for rational thought, communication, self-awareness, and so on. If these latent capacities are sufficient for moral status in the case of infants, then they must be sufficient in the case of pre-born human beings.

Embracing a potentiality principle of moral status might also be a way to justify the attribution of full moral status to human neonates but not, say, to adult chimpanzees, without laying oneself open to the charge of speciesism. Neonates are not more psychologically advanced or self-conscious than adult chimpanzees, but they have the *potential* for more sophisticated cognitive states than chimpanzees are able to attain. If potentiality is a basis for rights, this will be a morally distinguishing feature. As above, it could be argued that endorsing a potentiality-based theory of moral status is in fact the *only* way to justify extending a level of moral protection to human infants that surpasses that of nonhuman animals with equal or greater cognitive capacities without falling back on a mere species preference. For those who advance it, the potentiality principle is thought to entail that human beings possess full moral status from conception, since this is when an individual being with whom we can identify the relevant potential comes into existence (Stone 1987).

The potentiality principle suffers, at first glance, from an obvious logical problem. This is that there is no reason why being a potential person ought to endow a creature with the very same rights as an *actual* person. As some commentators have analogized it, the fact that someone is a potential president is no basis for awarding her the rights of an actual, current president (Benn 1984). More would therefore need to be said on behalf of the potentiality principle (PP) to explain why potential personhood qualifies a human being for all the rights that actual persons enjoy.

One particularly well-known iteration of PP seeks to do this by locating moral considerability in the possession of a distinctive kind of future, the sort of future that is typified by the capacities and traits we ordinarily associate with personhood. The philosopher Don Marquis has argued that reflecting about the wrongness of killing adult human beings leads us to the conclusion that the main reason killing is seriously wrong is because it deprives the person of the value of their future, typified by all of the forms of flourishing that are distinctive of persons (1989). Thus it is that we do not think killings carried out painlessly, in circumstances where the victim is wholly unaware, are any less seriously wrong qua killing than any other. The main wrong-making factor in killing is simply the deprivation of the victim's future life, and this holds regardless of how brutal or painless the killing is. However, Marquis argues that since embryos and fetuses *also* possess a future of the same distinctive value – a "future like ours" – killing such creatures is wrong for precisely the same reason that it is wrong to kill fully realized persons: it deprives them of a particularly valuable future, the future of a person.

Marquis's "future like ours" theory lends more substance to a potentiality-based account of moral status. But the potentiality principle still has some counterexamples and reductio challenges to contend with. Put briefly, depending on precisely how one constructs PP it seems to prove either too much or too little regarding who is afforded full moral protection. The principle states that it is really potentiality that matters for moral status. We must ask, though: potentiality *in what sense*? One answer is that creatures with the relevant kind of potential are just those creatures that are theoretically capable of becoming persons, whether they will in fact end up so becoming or not. But this kind of PP seems overinclusive. To take an example, Michael Tooley constructs an imaginary scenario in which a magical serum has been discovered that, when administered to kittens, turns those kittens into talking, reasoning persons (1972). As soon as the serum is discovered, then, it seems that *all* kittens have the latent potential to become persons, although they would have to go through the serum process first. If PP holds that full moral consideration extends to creatures that have the capacity to become persons, whether they do so or not, it will seem that once the serum is discovered, all ordinary kittens will possess as strong a right to life as you and me. But this seems far too liberal. Nothing about the interests or nature of ordinary kittens has changed simply because the magic serum has been discovered. It seems altogether wrongheaded to conclude that before the discovery they are just ordinary pussycats but that afterward their lives are as valuable as ours.

Alternatively, it might be suggested that the relevant kind of potential picked out by PP is instead *actual* potential. On this version of PP, only those creatures that will in fact become persons – in Marquis's terms, come to possess a "future like ours" – are worthy of full moral consideration. Creatures that *could* become persons are not full rights-holders unless they *will* become persons. This appears to give an odd result in the super-kitten scenario. It follows that whether or not any particular cat is worthy of full moral consideration depends on whether or not someone will, in the future, decide to administer to it the magical serum. Two kittens that are equal in terms of all their other qualities would stand on a completely different moral footing simply because luck has it that one of them will be the recipient of that serum. As well as yielding this strange result, the actual potentiality criterion also seems to be overly exclusive in a number of respects. It excludes, for instance, those human beings who, owing to congenital defects, will *never* have the distinctive future of a person. Perhaps some born human beings, such as those with radical cognitive deficiencies, are destined never to function rationally and embody the distinctive forms of person-like flourishing. They are not persons actually *or* potentially. The same can be true of infants and fetuses, depending only on their individual prospects. As Jeff McMahan points out, viable fetuses that suffer from severe cognitive abnormalities will lack an actu-ally realizable personhood potential, as might a severely intellec-tually disabled human infant.[20] Thus, it appears that a PP grounded in actually realizable potential will exclude from its ambit many individuals that defenders of that principle view as full moral rights-holders.

20 McMahan, J. (2002), *The Ethics of Killing: Problems at the Margins of Life* (Oxford: Oxford University Press), 154.

Importantly, the problem of overexclusiveness cannot be avoided simply by holding that being a potential person *or* being a born human being are both individually sufficient to qualify for strong moral rights. This is because the importance of potentiality is meant to avoid the speciesism challenge to human species membership as the basis of full moral status by further refining the rights-conferring property of all humans. A defender of PP cannot instead submit potentiality as an *alternative* basis for moral status, since it would then fail to meet the challenge it is developed to address.

The various problems of over- and underinclusiveness that we have encountered so far have led some supporters of PP to define the relevant kind of potentiality in a very specific way. It is suggested that the kind of potentiality that gives rise to full moral status is what has in different places been described as "radical" potentiality or the "radical capacity for rationality," which, in the philosopher Patrick Lee's description, is possessed by those "having a constitution or nature orienting one to active development to the stage where one does perform such actions – as opposed to an immediately exercisable capacity" (Lee 2013, 242). The "active development" condition in fact ends up being heavily qualified in such accounts, since it is clear that not all individual human organisms *will* be actively self-developing into rational, person-like beings. As we saw, this will not be true of fetuses, or, indeed, born human beings, with congenital defects that render them incapable of ever possessing reasoning ability or any of the other capacities distinctive of persons. On accounts such as Lee's, however, the "radical capacity" for personhood is possessed by all creatures with human genetic coding, whether or not they are ever able to realize that capacity. All human beings, however immature, possess that capacity through being the kinds of creatures that are "by nature" rational, regardless of whether they are or ever can be rational in actual fact. On this criterion, zygotes and embryos count every bit as much as fully functioning adult humans, regardless of whatever potential they can or will realize, because they too are creatures that, being human, are rational by nature.

The "Nature of the Kind" Argument

It seems to me that the radical capacity criterion of moral status in fact substitutes PP rather than salvages it. Once neither actual nor theoretical potentiality is any longer relevant to moral status, it can be questioned whether the principle under consideration is potentiality-based at all. Instead, it seems that the radical capacity criterion is intended to *replace* PP as the governing principle of moral status, and one that aligns more completely with human species membership.

The claim that all individual human creatures are rights-holders in virtue of possessing a "rational nature," regardless of which actual capacities they possess, is one that sits nicely with the notion that personhood is a matter of endowment rather than performance, and the idea that one cannot gain or lose one's personhood status – that an individual always is or is not a personhood-possessing sort of creature. The question remains, though, as to how creatures derive full moral status from their human genetic coding alone even when that coding does not furnish them with the traits distinctive of personhood (whether actually or potentially), as well as in what way all human organisms are thought to have a "rational nature," even when they can never be rational.

A common answer favored by proponents of the species membership criterion of moral status is that all human organisms are rational or person-like by nature because they have a *flourishing* that is defined by the characteristics typical of persons. As Kaczor has written, "rational endowment" is possessed by all individual human beings "whose flourishing consists in freedom and rationality" (2015, 106). He suggests that the kinds of flourishing which typify developed members of the human species, and distinguish them morally from other animals, constitute the nature of flourishing for *all* human organisms, immature, radically cognitively defective, or otherwise. As he elaborates, the inability to read or write or speak is a tragic failure to flourish for an adult human being, but not for a dog or cat or hamster (2015, 125). Speaking and communicating are part of what it means to thrive as a human but not as a cat. The same is true of reasoning ability. Kaczor argues that all human beings are properly described as beings that have a rational nature in having a good that is constituted by that nature. And having that nature makes all human beings full rights-holders from conception. Kaczor has called this the "flourishing like ours argument" (FLO) (2015, 124).

Kaczor's FLO argument is just one iteration of a broad way of thinking about moral status that has been termed the "nature of the kind" (NOTK) view (McMahan 2005). The defining feature of that theory is that it holds the moral status of a creature to be determined not by its individual capacities but by the moral significance of characteristics that are typically or generally true of the members of its kind. On Kaczor's NOTK argument, all human beings as of conception possess full moral status through being a member of a species the typical adult members of which are characteristic persons. On the NOTK view, human species membership is thus a sufficient condition for personhood status, although it is not a necessary one, at least not conceptually. A member of an intelligent alien species that is typified by the same forms of flourishing as are human beings might equally be owed full moral protection on this view, even if he does not individually bear out those capabilities.

In this way, defenders of NOTK arguments seek to evade the speciesism objection by showing that it is not human species membership as such, but rather an independent property to which it attaches, that is morally significant. Moreover, it might be suggested that belonging to a species the typical adult members of which are rational, intelligent, and so on is only one source of full moral status. Actually *possessing* the relevant capacities will also suffice. Thus, Tooley's superkitten that has been administered the magical serum will be a person once it is actually capable of speech and reason, even though these capacities are not typical of its kind.

The NOTK theory is appealing insofar as it extends moral status to all born human beings regardless of their current ability to express the cognitive traits distinctive of humans. Such a view has no trouble acknowledging the full moral status of infants or human beings with radical cognitive deficiencies, or those in deep sedation. However, the basic notion that every creature's moral status derives from its group membership has more than a few objections to contend with. The core objection, helpfully posed by Jeff McMahan, is that the NOTK view seems to accept that it is not really human species membership that matters to moral status at all, but rather the sorts of cognitive capacities that are foregrounded on developmental accounts. He explains:

> But the nature-of-the-kind argument itself presupposes that the essential properties for membership in the human species are not themselves status-conferring; for if they were, there would be no point in arguing that all human beings have a higher status than any animal by virtue of belonging to a kind whose normal or typical members have certain evidently or recognisably status-conferring intrinsic properties.
>
> (2005, 357)

Putting it differently, we might ask proponents of the NOTK theory what it is that really matters for moral status: human species membership or cognitive capacities? If the former, then why is the importance of human species membership only explicable in terms of the moral significance of capacities such as rationality and communication ability? If the latter, then surely a correct theory of moral status should pick out the actual possession of those capacities as the status-conferring property, rather than a certain relation to them through group memberships.

Pressing the objection against the NOTK view, McMahan also asks how it is that the morally significant properties of a particular kind get to be part of an individual's nature merely because that individual meets the basic conditions for membership of that kind. How is it that capacities absent in an individual are nonetheless part of her *nature* because they are possessed by others? They are not possessed by *her*; and a description of an individual's nature is ordinarily meant to trace what an individual is actually like.

Related to this point, we can also ask why the group membership that determines moral status on the NOTK view is species membership. Why not genus, family, or kingdom (moving up the biological taxonomic ranks), or, for that matter, membership of the local chess society? Some explanation must be given for why an individual's basic nature is determined by its species membership alone. The answer may be that what it would mean for an individual to flourish is determined only by her species membership. Our human biology sets the outer reaches and the limits of our morally significant qualities. But it is not true that there is nothing it means to flourish as a mammal, or as an animal, or, indeed, as a chess player. Even if individual moral status is determined by the typical features of the group of which we are a member, then, it remains an open question as to how that group ought to be identified.

The contrary view would hold that what constitutes flourishing for an individual creature can in fact only be read off her specific capacities. Once it has been administered the serum, what it means for the superkitten in Tooley's thought experiment to flourish surely changes, regardless of the nature of cats in general. As McMahan notes, NOTK arguments tend to have appeal when they "level up," awarding higher moral status to a creature in respect of its group membership, but far less so when they "level down" – that is, when they imply that a being with atypically advanced cognitive capacities still only possesses the moral standing of a typical mature member of its species (2005, 358). It seems erroneous to hold that the talking, reasoning superkitten is still only as morally important as the standard pussycat. It is not easy to see, though, how a theory that takes a creature's nature and moral status to be determined by its species kind can avoid such an implication.

Flourishing like Us: Cognitive Deficiency and Preborn Human Beings

The clear benefit of NOTK accounts of moral status is that they are not subject to the sorts of counterexamples that, as we saw, plague developmental accounts of moral status. Kaczor's "flourishing like ours" theory has no trouble accommodating the full personhood status of infants, comatose human beings, or mature human beings with radical cognitive deficiencies. But avoiding these reductios comes at the expense of propounding a theory of moral status that, while building on the moral importance of capacities that are typical of mature humans, somewhat dichotomously ties personhood to a different, conceptually distinct property: membership of a person-species.

It is worth pausing here to make an important comment about the counterexample based on human beings with radical cognitive deficiency (RCD). As we have seen, the standard reductio based on RCD claims that psychological capacities–based criteria for personhood are unable to account for the moral status of such individuals, which seems to be a repugnant conclusion. However, it is rarely acknowledged just how radical a human's cognitive deficiencies would have to be before we would struggle to fit them into the developmental concept of a person. And this in turn is liable to exaggerate the strength of the reductio based on RCD.

Consider again, for example, Mary Anne Warren's account of moral status, grounded in five core characteristics: reasoning, communication ability, self-consciousness, independent agency, and sentience (including the capacity for pain experience). Warren's claim, we saw, was that an individual need not possess all five capacities to properly be considered a person, but only that an individual possessing none of those traits could not qualify for personhood. But even human beings with severe mental deficiencies can, and typically do, possess a concept of themselves as an individual subject, reason and communicate (even if to a lesser degree), express independent agency, and experience sensation. The severely intellectually disabled human being whose psychological and emotional capacities are no more developed than that of a chimp may be more of a philosophical invention (useful for thought experiments) than a reality. As the philosopher (and mother of a seriously cognitively disabled woman) Eva Kittay argues, the capabilities and limitations of such people can almost never be simplified in such a way:

> We can retain some characteristically human capacities and lose others. What's lost and what is retained constrains the

extent to which, and how fully, we are able to partake in scope
of human existence and the panoply of human possibilities.

(2009, 615)

Chiding other moral philosophers for their broad-brush
descriptions of RCD humans and their capabilities, Kittay draws
on her experience as the mother of such an individual to point
out that severely intellectually disabled people are in fact far
different from their standard portrayal. In her experience, they
are able to experience aesthetic pleasure, understand the concept
of death and grieve for the death of their loved ones, and relate to
other human beings on a multitude of planes not available to
nonhuman animals. She writes:

> Most severely retarded people can speak at least a few words
> and can be and are involved in activities and relationships.
> Even "profoundly mentally retarded" individuals are far from
> being unresponsive to their environment and to other people.
> My daughter, Sesha, was diagnosed as having severe to pro-
> found retardation. She is enormously responsive, forming deep
> personal relationships with her family and her long-standing
> caregivers and friendly relations with her therapists and
> teachers, more distant relatives, and our friends. I have written
> quite a bit about her love of music, especially but not exclu-
> sively classical symphonic music, with the master of this form,
> Beethoven, being on the top of her list.
>
> (2009, 616)

Fully appreciating what human beings with RCD are actually like
is extremely important in discussions about moral status, and for
developmental accounts of personhood. Here, especially, it may
suggest that the RCD counterexample is much less problematic
for the developmental theory than first appears. On a theory such
as Warren's, only the most radical cognitive disabilities imagin-
able would seem to preclude full personhood status – the human
who wholly lacks the capacity to reason or communicate on the
higher level typical of human beings, to act independently *at all*,
and so on. In all but the most extreme cases, individuals with
cognitive limitations will still exemplify the kinds of characteristics constitutive of persons, even if in a compromised form.

The exclusivity of a developmental account such as Warren's is also tempered by the fact that it treats personhood as a cluster concept. Rather than setting out a strict set of necessary and sufficient conditions, Warren's account takes personhood to supervene on a cluster of core properties only an adequate selection of which are required for personhood status. While individuals with RCD may well lack one or more of the relevant properties either partially or wholly, it will be a far rarer case in which a human being lacks all or nearly all of the capabilities Warren deemed constitutive of personhood.

On a cluster concept approach to personhood, it might also follow that adequacy in one respect compensates for a deficiency in another respect. To illustrate, a human being with a normal level of self-awareness (that which is typical of humans) and the ability to communicate but who lacks reasoning ability could still qualify for personhood, since she will express a sufficient number of person-making characteristics to a sufficient degree. When treating the concept of personhood as both multi-criterial and fluid regarding the combinations of features that suffice for qualification, the RCD challenge again seems to weaken considerably.

So something like the "flourishing like ours" account of moral status may not be needed to account for the personhood status of human beings with radical cognitive disabilities. As I have tried to show, the reductio argument based on their exclusion from the personhood category under the developmental account is vastly exaggerated at the very least. Nevertheless, there is undoubtedly something residually appealing about NOTK theories such as FLO. Such accounts cater well for the common intuition that all born human beings are entitled to equal moral respect regardless of their capacities, and that even humans who bear out *none* of the constitutive features of personhood deserve moral consideration in excess of that owed to nonhuman animals. Put differently, NOTK theories support the judgment that beings standing in a *certain relation* to persons are worthy of a special kind of moral respect. In some places, that relation has been defined as being an individual who *could have* been a person but for some misfortune – someone for whom failing to be a person is a lament-able inability to embody everything they can and should be.

More precisely, the widely shared intuition to which NOTK theories speak is the notion that individuals who could have been persons ought to be treated in a way that is sensitive to everything they could and should be, even when they lack the capacities typical of personhood, and even when that proper treatment cannot be explained by reference to their individual interests. The belief that such individuals are entitled to our moral respect regardless of individual capacities is evidenced by our judgments about the wrongness of assaults on patients in permanent vege-tative states (including in circumstances where we stipulate away the potential for any harm or discovery), or the moral repug-nance of mocking individuals with limited cognitive capacities even when they are unaware of, and hence unharmed by, the affront.

The moral imperative to award those with RCD all of the moral respect due to typical mature humans could be explained and defended in terms of a range of moral considerations. However, tracing the FLO account considered above, one such consider-ation might be that RCD individuals are owed respect in virtue of being person-types. Cultivating an attitude of sensitivity and rev-erence for all individuals who *could have* been persons, and whose failure to embody the characteristics of personhood is a sad mis-fortune, may be part and parcel of maintaining the proper moral attitude toward persons themselves. Equally, relating to such individuals thusly might be particularly appropriate in light of the fact that their misfortunes are ones we might have shared, since we too might have (or still might) fail to realize our poten-tial as persons, through accident or deterioration. As the philoso-pher Stephen Mulhall writes, our duty to treat such human beings as fully our fellow humans does not come from mistakenly ascribing to them capacities that they lack, but partly from recog-nizing that their inability to share in our distinctive way of life – to flourish as persons – "is a result of the shocks and ills to which all human flesh and blood is heir – because there but for the grace of God go I" (2002).

Seeing in cognitively limited individuals our own unique frailties and possible misfortunes may give us special reasons to draw them into the fold and, as far as possible, help them realize their maximum potential. Importantly, these sorts of reasons are not a function of the specific, personhood-relevant capacities that such individuals do or do not possess. Rather, they seem to have to do with cultivating the appropriate sort of affective response to individuals whose failure to be persons is a misfortune, and one we might have shared.

This is admittedly a rather coarse-grained exposition of the sorts of considerations underneath the intuition driving FLO. But let us assume for the sake of argument that the kernel of the FLO account is correct, and that individuals whose flourishing consists in the goods associated with personhood – who, in some sense, *could have been* persons (Shelly Kagan describes such individuals as "modal persons"; 2016) – are owed full moral protection. Even when accepting an account such as this, I think it far from obvious that pre-born human beings qualify for full moral status on that basis.

Embryos and fetuses are differently positioned from developed human beings with RCD in that they are *not* failing to flourish by lacking the capacities constitutive of personhood. Reasoning ability, communication skills, and self-consciousness are not part of what it means to flourish as a fetus. Pre-born human beings *never* possess those capacities. The failure of fetuses to be rational is not owed to any calamity or shortcoming; it is perfectly consistent with flourishing as a fetus. Pre-born human beings do not, therefore, have a "flourishing like ours," insofar as they do not have a flourishing that consists in exercising the capacities constitutive of personhood. This is not to say that they lack a flourishing altogether. Clearly, there is something that it means to flourish qua fetus, and that must include continuing to survive and develop healthily. But elephant fetuses also have a flourishing that consists in these things, as do plants. This sort of flourishing is not distinctively enough "like ours" to engage the sorts of considerations that seem to explain the extension of moral status to individuals with an FLO.

It might be objected that embryos and fetuses *do* in fact have a "flourishing like ours" insofar as, as fellow human beings, what is involved in their flourishing is not just that they live and grow, but that they develop into thinking, speaking persons, like us. The question here, I think, is whether the same sorts of considerations that explain the extension of moral consideration to mature human beings who lack the core features of personhood apply in the same way to human beings in utero. There are at least some respects in which it seems they do not. Pre-born human beings are not versions of paradigmatic persons in the sense that they are not what we might call "person-types" – beings that *would* be persons but for some misfortune to which all mature humans might have fallen prey. To the extent that this is something that matters in our assessments about the morally proper treatment of RCD individuals, and for the intuitive appeal of the FLO account, embryos and fetuses are differently positioned.

Furthermore, some of the considerations for treating mature humans who lack personhood's constitutive features with serious moral respect may have to do not just with the good of those individuals themselves, but also with how our treatment of them influences and reflects our moral respect for all mature human beings and what is important in their lives. This may be true, for instance, of certain harmless behaviors directed at individuals with RCD that, although they inflict no detriment on the individual, demonstrate a pernicious disregard for the dignity and value of all developed humans. Again, inasmuch as fetuses are not equally "person-types" and do not echo our own good and ill, this concern will be far less pronounced when treating *them* as something other than persons. To be sure, there may be ways of treating fetuses that are morally improper and insufficiently sensitive to the goods we do share with them. But the relationship between our attitudes toward them and toward actual persons will be different, and in many places weaker. Having said all this, it warrants repeating just how severely limited an individual's cognitive capacities would need to be before it would be hard to reconcile her personhood with a developmental account of what it is to be a person.

1.7   Abortion and Infanticide

Infanticide and the Moral Insignificance of Birth

In the last section, I presented some objections to the claim that full moral status supervenes on potential personhood (the "potentiality principle") and against so-called nature-of-the-kind arguments, which state that creatures get to be persons through belonging to a species the typical mature members of which are persons. Both of these theories are possible routes to human species membership being a sufficient condition for personhood. If they fail to convince, we will therefore have reason to doubt that all human beings are persons from conception.

As we saw, however, both theories are often introduced as a response to apparent deficiencies in the antithetical view that personhood is constituted by a cluster of higher psychological capacities, such as self-consciousness and reasoning ability. These drawbacks, we saw, come in the form of reductio ad absurdum arguments to the effect that so-called developmental accounts of personhood fail to bestow full moral status on human beings who are obviously rights-holders. In the case of human beings with radical cognitive deficiencies, I pointed out that the degree to which such individuals are excluded by a capacities-based account could be miscalculated when there is insufficient knowledge of what people with cognitive limitations are actually like, and the kinds of interactions of which they are in fact capable.

Second, however, I suggested that the main intuition that renders the NOTK theory compelling may indeed be reflected in the moral considerations we have for treating all human beings who *could have* been persons, but through some misfortune fail to be, with the same moral respect that is owed to actual persons. Inasmuch as it encapsulates this moral imperative, the kernel of the "flourishing like ours" account of moral status might be correct. Crucially, though, I suggested that fetuses do not, on this rationale, stand in the same position as mature human beings who lack the constitutive properties of personhood. The nature of their flourishing is *not* "like ours" and they are not properly regarded as "person-types," that is, as individuals who would have been persons but for some defect or misfortune. Consequently, the moral considerations that apply in respect of mature humans with cognitive limitations are not exactly the same with respect to fetuses – at least, not for reasons supporting the FLO thesis.

But there is a significant problem still yet to be addressed. The issue concerns young infants and the "infanticide problem" set out earlier. For it is still difficult to distinguish young infants from fetuses on any of the relevant counts. They do not bear the distinctive features of personhood either – they are not rational, self-aware, able to communicate, and so on. Nor is it easy to see how they are distinguishable from fetuses in the respects that are salient to the FLO account of moral status. The nature of their flourishing is not much more like ours than is true of pre-born human beings. They are not failing to flourish *either* by lacking sophisticated cognitive capacities; like fetuses, neonates are still flourishing qua neonates when they fail to speak and reason and form a concept of the self. And like fetuses, neonates are not "person-types," in that they are not creatures that would have been persons but for a misfortune. The result is that if the FLO basis for according moral respect to RCD individuals does not extend to pre-born human beings, it will seem not to extend to young infants either. The infanticide problem is therefore still immanent. A theory of moral status that fails to recognize neonates as fully deserving of moral protection in their own right will be unacceptable to many.

So how does one begin to answer the infanticide problem? In many of its articulations, the problem is expressed alongside assertions about the moral arbitrariness of birth as a dividing line between creatures that fundamentally differ in their moral status, such that one could permissibly be killed for reasons that could never justify killing the other. Put crudely, what sort of moral difference can a few inches along the vaginal canal possibly make? In this vein, it is often claimed that the fact of birth is a mere matter of a human being's "location," and that where precisely an individual resides, inside the womb or outside it, cannot be the sort of fact that determines her right to life. This is not, it is said, an *intrinsic* moral difference. Some people remark on just how indistinguishable neonates are from late gestated fetuses in every meaningful way. Indeed, a prematurely born neonate, born, say, at 24 weeks, will be even *less* physiologically developed in many ways than a fetus at the later gestational age of 30 weeks. The idea that only one of these beings will be worthy of full moral protection through the fortune of having been born (which, in turn, might depend on any number of propitious circumstances) strikes many discussants as obviously indefensible, and a fatal flaw of any theory that is forced to embrace it.

Thresholds and Vagueness

In responding to this persisting problem, I want first to make a few further remarks about the particular nature of the infanticide issue. The infanticide problem is not exactly like the other counterexamples set against a capacities-based account of personhood, such as the case of human beings with radical cognitive deficiencies. The RCD counterexample is intended to challenge a certain view about the constitutive features of personhood. The infanticide counterexample does this too, insofar as it submits an example of human beings who do not bear out those constitutive features but who nevertheless seem to warrant inclusion in the class of persons. However, when focused on the moral arbitrariness of birth, the infanticide problem is also an issue about precisely where the *threshold* of personhood falls. That is, it is a question not just about personhood criteria, but also about cutoffs and line-drawing.

The issues surrounding the threshold of personhood and its constitutive properties are related but also distinct. Where one locates the threshold or the beginning of personhood will naturally depend a great deal on the conditions for personhood one supports. For example, someone committed to the view that independent living ability is a sufficient condition for personhood might support the point of fetal viability as personhood's threshold. Alternatively, someone who endorses consciousness as the core condition for personhood might defend a threshold somewhere late in gestation if that is when consciousness is thought to arise. In one way, though, the problem concerning the moral arbitrariness of birth reflects an independent problem about the threshold of personhood and what it ought to be like. As well as being salient to the question of what makes a person a person, it is a matter of where the line falls which divides those who are considered persons from those who aren't. In the ordinary course of things, when exactly does a person arrive on the scene, and how might we defend drawing the line in one place rather than another?

Even for those convinced that the constitutive features of personhood are psychological capacities, the issue concerning the *exact* threshold of personhood can still be pertinent. If birth does not mark a change in any of the personhood-relevant properties, on what ground ought we to identify it with the threshold of personhood? There is something slightly incongruous seeming, however, about the moral arbitrariness of birth objection as it is presented by defenders of the species membership criterion of personhood, which supports conception as the corresponding threshold. This is because the objection that birth marks no "intrinsic" moral difference and hence cannot change a being's moral status only really makes sense against the background assumption that differences in developmental capacities, such as reasoning ability or consciousness, *would* count as intrinsic, morally relevant differences if they could be pointed out. If neonates came directly out of womb suddenly able to reason and speak, we would not doubt that birth is a morally significant event. Yet defenders of the species membership view do not, in any case, believe that capacities such as these are determinative of personhood status. They hence cannot impugn the birth threshold for failing to map onto changes of *that* kind. This would be to lay down a challenge that, even if surmounted, would make no difference to their rejection of birth as the benchmark for personhood.

So we cannot understand the objection to the birth threshold by defenders of the species membership view as the complaint that birth makes no difference to any cognitive capacities, and must seek to understand it in different terms. Those terms, I think, reflect the same reason why *all* post-conception thresholds are deemed to be unacceptable to some discussants arguing in favor of the conception threshold. This is the supposed problem that all post-conception thresholds are unavoidably arbitrary in the sense that they must pick out a nondefinitive point in the fluid continuum of human development. For example, taking the birth threshold, one might ask at precisely which moment in that process a person is thought to arrive on the scene. Is it when the newborn first begins to emerge from a woman's body, or when it is halfway out, or not until it is fully separated from the woman? Whichever point one picks will not seem to be meaningfully distinguishable from the developments occurring immediately on either side. There is no reason for thinking that a person has not yet come into being when a baby's head and shoulders have emerged but *has* come into being once it emerges just past the navel. These are insignificant variations that cannot be responsible for cataclysmic changes in moral status.

The same sort of objection might be levelled at any number of suggested thresholds of personhood. Say someone claims that human beings become persons at 25 weeks of gestation. Well, one might ask, why not 24 weeks and 6 days? Surely there is no feature borne out by fetuses at 25 weeks that is considerably less present one day, or, indeed, one hour earlier. How, then, might one support the later threshold without conceding that there is every bit as much reason to support the earlier one? Because of the incremental nature of human development, the same arbitrariness problem will simply resurge as soon as one moves the threshold backward one fraction: if 24 weeks and 6 days, why not one day earlier than *that*? The conclusion by opponents of developmental views is that only the conception threshold constitutes a definitive and nonarbitrary benchmark that is not incremental in nature and does not mark merely one point on a continuum of development, indistinguishable from other closely neighboring developments. Conception, it might be argued, marks a discrete, transformative event when a new human being comes into existence, and which is clearly nonarbitrarily distinguishable from all other points on the spectrum of early human life.

Relatedly, it is sometimes argued that the arbitrariness of all post-conception thresholds of personhood gives rise to a slippery slope problem, since in every case there will be no clear reason against placing the threshold fractionally later. If 25 weeks, why not an hour or a day later? But then, why not a day later than that? And so on and on. Only conception, the claim goes, marks a definitive threshold that cannot logically be extended further and further forward, perhaps even beyond birth and into infancy.

There are a number of problems with this arbitrariness critique of all post-conception thresholds. First of all, it is not correct that conception is a definitive "moment" in human development. In fact, conception is a process like everything else, comprised of numerous successive and nonarbitrarily distinguishable increments. We might equally pose the question as to which of the many numerous developments in the process of conception is the *exact* moment when a person comes into being. Is it the second when the sperm first makes contact with the egg, or the next second when it begins to penetrate it, or one of the seconds or milliseconds during which the pronuclei are fusing? It might equally be asked what nonarbitrary reason one could possibly have for settling on one of these moments over any of the others. Supporters of the conception threshold who eschew developmental thresholds for being "arbitrary" and nondefinitive must believe that conception *does* mark a moment that has the quality of being nonarbitrarily distinguishable from all adjacent ones. But this is simply not so. Furthermore, if there is no nonarbitrary reason to settle on one microscopic development over another, the logical slippery slope in the direction of moving the threshold later and later ad infinitum looms just as large when adopting the conception threshold.

Defenders of personhood-from-conception might retort that the objection misfires, for even though it is true that conception, like everything else, is comprised of successive moments, there is a time very early in human development when it is clear that conception has been completed, and after which we can therefore say with certainty that a new person is present and abortion is morally impermissible. But advocates of post-conception thresholds of personhood can respond to the arbitrariness problem in exactly the same way. Birth, viability, or the onset of consciousness are all developments that occur incrementally and that admit of no nonarbitrarily distinguishable "moments." Still, there are clear cases on either side where it is indisputable that an individual has become conscious, or viable, or has been born. If the arbitrariness problem can be surmounted in respect of conception just by pointing out that there is a time by which the process is definitely complete, the same consideration must come to the defense of other benchmarks.

More importantly, however, it might be thought that the entire thrust of the arbitrariness critique as it is presented here rests on some very contestable presuppositions about what the beginning of personhood is like. Specifically, it appears to embrace a fallacy best brought out by thinking about a classic problem in philosophy, known as the "sorites paradox," or the paradox of the heap. The sorites paradox asks us to consider a heap of sand. More than a few grains are clearly required to constitute a "heap." But how many exactly? Suppose I start drawing grains together, one minuscule grain at a time, and ask you to tell me the exact addition with which a heap has appeared. It seems that no answer will be satisfactory. For it does not appear true to say of any individual grain that *it* makes the difference between a heap and a nonheap. If the millionth grain, why *this* one, and not the grain immediately before or after? There will be no good answer to that. There are, in other words, no nonarbitrarily distinguishable grains with which it seems reasonable to identify the coming-to-be of the heap.

Nevertheless, it is still clear that there is a difference between a heap and a nonheap and that whereas no heap is in existence in the beginning, one has clearly materialized by some later stage. It would be an unreasonable response to the sorites problem to claim either that no heap has come to exist, even where there are millions of grains, *or* that we must conclude a heap was in existence from the very first grain. Rather, the truth is that a nonheap has indeed turned into a heap but that there is no nonarbitrarily identifiable moment when this happened. We know that the grains of sand become a heap at some point, even though we cannot pinpoint an exact moment when this occurs. In other words, the beginning of the heap is vague, with no sharp beginning.

The arbitrariness critique of post-conception thresholds seems to replicate the fallacious response to the sorites paradox, implying that there must be a nonarbitrarily distinguishable moment at which persons begin, and that if we cannot pinpoint such a moment, we must conclude either that a person has not yet come into existence (even by birth or infancy) or that a person has always been in existence from the very first developments in conception. Put differently, it assumes that the beginning of personhood must be a sharp borderline – a single, identifiable moment that is morally transformative – and cannot possibly be vague. On this view, a proposed threshold of personhood will be unsupportable if it does not constitute a sharp borderline of the kind, which will be so if one cannot adduce good reason to distinguish it from its closest neighboring points.

I have elsewhere referred to the view that the beginning of personhood is a sharp borderline as "punctualism" (2017). Punctualism states that early human life is somewhere punctuated by the decisive beginning of personhood. Only a view such as this could, I think, defend the need to adduce a completely nonarbitrarily distinguishable point with which to identify the beginning of personhood. As we have already seen, conception is actually no better able to meet this very exacting standard than any other benchmark in human development. However, as soon as we reflect on what a belief such as punctualism commits us to holding about the nature of personhood, I think it apparent that we cannot accept it. If punctualism is true, then for any case in which an individual clearly goes from lacking personhood to possessing it (or, equally, back the other way), we must be prepared to say that there *is* a precise, nonarbitrarily distinguishable moment that is transformative of moral status. Yet this is extremely difficult to believe.

Take again, for instance, Michael Tooley's imaginary example of a serum invented that can give kittens the power to reason and speak. It seems incontrovertible here that before a kitten is injected it is not a person, but that once it is injected and has acquired the new powers, it is. But the punctualist thesis must hold that there is a sharp borderline when the kitten goes from being the one thing to the other. Say, for example, that there are 100 drops of serum in the injection dose. How many drops precisely make the difference between personhood and its absence? On the punctualist thesis, there must be a determinate answer to this question, that is, to the question of whether the kitten becomes a person after the addition of the fifty-sixth drop of serum, or the eightieth. But this will not seem reasonable to hold if there is no individual drop of serum with which it is reasonable to identify the beginning of personhood. No individual increment is significant enough to make that difference. Still, it is beyond doubt that a change in moral status has taken place. The problem with punctualism is that it entails something that simply appears false: that if there is no exact and nonarbitrarily distinguishable moment with which to identify the emergence of personhood, we have no basis for thinking that a person has come into being. The superkitten scenario is just one thought experiment which shows this to be untrue.

Stipulation and Law

Let us accept, then, that the beginning of personhood in early human life is indeed vague. Remaining with a capacities-based view of personhood's constitutive conditions, this means that there is no absolutely precise point at which a human being acquires sufficient consciousness or self-awareness or any other higher cognitive capacity to meet those conditions. This does not change the fact that there are clear cases on either side. Rejecting the punctualist thesis is merely to reject the claim that there is a decisive moment of a morally transformative nature.

However, the law cannot simply accept that the beginning of personhood is vague and offer no more guidance than this. Especially given the normative implications of personhood status, it is crucial that the law stipulates an adequately precise threshold that is clear, practical, and capable of guiding behavior. The reasons the law has for stipulating a clear and absolute boundary line between nascent human beings and fully rights-holding persons are partially independent from our commitments regarding the constitutive properties of personhood. The need for legal bivalence is pressing, whatever those properties are taken to be. Clarity in the law concerning where the borderline falls is essential for a plethora of reasons, both legal and moral. Some of those reasons reflect rule of law considerations of predictability, consistency in law, and the importance of treating like cases alike. When reproductive freedoms and the permissibility of ending human life turns on the applicable threshold of personhood, fairness and consistency in the law requires as much guidance as is practicable.

There are other reasons of a special kind for the law to settle on a clear benchmark and to treat personhood as absolute once that threshold is crossed. One such reason might be the avoidance of a degree moral slippage that might ensue were the beginning of personhood to be left indeterminate under the law. Particularly because of the vague and incremental nature of early human development, including of the capacities salient to personhood, one might worry that absent a clear legal boundary, the affording of full moral protection might be pushed increasingly far forward into early human life, past a point that is justifiable. In other words, vagueness surrounding the beginning of personhood is itself a reason for clear legal stipulation.

It might also be thought that a legally recognized baseline beyond which moral status is taken to be full and absolute under the law is an essential feature of a polity in which all members are regarded as equally valuable. As has been suggested in places, maintaining a coarse-grained approach to varying agential capacities could be instrumentally indispensible to sustaining a community in which all are treated with dignity (Carter 2011), and for avoiding the sorts of subclassifications and discriminations that can threaten a common citizenship. It is arguable that a legally sanctioned threshold beyond which personhood status is complete and equal, regardless of variable individual capacities, is a necessary condition of the valuable sorts of social relations in which the participants treat one another with equal dignity and do not unjustly subordinate certain groups.

If this is correct and if there are, in fact, compelling moral and pragmatic reasons for the law to settle on an absolute threshold for personhood status, the only questions remaining are where the acceptable range of answers lies, and what, within that range, would count as a good reason to draw the absolute dividing line at one particular point rather than another. On this thinking, a boundary line will be unacceptable if there is a decisive reason *against* stipulating the threshold there. This would be true if a threshold failed to capture clear cases of persons, or if it extended full moral protection to nonpersons at the significant expense of full rights-holders. Crucially, though, the fact that a legal threshold is arbitrary in the sorites sense – that is, is nonarbitrarily distinguishable from its immediately neighboring points – *cannot* count as a reason against a suggested threshold, given that the need for clear stipulation is part of the justification for stipulating a threshold to begin with. Consequently, the fact that no principled moral distinction can be found between full-term fetuses and neonates would not count as a reason against stipulating the threshold at birth, assuming that birth was still within the range of acceptable answers. Likewise, should the law, for the sake of clarity, set the limit at 25 weeks' gestation, then the fact that there is no transformative change between 25 weeks and 24.5 weeks is no reason to move the threshold earlier, assuming that 25 weeks is still a reasonable place to draw the legal line. For the kind of arbitrariness implicated here is only that which goes along with stipulation at any point.

In response to this, it might be objected that deciding a personhood threshold by decision or stipulation, informed in part by what is pragmatically desirable or appropriate, effectively claims that there is no real or right answer to the question when personhood obtains. Yet this sounds far too relativistic. If there is no right answer whatsoever, it follows that it is perfectly justifiable to set the threshold at five or ten years old, if only there were good pragmatic reason to do so. And that cannot be right.

But this objection fails to appreciate the particular nature of the stipulation issue and also appears to smuggle in the punctualist view about the beginning of personhood. I am presuming here that there is a period of human development during which personhood vaguely materializes, and that there is no precise moment during that development which corresponds with the sudden onset of personhood. Given that this is the case, I have suggested that there is a practical and moral necessity for the law to stipulate a threshold within the acceptable range that is as specific as possible, while still capable of being followed. But none of this implies that there is simply no truth of the matter whatsoever about when persons begin, only considerations of convenience; that any answer is as good as any other; or that the question about the beginning of personhood is ungoverned by rules. Placing the threshold in one place or another can still be patently erroneous in light of what we take the constitutive features of personhood to be. For example, if we are committed to the view that personhood inheres in the psychological capacities distinctive of mature humans, it will be plainly unreasonable to identify the legal threshold in early pregnancy, when no cognition of any kind is possible, or at ten years of age, when the relevant capacities have already materialized significantly earlier. The fact that there is nothing to choose between multiple adjacent thresholds within the accepted range is part of what necessitates stipulation by law. It is a need borne out of vagueness surrounding the emergence of moral status. But this is not at all the same as total relativism regarding when and how personhood emerges. Likewise, the decision whether to classify Pluto as a planet or a big asteroid might ultimately need to be a matter of stipulation. But this does not mean we might as well call a small piece of space debris a planet or Earth a big asteroid.

The Virtues of Birth

I have contended that there are sound reasons for the law to stipulate an absolute threshold of personhood within what is thought to be the margin of acceptable benchmarks. Still, it might be asked what there is to recommend birth in particular. Why place the absolute threshold there, and not a little earlier, or, indeed, later? The justification for stipulation does not point exclusively and directly to birth. The concerns about clarity and consistency under the law would be equally met by a law that picked out 25 weeks' gestation, or 2 weeks post-birth, as the absolute minimum. So too would be the moral and political necessity for regarding all human beings past a qualifying threshold as equal in respect of their personhood.

Thus the question remains: why birth? Pursuant to the familiar argument about the moral insignificance of birth, it might again be pointed out that neonates do not exit the womb suddenly endowed with the sophisticated cognitive capacities that are germane to our concept of a person. Since these only develop gradually throughout maturation after birth, it might be doubted that birth even falls within the margin of defensible legal thresholds. On a capacities-based account of personhood's constitutive conditions, it could be argued that birth in fact falls firmly outside that range. Between late gestation and birth, moreover, it is claimed that the early human being does not undergo any clearly significant change in its intrinsic nature, such as would mark it out as an obvious or natural point to draw the line.

But someone would be mistaken to claim that there are absolutely no significant changes that take place during birth. Early human beings in fact undergo extremely dramatic biological and physiological changes in the birth process itself to prepare them for survival in the extrauterine environment. These include numerous biological adaptions, such as changes in the circulatory system and the clearing of fluid from the lungs, which enables the newborn to breathe in air for the first time. Surges of hormones are released to regulate temperature outside the womb, new enzymes are activated, and the digestive system undergoes considerable adaptations. Neonatologists Noah Hillman et al. describe the transition from intrauterine to extrauterine life as "the most complex adaptation that occurs in human experience" (2012).

Birth also triggers a number of dramatic behavioral state changes, including crying for the first time, heightened wakefulness, and much increased responsiveness to external stimuli such as noise, light, and touch (Littleton and Engebretson 2005, 757). Some experiments have documented the capacity for neonates to imitate other people's facial expressions as early as 42 minutes after birth.[21] Challenging the view that birth changes only the "spatial position" of the new human being, Jose Bermudez describes a series of experiments revealing that the ability to imitate facial expressions such as tongue protrusion develops extremely quickly after birth, at an average age of 32 hours, and a lowest recorded limit of only 42 minutes post-birth. Bermudez argues that the capacity for facial imitation requires at least a primitive understanding of the difference between self and other, a rudimentary form of self-consciousness that full-term fetuses do not possess.

Some psychologists have even argued that entry into the extra-uterine world is a condition for the development of subjective conscious awareness. Psychologist and pain specialist Stuart Derbyshire has suggested that the mass of mental content to which the neonate is immediately exposed on exiting the womb – the sights, sounds, smells, and tastes of the world – are in fact essential components for developing conscious experience, memory, and emotion (2006). These stimuli, Derbyshire has suggested, form the basic material for conscious thought and experience – they are, in other words, the objects of conscious life to which the new human being must be exposed before it can develop sensory reaction and a sense of itself as opposed to the rest of the world. In particular, Derbyshire suggests, young infants begin to develop representational memory (what he calls the "building blocks of consciousness") through being presented with a wealth of content, enabling them to "tag" as "something" "all the objects, emotions, and sensations that appear or are felt" (2006, 911). Thus it is that the newborn's mental state changes

21 Bermudez, J. L. (1996), The Moral Significance of Birth, *Ethics, 106*, 378, 398. See also Meltzoff, A. N., and Moore, M. K. (1977), Imitation of Facial and Manual Gestures by Human Neonates, *Science, 198*, 75, and Meltzoff, A. N., and Moore, M. K. (1983), Newborn Infants Imitate Adult Facial Gestures, *Child Development, 54*, 702. See also Burin, A. K. (2014), Beyond Pragmatism: Defending the Bright-Line of Birth, *Medical Law Review, 22*, 494, 500–504.

immediately on birth, entering a period of intensely heightened alertness, contrastable with the more sedate mental states of fetuses at the same or later gestational age. He writes:

> Before infants can think about objects or events, or experience sensations and emotion, the contents of thought must have an independent existence in their mind. This is something that is achieved through continued brain development in conjunction with discoveries made in action and in patterns of mutual adjustment and interactions with a caregiver ...
>
> When a primary caregiver points to a spot on the body and asks "does that hurt?" he or she is providing content and enabling an internal discrimination and with it experience. This type of interaction provides content and symbols that allow infants to locate and anchor emotions and sensations. It is in this way that infants can arrive at a particular state of being in their own mind.
>
> (2006, 911)

Birth also brings about the obvious radical changes in a human being's physical and social situation that are entailed by its separation from the pregnant woman. Individually and separately embodied in the world for the first time, the neonate no longer draws its basic life support from the pregnant woman and depends on her for survival. This separate embodiment also affects the relations between the neonate and other people besides its biological mother. Its presence in the world is no longer mediated through the body of the pregnant woman, and so too its opportunities for inclusion in the world of others. Once born, other people may nurture and respond to the new human being as an individual in its own right, no longer restricted to access only through the pregnant woman's body. This separate embodiment enables the neonate to be drawn into the social world of others in ways previously not possible – to be touched, fed, spoken to, and heard; in short, to be treated as a member of the social community in ways that are precluded by its social estrangement when enclosed in the womb.

Birth is therefore far more than a mere matter of location. Still, it will be objected that none of these changes is an *intrinsic* change, meaning the sort of change that makes all the difference between the possession of personhood and its absence. Neonates do not exit the womb immediately self-aware, rational, communicative, and so on. Once we have rejected the view that I call "punctualism," however, it should be clear that we ought not to expect a legal threshold of personhood to trace a single moment of complete transformative change. Rather than searching for a precise point that corresponds with the beginning of personhood, the law need only look for a reasonable place to set an absolute boundary line, reasonable in the sense that it is within the range of reasonable limits and bears out the legal virtues of clarity, predictability, and transparency.

On these counts, I think there is much to recommend birth over closely neighboring thresholds. Birth has a high visibility and unmistakability that cater well to the need for clarity and consistency in the law. The birth event is utterly transparent and undeniable, and does not blend as seamlessly into earlier and later phases of development as do other benchmarks before and after birth. This means that there is no scope for uncertainty or mistake about whether the pertinent threshold has indeed been crossed, lending birth a practical workability that other thresholds may lack. Birth also has a universal social salience that makes it especially suitable as a legal boundary line. The fact of having been born has, in almost every society, enormous cultural implications regardless of the law. This again might be thought to render the birth threshold uniquely appropriate within the range of acceptable legal borderlines, since it mirrors the marker of unequivocal social personhood and leaves even less room for ambiguity or ignorance.

Finally, I have conceded that birth does not amount to a transformative moment in which the moral status of the early human being is radically altered, although I have argued that no moment of the kind in fact exists in any event. Still, birth does mark the beginning of many of the processes and conditions required for the progressive development of capacities salient to moral status. As is outlined above, birth is an event that places the new human being in the necessary context for the development of conscious awareness and the higher forms of self-consciousness typical of mature human beings. On emerging into the world, the new human being is confronted with the wealth of stimuli and content through which it will experience sensation and about which it will gradually develop conscious thought, the basis of all higher forms of cognition. Although this new context is not itself transformative of intrinsic moral status, it is an essential precondition for personhood's constitutive features, and as such, lends the birth event even greater meaning. To clarify, it cannot count against the birth threshold that it is comprised of numerous small increments, since, as we now know, this is true of all thresholds. However, no threshold in late gestation or early infancy corresponds with such a discrete and naturally consequential event in the lives of early human beings.

Late Abortion

To recap once more, I have suggested that there is genuine vagueness surrounding the beginning of personhood in human beings, and that persons do not begin instantly and completely on a sharp borderline as (what I have termed) the "punctualist" view suggests. Nevertheless, there are vitally important reasons for the law to settle on a clear and absolute benchmark, and the recognition of these reasons does not in any way plunge us into relativism about when persons begin. There remain clear conceptual constraints on what sorts of creatures can and cannot be persons, and those constraints will inform the margins within which it is reasonable to stipulate the minimum threshold. Finally, I suggested that, assuming that it is within this reasonable margin, there is much to recommend birth as the threshold of qualification for personhood.

What are the implications of these arguments for abortion permissions? The prima facie conclusion is simply that the termination of human life will be justifiable before birth but not afterward, since we are taking possession of personhood to track the fundamental right to life. Yet this will still be disconcerting for many. Does it entail that abortion is defensible for absolutely any reason, including in late gestation, all the way up to birth?

Especially given that I have not contended that birth corresponds with a dramatic metaphysical leap into full moral status, it may be somewhat difficult to accept that fetuses are owed next to no moral protection immediately before birth yet could become full rights-holders immediately afterward. This conclusion cuts against the very prevalent notion that abortion of fetuses late in gestation is a more morally sobering affair than those carried out earlier in pregnancy, and ought to be subject to more stringent conditions. Even those who are generally supportive of abortion rights often express a certain amount of disquiet about the practice of "late" abortion, and especially at the prospect that developed fetuses may have their lives terminated for what are deemed to be insufficiently weighty reasons, such as that a woman has simply changed her mind about becoming a mother.

Late abortion is, we then might say, a hard case for proponents of abortion rights. The resemblance between late fetuses and neonates is still remarkably close, despite the physiological changes that birth occasions. Such human beings can be little more than a hair's breadth away from babies whose vulnerabilities are regarded as so important and move us to care for them. It strikes us as somewhat incongruous, then, that their lives should be so readily dispensable only weeks, or, potentially, moments, earlier. The particular methods employed in late-term abortion procedures can feed into this sense of unease. Abortive methods that proceed by attacking the body of the fetus either prior to or during its extraction are regarded as particularly horrifying and have led some to raise concerns about the possibility of fetal pain. Concerns of this kind largely motivated the US Congress's decision to pass the Partial-Birth Abortion Ban Act of 2003, which prohibited almost exclusively a particularly controversial method of late abortion.

An account that claims fetuses are not worthy of moral protection even late in gestation will be problematic insofar as it fails to reflect the widely held judgment that late abortion, even if it is not homicide, is far more grave than abortion in early pregnancy, involving the loss of something of great value, and to be avoided in all but the most dire circumstances.

There is little space remaining to discuss the problem of late abortion thoroughly, so I will make just a few points about how we can approach that issue on the theory I sketched out. First, there is no logical tension between stipulating the absolute beginning of personhood at birth while still affording some measure of protection to late fetuses, including restrictions on abortion. There may be good reason to accord a great deal of moral respect to human beings late in gestation, even if birth is a more suitable point at which to stipulate the beginning of personhood, with its entire package of normative and legal implications. Two questions arise here, however. First, how can adverse reactions to late abortion be made intelligible on a capacities-based view of moral status? Developed fetuses may be chronologically closer to becoming persons than early ones, but they do not seem to embody the constitutive properties of personhood very much more, if at all. Second, if we are to assume that late-gestated fetuses enjoy a significant degree of moral status, what constraints on abortion rights does this suggest, given that they still do not enjoy the status of persons, and, bearing in mind what was discussed in Section 1.2, given the potentially high costs of unwanted pregnancy for women?

One might think that the avoidance of fetal pain is a serious moral consideration in abortion regardless of personhood status. We have general reason to avoid inflicting serious pain on other creatures, human or nonhuman, without just cause. The capacity of fetuses to feel pain is in fact a fairly controversial matter. Contrary to the congressional findings cited in the Partial-Birth Abortion Ban Act, medical and scientific opinion is divided on the question, with some psychologists claiming that subjective pain experience is distinct from purely physical responses to stimuli, such as flinching and the release of stress hormones, and is not possible in the absence of self-consciousness (Derbyshire 2006). However, it might be questioned whether pain capacity, in and of itself, explains common aversion to late abortion. If that were so, the objection would arguably be neutralized by the enactment of laws that require the administration of fetal anesthesia prior to abortion. Yet I doubt that measures of this kind would go very far toward placating reservations about late abortion.

Late abortion is especially troubling to many because developed fetuses so closely resemble babies. They share a huge amount of the embodiment of born human beings, and, indeed, of our own embodiment. As I argued in Section 1.4, the constitutive properties of personhood do not exhaust the considerations relevant to according moral respect to other creatures. The violent destruction of beings that possess so much human embodiment – a mode of embodiment shared with person-types – may be unsettling not only because it contravenes their interests, but because it manifests serious disrespect for the human form, which has significant meaning in being the requisite physical substratum for persons as we know them. Once appreciating this, we might understand why late abortion is unsettling irrespective of the question of fetal pain. Late abortion can involve the sort of attack on the body of a fetus that, if directed at a baby, would be deeply disturbing. Given the anatomical closeness of the two, one could suggest that our moral sensibilities are appropriately affected by the destruction of pre-born human beings, which share so much of an infant's form and vulnerabilities. The point here is not that late-term abortion merely *looks* distasteful, but that the knee-jerk aversion to it could be part and parcel of maintaining appropriate moral respect for the human form as such.

What all of this means for the right to abortion late in pregnancy is not entirely straightforward, though. When framing legal abortion permissions there are always multiple considerations to take into account, including efficacy and possible counterproductivity of restrictions. If a legal system does not equate late abortion with homicide, these considerations will be operative. The importance of demonstrating respect for human embodiment as such might well support limitations on nonchalant or frivolous terminations of developed fetuses. But these are not the sort of terminations that the law is typically needed to deter; late abortion is a process hardly ever undertaken for trivial considerations. The fact that women on the whole appreciate and respond to the strong reasons against late abortion is evidenced by the comparatively low rates of abortion in the second and third trimesters (British Pregnancy Advisory Service 2015). The effects of this broad self-censure must be weighed in the balance, along with the potential harms of restriction or prohibition. These may include a broad chilling effect on late abortion which could hamper the abortion right even in obviously justifiable cases, such as abortion for fatal fetal abnormality or where a woman's health or life is seriously put at risk by the pregnancy.

2 Abortion as Human Rights Violation

Christopher Kaczor

Everyone capable of reading this book has a view about abortion already. Some readers are strongly pro-choice, others are strongly pro-life, and others are somewhere in between. Why bother talking about this topic when every reader already has likely well-formed fundamental beliefs about the topic?

Whatever view one has on this difficult issue, it is always possible to understand one's own view or someone else's view better. Mutual understanding helps create a more civil, more respectful, and more rational society. My goal is to help readers of all perspectives to better understand *why* people hold the pro-life view. What reasons can be put forward in its favor? What are some of the strongest objections against this view? What are the alternatives? Increased mutual understanding is a goal worth pursuing by all people of good will, for all people of good will desire a more civil, more respectful, and more rational society.

So, let us begin with something relatively uncontroversial. If someone were to intentionally kill you right now as you read this book, that person would do something seriously wrong. If other people have a duty not to intentionally kill you, then you have a right to life. Most people also believe in equal rights, so that what holds true for you also is true for other human beings like you.

When did your right to life begin? You had it yesterday, and the day before that, and the year before that. But when did it begin?

The answer to this question plays an important role in discussions about abortion. We will see in the course of this chapter various answers to this question. Perhaps you began to have a right to live when you began to value your own life, or when you were born, or when you first had any desire in utero, or when you became viable, or even earlier when twinning became impossible.

The pro-life view holds that *all* human beings – regardless of race, religion, age, disability, or birth – have the same fundamental dignity from which arise basic, equal rights. On this view, your right to life began when you began, and you continue to enjoy basic rights as long as you exist. To intentionally kill you, therefore, is ethically wrong today, it would have been wrong yesterday, and all the way back to when you first began to exist.

What is meant by "abortion rights"? Rights are often distinguished into legal rights and moral rights. Abortion rights could be understood as the claim that getting or doing an abortion is morally permissible (contrary to no ethical duty) or is legally permissible (contrary to no law). The law on abortion throughout most of the Western world permits abortion early in pregnancy. In some countries, such as the United States, abortion is legally permitted all the way through pregnancy to birth for any reason. There is no debate about whether or not there is a legal right to abortion in these jurisdictions, although there is debate about whether there should be a legal right to abortion. Obviously, the legality of a practice does not entail its ethical permissibility. Slavery was legal throughout most of human history, but slavery was always ethically wrong.

This book focuses primarily on the question of abortion as an ethical issue or a moral right. I hope to help the reader to better understand why some people hold that (almost) all abortions are ethically impermissible. On this view, there is no moral right to an abortion in the vast majority of cases. Whether or not abortion should also be a legal right is not the main focus of this work, though the discussion will touch on legal issues. So, unless the context clearly indicates otherwise, I will be addressing abortion as an ethical rather than legal issue. Of course, the ethical conclusions a person draws about abortion often also have legal implications, supporting or calling into question legalized abortion.

In this work, a man is presenting the pro-life side of the debate and a woman is taking the other side. What right do men have to speak about an issue that is a woman's issue? Obviously, abortion affects women who seek or get abortions in ways that abortion does not affect men. Does it follow that men should remain silent on the issue of abortion?

The ad hominem fallacy seeks to discredit a view because of the identity of the person who advocates the view, and to claim that men have no right to speak about the abortion issue exemplifies the ad hominem fallacy. The view that women alone should address the issue of abortion also begs the fundamental questions at issue. Abortion does not concern women alone – unless one presupposes that the human being in utero does not have a right to live. If there are at least two persons involved in abortion, rather than just one, then abortion does not concern women alone but also a human being prior to birth. In fact, abortion also affects men who cause pregnancy, taxpayers who fund it, social service programs who depend on future workers, and the society at large. To say women alone have a right to discuss abortion is like claiming that men alone have a right to discuss mandatory drafting of men for military service or funding for prostate research. Indeed, if we all have a right to freedom of speech, then we all have a right to talk about any issue we would like.

Abortion is an issue of justice that concerns all people of good will. If the pro-choice side is correct, it is unjust to restrict or inhibit those who want to get abortions. If the pro-life side is correct, abortion itself is an injustice to the human being prior to birth, violating the right to life. Anyone who cares about creating a more just world should care about the issue of abortion.

Although abortion is a matter of justice, a certain danger can arise in discussing the issue. If the pro-choice side is correct, the danger arises that advocates for this position might depict those who have a different view as unjust, bad people since they wish to stop women from exercising their fundamental right to get an abortion. On the other hand, if the pro-life side is correct, the danger arises that advocates for this position might depict pro-choice advocates as unjust, bad people since they defend actions that violate the fundamental rights of human beings prior to birth. I think both views are mistaken.

We must distinguish between the objective morality of an action and the subjective culpability of the agent. Conscientious, good people can do things which – objectively speaking – are seriously wrong, and yet they do so without full knowledge and consent to their action. So, even if every woman has a moral right to an abortion, it could turn out that those who oppose this right are honestly and inculpably mistaken in their view that abortion is wrong. Even if every fetal human being has a right to life, it could turn out that those who get abortions or support abortion are honestly and inculpably mistaken in their view that abortion is ethically permissible. I believe that we should not make judgments about agents since we do not, in general, know what was in the mind and heart of any particular agent, and so we cannot know whether an agent is fully responsible for the action performed. So, unless otherwise noted, my remarks exclusively address the objective morality of the action of abortion. I am not addressing the subjective culpability of those who get abortions or who oppose abortions, since I believe no one can (or should) judge these people.

One of the challenges of discussing any difficult topic is the choice of words to use in the discussion. The choice of one set of terms in which to conduct the discussion biases the conversation in one way or another. I agree with former President Barack Obama, who said:

> I do not suggest that the debate surrounding abortion can or should go away ... Each side will continue to make its case to the public with passion and conviction. But surely we can do so without reducing those with differing views to caricature. Open hearts. Open minds. Fair-minded words.
>
> (Obama 2009)

Although the various sides in this discussion (and there are more than two) may not eventually reach complete agreement with each other, what is certainly possible is a greater understanding of various positions taken in the discussion as well as greater clarity about how precisely these sides differ from one another.

This process is aided by the use of fair-minded words and the avoidance of question-begging epithets, such as "pro-abortion," "anti-choice," "unborn child" and "fetus." At the "Open Hearts, Open Minds, Fair Minded Words" conference inspired by President Obama and held at Princeton University, John Finnis said:

> About the moral status of the phrase "the fetus," I will just say this. As used in the conference program and website, which are not medical contexts, it is offensive, dehumanizing, prejudicial, manipulative. Used in this context, exclusively and in preference to the alternatives, it is an F-word, to go with the J-word, and other such words we know of, which have or had an acceptable meaning in a proper context but became in wider use the symbol of subjection to the prejudices and preferences of the more powerful. It's not a fair word, and it does not suggest an open heart.
>
> (Finnis 2010)

The term "fetus" is a medically accurate term just as is the corresponding term "gravida" for the pregnant woman. But outside of medical contexts, no one uses the term "gravida" in speaking of expectant mothers. So too, outside of medical contexts (and the justification of abortion), people talk about the "baby shower" not a "fetus shower" or ask pregnant women, "When is your baby due?" not "When is your fetus due?"

So, how then shall we speak about the being who is called "fetus" by some and "unborn child" by others? Until more is said about the moral status of this creature, it is perhaps best to use words that are scientifically accurate but also not dehumanizing, such as prenatal human beings, human being in utero, or fetal human being.

But these terms too, it might be said, are question begging, since part of the debate surrounding abortion is whether or not the creature in question is a human being, or for that matter, is even alive. Before we can answer questions about the ethics of abortion, we must first explore (rather than dogmatically assert answers to) the questions, "When does life begin?" and "When does a human being begin?"

Although these questions are commonly posed in nonscholarly debates about abortion, sophisticated defenders of abortion as well as critics both generally presuppose the same answers to these questions. Both the life and the humanity (in the genetic sense of belonging to the species *Homo sapiens*) is conceded by informed defenders of abortion, such as Peter Singer, who writes:

> It is possible to give "human being" a precise meaning. We can use it as equivalent to "member of the species *Homo sapiens*." Whether a being is a member of a given species is something that can be determined scientifically, by an examination of the nature of the chromosomes in the cells of living organisms. In this sense, there is no doubt that from the first moments of its existence an embryo conceived from human sperm and eggs is a human being.
>
> (Singer 2000, 127)

Is this individual being a living being? The scientific evidence is overwhelming and conclusive that a human fetus is a *living* organism growing proportionately, assimilating nutrients, maintaining homeostasis, and developing toward maturity. The human fetus is a being that can die, and only a living being can die.

Moreover, the prenatal human being is a clearly human being (member of the species *Homo sapiens*), arising from human parents, having a human trajectory of growth, and having a human heart, human blood, and other human organs typical of the human species. In terms of biological classification, the offspring of two human beings is never a dolphin, an orangutan, a cat, a dog, or any other kind of creature other than a human being. Among informed participants, the debate about abortion is not about "when life starts" or "whether the fetus is human." Rather, the debate focuses on whether the prenatal human being has a right to live, and if so, whether the fetal right to live means that abortion is not ethically permissible.

2.1 Does a Human Being Gain the Right to Live after He or She Is Born?

The most famous recent article about abortion is Alberto Giubilini and Francesca Minerva's "After-Birth Abortion: Why Should the Baby Live?" (2013). Following a standard line of argument, the authors distinguish between a "person" and a "human being" as terms with a technical sense in this discussion. A person is a being with moral worth, with basic rights, with equal status in the moral community. A human being is a member of the species *Homo sapiens*, a biological category, an organism of the same species as Hillary Clinton.

Simply to be a human being is not, on their view, sufficient for having a right to life, as acceptance of embryonic research, abortion prior to birth, and capital punishment indicate. To have the right to live, what counts is not being a *human being* but being a *person*.

Giubilini and Minerva point out that the same conditions that advocates of abortion say justify abortion may also exist after birth. Before birth, someone may seek an abortion because of poverty, but loss of job or dramatic reversal of economic fortune may also take place after birth. Abortions may be sought because the man who impregnated the woman is a cad. But after a baby is born, a woman may discover that the father is cheating on her or otherwise is an unfit partner. Abortion may be sought because of fetal anomaly, but some infants become handicapped in the process of being born, while the handicap of others is discovered only after birth. Giubilini and Minerva suggest that, "when circumstances occur after birth such that they would have justified abortion, what we call after-birth abortion should be permissible" (Giubilini and Minerva 2013, 2). Killing newborn human beings is permissible whenever abortion would be permissible. Their argument is that there are no morally significant differences between a newborn and a fetal human being in utero, neither one is a "person" in the moral sense of the term. So, if abortion is ethically permissible, then post-birth abortion is also ethically permissible.

Giubilini and Minerva hold, "Both a fetus and a newborn certainly are human beings and potential persons, but neither is a 'person' in the sense of 'subject of a moral right to life'" (2013, 2). What then is a person? "We take 'person' to mean an individual who is capable of attributing to her own existence some (at least) basic value such that being deprived of this existence represents a loss to her" (2013, 2). Now a newborn baby does not know that he or she exists, and so cannot attribute value to his or her existence. If a person does not exist even after birth, a fortiori there is no person at any time during gestation. Yes, it is true that the newborn is a potential person, that is, a being with the intrinsic orientation to develop into a person who values her own existence just as we do. But a potential person does not have the rights of an actual person, even as a potential president does not have the rights of an actual president.

But, they imagine someone objecting, isn't a newborn (or a human fetus) harmed by being destroyed and losing life? They reply that "it makes no sense to say that someone is harmed by being prevented from becoming an actual person. The reason is that, by virtue of our definition of the concept of 'harm' in the previous section, in order for a harm to occur, it is necessary that someone is in the condition of experiencing that harm" or being capable of experiencing the harm. They continue:

> So, if you ask one of us if we would have been harmed, had our parents decided to kill us when we were fetuses or newborns, our answer is "no," because they would have harmed someone who does not exist (the "us" whom you are asking the question), which means no one. And if no one is harmed, then no harm occurred.
>
> (2013, 3)

The interests of actual people (parents, family, society) override the nonexistent interests of potential people (newborns, prenatal human beings). The financial expense and personal burden of infants can detrimentally affect the interests of actual people. So, killing a newborn is morally permissible. "In these cases, since non-persons have no moral rights to life, there are no reasons for banning after-birth abortions" (2013, 3). Some people may wish to place unwanted infants in families by adoption, just as some women with unwanted pregnancies arrange to do, but this choice may be difficult or unwanted and should not abolish the choice of ending the life of the unwanted infant.

Giubilini and Minerva's argument can now be summarized. If we accept the principle that abortion is ethically permissible in certain social, economic, or psychological circumstances, then consistency demands that in similar circumstances post-birth abortion also be accepted. The same reasons that justify abortion of the human being prior to birth also justify killing a newborn after birth. Since in neither case does killing destroy a "person," both pre-birth and post-birth abortion is ethically acceptable and should also be legally acceptable.

Giubilini and Minerva decline to state at what moment after-birth abortion becomes ethically wrong. But psychologists indicate that self-awareness in children typically begins around two years of age (Rochat 2003, 718). Since you cannot *value* your own existence until you are *aware* that you exist, if these psychologists are correct, then post-birth abortion is permissible until around two years of age. Until human beings become aware of their own existence, they cannot take an *interest* in their continued existence. So, if Giubilini and Minerva's account is correct, infanticide is ethically permissible and should also be legally permitted until the child is around two years old (unless the child is intellectually disabled, in which case the right to live would arise even later or never arise at all in cases of severe intellectual disability).

If their conclusion is unacceptable, then something is wrong with Giubilini and Minerva's argument. Indeed, I believe their argument is riddled with questionable assumptions and false assertions. Giubilini and Minerva assume that killing a human being is wrong because the human being *desires, takes an interest in,* or *values* their continued existence and not being killed. But suicidal human beings (such as those who are deeply depressed, addicted to drugs, or brainwashed cult followers) do not desire their continued existence, but it would still be wrong to kill them.

In fact, we desire things (like continued living) because we (rightly or wrongly) think that such things are good. So, what is relevant in determining whether someone has been wronged is not simply whether they were deprived of something they *desired* but also whether they were deprived of something *good*. After all, no one thinks it is wrong to deprive the suicide bomber of the explosive vest he desires in order to kill judge, jury, and everyone else in a courtroom. What we desire can be insane, tyrannical, unjust, uninformed, sexist, or racist. What is relevant ethically is not undermining someone's desires but undermining someone's good.

Moreover, Giubilini and Minerva assume "harm" is possible only if someone *experiences* (or is capable of experiencing) it as a harm. However, the lobotomy of a normal person may so damage the brain that the person does not experience the loss of brain power as a harm. Likewise, someone rendered permanently unconscious is harmed, but does not experience her condition as a harm and is not capable of experiencing her condition as a harm. Imagine a killing that is totally unexpected and instantaneous, like getting incinerated in a surprise nuclear blast by terrorists. In this kind of killing, unless we assume that people consciously survive their own deaths (which Giubilini and Minerva surely reject), the victims do not *experience* their death as harm, since they do not *experience* anything at or after death. So mass murder (as long as it is unanticipated and instantaneous) does not wrong the victims killed.

Giubilini and Minerva assume that no one has been *wronged* if no one has been *harmed*. This assumption is false because a wrong can be done even if no one is harmed. A failed assassination attempt may harm no one, but the target is wronged nonetheless. Malicious slander of someone's reputation (even if no one believes it) wrongs the person slandered.

Another questionable assumption of Giubilini and Minerva's view is its implicit body–self dualism. On their view, "you" are your aims, desires, awareness. Your body (the organism that was born and that your mother had in her womb) is not you. A human organism – not you – was born, and then months later "you" began to exist, when your thoughts, desires, and self-awareness began. If this view were true, you would not have a birthday, since you actually arose around two years after the human organism that you make use of was born.

The problematic nature of body–self dualism is illustrated by considering the case of twin three-year-old girls. Let's call them Sophia and Madison. The girls survive a car crash, but both have memory loss. Sophia will eventually recover most of her memories, but Madison will never recover hers. If the right to live depends on psychological connections, to kill Sophia is seriously wrong, but to kill Madison is not. The identical twins have radically different moral statuses because one will recover a few memories and the other will not. This is hard to believe. Moreover, the car accident both destroyed a person (Madison before her crash) and led to the creation of a new person (Madison after her crash). This is very hard to believe. It is much easier to believe that there is just one individual person (Madison) who survived her crash but was injured as a result of her crash. Indeed, this is what everyone not in the grip of a theory called body–self dualism believes.

If we accept body–self dualism, then one individual human being may in fact be several persons. Consider someone who suffers from dissociative identity disorder, formerly called multiple personality disorder. One individual human being may be both Dr. Jekyll and Mr. Hyde, with two sets of memories, desires, and loci of conscious awareness. Sometimes people suffering from dissociative identity disorder report not just two but sixteen different sets of identities. Each "alter" has his or her own memories, desires, and conscious awareness. If body–self dualism is correct, one human being with dissociative identity disorder is actually sixteen persons, and every person has a right to live. Thus, to kill one human being with dissociative identity disorder is to murder sixteen people. This is implausible.

Let's suppose a psychiatrist invents a breakthrough serum that completely and permanently cures dissociative identity disorder. Within one hour of injection into the back of the head just above the spinal column, the human being who had sixteen different personalities has only one personality. If body–self dualism is correct, administering the injection destroys fifteen persons. It is very hard to believe that the psychiatrist curing multiple personality disorder is not a compassionate healer but rather a mass murderer. (For more challenges to this assumption of Giubilini and Minerva, see Lee and George, *Body–Self Dualism*).

Some defenders of post-birth abortion appeal to John Locke's definition of a person, namely, a being with (1) an awareness of his or her own existence (2) over time and in different places with (3) the capacity to have wants and (4) plans for the future (Singer 1994, 218). A newborn baby (let alone a prenatal human being) does not satisfy these conditions, so post-birth abortion does not destroy anyone with a right to live.

No one disputes that Locke's conditions are *sufficient* for being a person, but why should we think of these conditions as *necessary* for the right to live? Picking out sufficient conditions for personhood is fairly easy. Everyone who can read *Leaves of Grass* or calculate the interior angles of a triangle is a person. But it does not follow that those who cannot appreciate Walt Whitman or Euclid's proofs do not have a right to live.

Why does Locke think of a person in this way? For Locke, on at least one plausible interpretation (Waldron 2002), our rights arise from our duties. According to Locke, we have a duty to obey God, a duty that we cannot discharge if others kill us or interfere with us, so we also have a right to life and liberty. Everyone who has the same capacity to act as a moral agent has equivalent duties to us, and therefore equal rights to us. The theological basis for Locke's view is a basis that I suspect many defenders of abortion (as well as many critics) would not accept.

But even if we were to strip away Locke's theological basis, and redefine Locke's person as a being that can discharge his or her duties (whether or not the moral obligation comes from God), this basis too proves problematic. Although there are a few defenders of post-birth abortion, no one defends the idea that *only* those who can act as moral agents discharging their duties merit respect as persons. If the right to live is enjoyed only by those who can act ethically, then the right to live arises only when a human being can be held morally accountable, namely, at the "age of reason" usually thought to be around seven or eight years of age. So, the basis for Locke's view of personhood is implausible, both as originally formulated theologically and as reformulated nontheologically. Unless we are provided another basis for thinking that all persons must have self-awareness etc., we have no reason for thinking Locke provides the necessary conditions for personhood.

Other aspects of the Lockean definition of a person are also problematic. Is self-awareness really necessary for personhood? *Actual* self-awareness cannot be necessary, unless we suppose that the right to live vanishes and reappears whenever someone loses consciousness in sleep. Nor is the *immediately exercisable* capacity for self-awareness necessary for basic rights, since no one thinks that a normal adult who is heavily sedated may be killed, yet such adults do not have an immediately exercisable capacity for self-awareness. Maybe the "mental hardware" or *current neural architecture* (or something functionally equivalent) that enables self-awareness (Savulescu 2002) is what is necessary for the right to live. But consider someone who has been in a car accident with temporary swelling of the brain that makes self-awareness temporarily impossible. The current neural architecture of such a swollen brain is incapable of self-awareness, but it is difficult to believe that such people in temporary comas have lost their right to live.

One proposed solution to the temporary coma case is to think of the right to live as a right that once attained with initial consciousness is retained for the rest of the being's life. However, this would mean that a human being in a permanent coma, a persistent vegetative state, maintains a right to live, which many defenders of abortion do not believe. Moreover, it is unclear why someone who attained self-awareness briefly and then lost it merits more protection than someone just about to attain self-awareness and who will have it for a long life. Why should an individual who had self-awareness once and never will again deserve more protection than another individual who will (if not killed) enjoy a full lifetime of self-awareness?

2.2   Does the Right to Live Begin at Birth?

Some people distinguish human beings who are not persons from human beings who are persons by means of birth. Prior to birth, even just moments before, the full-term human fetus does not have the right to live. After birth, even just moments after, the newborn baby has a right to live. Judith Jarvis Thomson in the violinist argument conceded that the right to life begins prior to birth but held that abortion is justified anyway. Arguments of this type will be explored later in this chapter.

In this section, however, I'd like to consider the view that birth itself confers the right to life on the human being. On this view, abortion is ethically permitted but infanticide or post-birth abortion is ethically forbidden. The question arises why should birth be the "magic moment" giving rise to the right to life.

Does birth itself transform an individual's moral status, granting the individual a right to live? Many animals, including rats and vipers, are born. Unless we hold that rats and vipers have a right to live, then birth itself is not sufficient to grant the right to live. Perhaps both being born and being a human being are necessary in order to have a right to live. This view is incompatible with standard defenses of abortion and infanticide that assert that being a human being is merely a biological category that is ethically irrelevant for determinations of an individual's moral status. Nor is "being born" necessary to have a right to live. Imagine creatures like us in every way save that they are hatched from eggs. Such creatures, though not born, would be every bit as much persons as we are. The right to life of an individual does not depend on whether the individual is born, hatched, or for that matter pops into existence full grown as the ancient legend of Athena springing from the head of Zeus.

It could be that being inside someone else's body is the reason that the human being has no right to life and that being outside someone's body grants the right to live. But why should this be true? Defenders of abortion typically do not think that human beings conceived outside the womb in vitro have a right to live, so simply being human and being outside the womb doesn't grant a right to life. If you were (without your consent) placed within someone else's body or on someone else's property, you would not simply by your location lose your right to live. Let's say a normal adult human being, let's call her Lisa, is (somehow) inside another person's body. Would this fact of itself mean that Lisa is not a person? Certainly, having parts of herself – let's say, Lisa's hands are within the body cavity of a person during surgery – would not render her a nonperson. In the movie *Honey I Shrunk the Kids*, persons are shrunk down to tiny size and are unknowingly placed into the mouth of a regular-sized person along with a bite of breakfast cereal. It is hard to see why they would lose their rights to life by this unfortunate accident.

In some cases of fetal surgery, a human being in utero is removed from the woman's body for the surgical procedure and then placed back in the woman's body for the rest of pregnancy. Are we to supposed to believe that the human being in this case did not have right to life, then gained a right to life during surgery since he or she was outside the body of the woman, and then he or she lost the right to live again after surgery, only to gain the right to life again if there is another surgery? It is hard to believe the right to life is episodically related to us based on our current location.

And precisely what location is it that gives us a right to live? Did we gain the right when any part of our body exited our mother's body? If half our body is outside our mother, say past our hips, is this sufficient for the right to live? Must our whole body be outside our mother? Would we not yet have a right to live until the umbilical cord that connects us to our mother is clamped?

Unfortunately, such questions are not merely rhetorical. Partial birth abortion, in which a human being is delivered feet first, but the human being's head remains within the mother, remains a question of contention both ethically and legally. Lawrence Tribe defends partial-birth abortion by arguing:

> The proposed statute therefore seeks to make the legality of the physician's conduct in facilitating the woman's exercise of her

reproductive freedom turn not on the viability of the fetus or on its capacity to perceive or on the health of the woman but, strangely, on the physical location of the fetus between the uterus and the vagina at the moment its development within the woman is deliberately halted – as though the fetus that is being aborted were suddenly to acquire the capacity to experience sensations of pain, or were to acquire other traits of personhood, simply by virtue of having been moved from one point to another within the woman's body prior to completion of the abortion procedure, rather than by virtue of its own state of neurological or other development. Evidently unable to identify in any other manner the procedure they wish to outlaw, the statute's authors have thus fastened upon anatomical details that bear no relationship whatsoever even to the concern with fetal dignity or sensation that supposedly animates both the statute's title and its structure.

(Tribe 1997, 1)

There is also no difference in the neurological development or the capacity of experiencing sensations of pain, or any other traits of personhood that emerge in the few moments that separate the partial birth of a human being and the completed birth of a human being. So, if Tribe is correct that the human being lacks a right to life when he or she is half-born, and that location is irrelevant to the moral status of the human being, then not just partial-birth abortion but also after-birth abortion is ethically permissible.

A conventional pro-choice view (as represented by writers such as Mary Anne Warren) defends abortion all the way through the process of completed birth but condemns after-birth abortion. On Warren's view, there is no intrinsic ethically relevant difference between the human being before and after birth. Nevertheless, we should condemn infanticide but defend abortion. A variety of defenses have been offered for condemning post-birth abortion but approving even late-term pre-birth abortion.

According to this conventional view (see Englehardt 1999), we should condemn post-birth abortion in order to promote the virtues of caring for the weak and vulnerable in society. It would also disturb many children to know that their infant brother or sister was killed after birth. At the same time, we should defend pre-birth abortion because without it the convenience of women and their families would be greatly hampered by too many children. Abortion is needed to fight overpopulation, and abortion also helps eliminate genetic diseases discovered in prenatal diagnosis.

The conventional view suffers from inconsistency in that the arguments given to defend prenatal abortion apply also to postnatal abortion and the arguments against post-birth abortion apply also to pre-birth abortion. Yes, abortion can eliminate fetal disability by means of eliminating the fetal patient. But postnatal abortion, the killing of disabled newborns, also eliminates disability by eliminating the newborn patient. Indeed, killing after birth is even more effective in that there is no risk to the mother's physical health whatsoever in this kind of killing and the exact extent of anomalies and disabilities can be determined more accurately after birth than before birth.

Yes, prenatal abortion reduces population, but postnatal abortion can reduce population even more effectively. Imagine two desert islands with stranded collegiate track teams. On Man Island, you have twenty members of the men's track team and just one young female trainer. On Woman Island, like the Island Lemnos in the Greek legend, you have twenty members of women's track team and a lone young male trainer. Assuming everyone is fertile and attempts reproduction, will Woman Island or Man Island have a greater population? Even if the woman on Man Island tries to have as many children as physically possible, it is highly unlikely she could have more than 20 babies over the course of her lifetime. By contrast, the females on Woman Island could have 20 babies born in a single year because the lone man on Woman Island can impregnate all twenty females in one month. The differences between male and female reproductive capacity will lead to fewer children being born on Man Island than on Woman Island. Given these differences in reproductive capacity, reductions in population are more effectively accomplished by the elimination of a greater percentage of females than by elimination of equal numbers of males and females. Reduction in the percentage of females born can be accomplished through sex selection abortion. But in poor areas, where ultrasound is not available, sex selection abortion of females may not be possible. In such circumstances, infanticide of female infants is an effective route to population control. So, if population control justifies prenatal abortion, population control also justifies infanticide, particularly of baby girls.

It is true that pre-birth abortion aids in the convenience of women and their families, but it is also true that post-birth abortion aids the convenience of women and their families. It is only after a baby is born that certain inconveniences arise, such as the need for diapers, for feeding the baby, for strollers, and the baby making noises at inopportune moments. Indeed, only after birth might a baby inconvenience other family members by throwing up, waking up in the middle of the night, and so forth. So, if prenatal abortion is justified because of convenience, and post-birth the baby is in some ways even more inconvenient, then post-birth abortion is justified by the same reasoning.

Likewise, it is true that abortion can eliminate the existence of prenatal human beings with serious genetic defects, but the same justification also applies to babies who are born. In many cases, the process of birth itself leads to serious handicap in the newborn infant. Pre-birth abortion is not able to deal with such cases, but infanticide can make sure that infants with serious handicaps do not continue to exist.

Now let us turn to the reasons given to oppose infanticide. Engelhardt says that we should not kill newborns because there is virtue in caring for the weak and vulnerable among us. But the same reasoning can be applied to pre-birth abortion, since every prenatal human being is weak and vulnerable (indeed, often more weak and vulnerable than a newborn baby). Engelhardt provides no explanation of why virtues of compassion and care for the vulnerable are relevant in the case of human beings after birth but not human beings before birth.

Similarly, Engelhardt invokes the horror that many older children would feel if their younger brother or sister were killed after birth. He is right. But Engelhardt does not explain why the revulsion that many older children feel if their younger brother or sister in utero is killed is not also relevant. Nor is it clear why the feelings of older children in either case are determinative of the ethics of parental action. In many cases, older children are upset by the existence of a new brother or sister, but this does not mean that parents have an obligation to have only one child. Although Engelhardt and Warren hold that killing after birth differs ethically from killing before birth, the arguments given against after-birth abortion apply also to pre-birth abortion and the arguments given in defense of pre-birth abortion apply also to post-birth abortion.

The conventional view defending prenatal abortion and condemning postnatal abortion is inherently unstable. The arguments in favor of prenatal abortion often also apply to infanticide. The arguments against infanticide often apply to abortion. It is more consistent to be opposed to killing both before and after birth or to be in favor of killing both before and after birth. Birth, in other words, is not a magic moment that transforms an individual who can be killed at will into someone like us who has a right to live.

Let us consider one more argument that birth is the magic moment that grants human beings a right not to be intentionally killed. In "The Moral Significance of Birth" (1996), Jose Luis Bermudez acknowledges that there is no intrinsic difference in the capacity of all newborns that distinguishes them from all prenatal humans. But he argues there is a difference in the exercise of a capacity, namely, the exercised capacity for social interaction. Newborn babies can imitate another human being, which indicates a rudimentary distinction between self and other, a rudimentary self-awareness. The exercise of the social capacity for interaction grants the newborn a right to life.

The Exercised Capacity to Imitate account of the right to life faces serious challenges. In fact, some newborns do not exercise any social capacity for imitation. As a newborn baby, Stevie Wonder could not see anyone, so he could not imitate anyone until much later in life. Indeed, an agent could damage the eyes of a baby just after birth before the newborn had a chance to exercise the capacity for imitation, and thereby extend the period in which killing the human being in question is permissible. Moreover, twins in utero exhibit social interaction (Weaver 2013). It is hard to believe that the basic rights of a particular human being depend on whether or not that human being happens to have had a twin brother or sister. Is abortion of twins impermissible but abortion of just one human being permissible? Even if we granted the bizarre conclusion that abortion of twins is wrong but abortion of a singleton is right, the Exercised Capacity to Imitate account does not differentiate all post-natal from all prenatal human beings. So the account given by Bermudez cannot differentiate cases of infanticide from cases of prenatal abortion.

Finally, why should the Exercised Capacity to Imitate grant a being a right to live? The argument given by Bermudez is that imitation requires at least implicit self-awareness, and that self-awareness grants the right to life. I'm skeptical of this conclusion in part because I'm not sure that imitation requires self-awareness of the kind that grants a right to live. Polly the Parrot has an Exercised Capacity to Imitate. A trainer can get her to echo a human being saying, "I love your brown eyes" or "My red, yellow, and blue feathers are lovely." But, despite possessing the Exercised Capacity to Imitate, it is doubtful Polly has self-awareness. Even if Polly did have self-awareness of some rudimentary kind, surely Polly does not have a right to life equal to a newborn, let alone equal to your right to live. The example of Polly the Parrot shows us that the Exercised Capacity to Imitate is not a sufficient condition for being a person. Assuming post-birth abortion isn't permissible, the example of baby Stevie Wonder, who was blind at birth, shows us this capacity is not a necessary condition for being a person.

Maybe the fact that the prenatal human being is within the body of another human being is the fact that allows us to consistently hold that abortion is permissible and infanticide is impermissible. Again, some defenses of abortion hinge on the right of a woman to control her own body, and therefore her right to get an abortion. But this kind of defense of abortion need not (as Judith Jarvis Thomson showed in her violinist argument defending abortion) involve the denial of fetal personhood. I examine these defenses of abortion at the end of this chapter.

2.3   Does the Right to Live Begin during Gestation?

Perhaps the most sophisticated defense of abortion is offered by David Boonin's *A Defense of Abortion* (2003). Boonin not only critiques prominent pro-life positions but also offers a view of his own of when the right to life begins, the Conscious Desires Account. According to Boonin, the right to life of a human being begins when that human being has a present desire for anything whatsoever. The desire to live is not necessary but the desire for anything whatsoever, perhaps to hear something like his or her mother's voice. Any actual desire presupposes what he calls implicit desire. An implicit desire is for all the conditions that must obtain in order to get an explicit desire. So, if I explicitly desire to win an Olympic gold medal in cross country skiing, I implicitly desire that my red blood cells efficiently carry oxygen to my muscles, even if I do not explicitly know that red blood cells efficiently transferring oxygen is necessary for me to win the gold medal. So, once a human being has a desire for anything (including, say, to hear her mother's voice) this explicit desire brings with it an implicit desire for a future of value. No present explicit desire can be satisfied in the future unless the being in question has a future. Moreover, explains Boonin, this implicit desire to live can be merely ideal, rather than actual. The suicidal teenager who has been dumped by her boyfriend may actually desire to die. However, her ideal desire (what she would desire if she were fully informed, not emotionally distraught, and of sound mind) is to live. The implicit, ideal desire may also be dispositional rather than occurrent. An occurrent desire is a desire that is present to the conscious mind; a dispositional desire need not be present to the conscious mind. A hungry football player waiting at McDonald's for a Big Mac has an occurrent desire for a double cheeseburger. The same man has only a dispositional desire not to be attacked by a ninja wielding a samurai sword, since the football player is thinking only about his stomach and not about a possible attack. If the ninja attacks, the player's dispositional desire for safety becomes an occurrent desire for safety.

So, on Boonin's view, when does a human being gain a right to live? When a human being first has any actual desires, a human being gains the right to live because at that point the human being in question has the implicit, ideal, and at least dispositional desire to continue living. And when does this take place? On Boonin's view, the human brain is not sufficiently developed to have desires of any kind (say, to hear mother's voice) until between 25 and 32 weeks after conception (Boonin 2003, 127). Since 99 percent of abortions take place before 25 weeks, no being with a right to life is killed in the vast majority of abortions.

How might a defender of equal rights for all human beings critique this argument? The Conscious Desires Account fails to differentiate, as Boonin hopes it will, abortion from infanticide. Some premature babies are born before 25 weeks and many more are born before 32 weeks. So, if we accept Boonin's account, intentional killing of babies after birth does not violate the right to life of these prematurely born babies.

Moreover, it is unclear whether even full-term infants would have a right to life on the Conscious Desires Account. To desire involves something more than simply to experience enjoyable or painful sensations. To desire is to project out into the future and wish for fulfillment in this future. Desiring involves the exercise of imagination of some good not yet had but possibly to be had in the future. Since we only desire what we take to be in some respect good, desires also involve a judgment that whatever it is that we desire is good in some respect. But it is doubtful that even full-term infants have a sense of time, and so they have no sense of the future. Moreover, newborn babies seem incapable of making any kind of judgment about some state of affairs as good or bad. So, since even healthy newborn babies cannot imagine the future and cannot make judgments, they might enjoy nursing or being cuddled by dad, but they do not (until later) desire to nurse or to be cuddled by dad. If healthy newborn babies have a right to live, then the Conscious Desire Account is mistaken.

Moreover, it is questionable whether desires of any kind are necessary for a right to live. Consider a Buddhist master in the state of nirvana in which (at least according to some) all desires, even the desire to continue in the state of nirvana, are extinguished. It is hard to believe that a Buddhist master in the state of nirvana has no right to live. Perhaps scientists invent a drug, Nirvana Now, which chemically induces the state of being free of desire. Obviously, a person taking this drug maintains equal basic rights with all other persons. Or imagine someone who has a serious brain injury that damages the part of the brain responsible for conscious desires. Is such a person, like us in all ways but one, lacking in a right to live?

Finally, it is unclear on the Conscious Desires Account why persons would have equal rights. The foundation for their rights – having conscious desires – is clearly unequal. Some people greatly desire to keep living so they eat a large bowl of green kale each morning for breakfast, walk an hour a day, and ingest fish oil pills for their heart. Other people would rather smoke two packs of cigarettes, drive drunk, and eat donuts daily even though they know such practices increase the probability of an early death. So if what gives us our rights is radically unequal, namely, our desires, on what basis can we hold that all people have equal rights?

Viability

Another view that the right to live begins during gestation claims that viability is the characteristic that grants the right to live. Viability, as defined by the US Supreme Court, is when a prenatal human can survive outside the uterus with artificial help. The Court in *Roe v. Wade* declared the importance of viability: "With respect to the State's important and legitimate interest in potential life, the 'compelling' point is at viability. This is so because the fetus then presumably has the capability of meaningful life outside the mother's womb" (*Roe v. Wade* 1973). The Court did not hold that abortion was prohibited after viability, but only that the states could, but did not have to, enact some restrictions on abortion after viability, so long as such restrictions did not adversely affect the life or health of the mother. In the companion case to *Roe v. Wade* issued the same day, *Doe v. Bolton* clarified that "health" is understood broadly to include all physical, mental, and emotional factors. So, the possible limitation on abortion that states could enact after viability was rendered in practice no limitation at all. The health of the mother can be construed as including her desire not to be pregnant, so any restriction of abortion that contains a health exception is no restriction at all.

Why does the US Supreme Court consider viability important? Viability is important, the Court declares, because viability is when the fetus has the capability of meaningful life outside the womb. Aside from the addition of the word "meaningful," this justification simply restates the definition of viability. In saying that viability is important because that is when the human fetus is viable, the Court provides no justification for abortion but rather reasons in a circle.

As the US Supreme Court later pointed out in *Planned Parenthood v. Casey* (1992), given technological progress, the importance of viability as expressed in *Roe v. Wade* is on a crash course with itself. The age of viability is a function of our scientific capabilities, and technology continually advances. Right now, scientists are working to create artificial uteruses, highly advanced incubators in which a human embryo could be viable throughout the typical time of gestation. It is hard to believe that defenders of the moral importance of viability would suddenly become pro-life if these scientists successfully created such incubators.

Defenders of abortion and infanticide point out other problems with considering viability as the moment when fetal rights begin. Peter Singer notes that a fetus might be viable if near a hospital, but not viable if far away from a hospital (1993, 102). So the fetal right to life would exist when a woman was at work in a city, and disappear when she went deep into the woods on a camping trip, and then suddenly reappear once back in the city. Michael Tooley (1999) notes that in some cases of conjoined twins, one twin will depend on the other for continued life. Conjoined twins Abby and Brittany Hensel are graduates of Bethel University, and uncontroversially persons. The fact that one twin depends on the other for continued life makes no difference for their basic rights. So, viability – the ability to live independently from other people with or without technological help – is not necessary for personhood.

Quickening/Fetal Movement

Another proposed criterion for dividing those human beings who enjoy basic rights from those human beings who do not enjoy basic rights is quickening, or fetal movement. Quickening is when the expectant mother first feels the movement of the human fetus in her body. Fetal movement itself begins much earlier, but it is only later when this movement is felt by the pregnant woman. Abortion at English Common Law was, at one point, permitted prior to quickening and then forbidden after quickening. Since internally generated movement in location of an organic body is a sign of life, quickening can be construed as the moment at which the human fetus becomes alive.

While it is true that internally generated movement of location in an organic body is a sign of life, such movement is not a necessary condition for being alive. A normal adult under anesthesia shows no signs of internally generated movement in location, yet such a person is obviously alive. For an organism to live does not require local motion. Moreover, the standard of quickening was abandoned in the law after scientific discoveries in the nineteenth century showed that conception marks the beginning of a human life. (For more, see John Keown, *Abortion, Doctors and the Law*, and Joseph W. Dellapenna, *Dispelling the Myths of Abortion History*.)

Sentience

Yet another view about when a human being gains the right to live or when a human being gains basic status is sentience – the ability to experience pain. Peter Singer argues that the capacity to suffer is both the sufficient and necessary condition for an individual to have moral status. Singer writes:

> If a being suffers there can be no moral justification for refusing to take that suffering into consideration. No matter what the nature of the being, the principle of equality requires that its suffering be counted equally with the like suffering – insofar as rough comparisons can be made – of any other being. If a being is not capable of suffering, there is nothing to be taken into account. So the limit of sentience (using the term as a convenient if not strictly accurate shorthand for the capacity to suffer and/or experience enjoyment) is the only defensible boundary of concern for the interests of others.
>
> (Singer 2016, 32)

A being without interests – such as a rock – does not have any moral status. When a being can experience pain, the being in question has an interest in not feeling pain. So, prior to sentience emerging in a fetal human being, the human being in utero does not have any interests, and therefore also has no rights. Now, when exactly sentience arises in fetal human beings is a matter of dispute, some people claiming early in pregnancy and others only at the end of pregnancy, but the Sentience Account holds that whenever the ability to experience pain arises, fetal interests arise.

Questions arise for the sentience view. Why should suffering *alone* count in our moral judgment of what is right and what is wrong? Let us say that people try to blacken your reputation by saying that you are an unfair person who harasses other people, but that you never learn of their calumny. Fortunately for you, no one believes their charges, so your reputation with other people does not change at all. So, no suffering whatsoever occurs. But the people who lied about you did something wrong in trying to blacken your reputation. So, more than suffering is at stake in coming to our moral judgment. Jonathan Haidt provides another example:

> Jennifer works in a hospital pathology lab. She's a vegetarian for moral reasons—she thinks it is wrong to kill animals. But

one night she has to incinerate a fresh human cadaver, and she
thinks it's a waste to throw away perfectly edible flesh. So she
cuts off a piece of flesh and takes it home. Then she cooks it and
eats it.

(Haidt 2013, 45)

If cannibalism in this case is wrong, suffering does not explain
why it is wrong. The corpse doesn't suffer. We can posit that
Jennifer tells no one of her action, so no one else suffers from
being disgusted.

Unless we are utilitarians supposing that the *only* thing that
ultimately matters morally is suffering and pleasure, why should
we think that moral status necessarily depends on the capacity for
suffering and enjoyment? Indeed, if we accept the value of
human rights, then we should not be utilitarians. If maximizing
pleasure and pain are all that matters, then the founder of utilitarianism Jeremy Bentham was right that pre-legal human rights
are "nonsense on stilts." For we can never exclude the possibility
that to bring about the "greatest happiness of the greatest
number," we not only *can* but *must* torture, rape, and even
murder some minority of human persons. As Stalin said, you
can't make an omelet without breaking a few eggs. Nor can rule
utilitarianism get us around this problem. We have no reason to
think that following the rule "don't torture, rape, and murder
innocent human beings" must always bring about the greatest
happiness for the greatest number, so we have no reason to
always follow this rule.

Moreover, utilitarianism presupposes psychological hedonism,
that the only thing that we desire as good in itself is pleasure and
the only thing that is bad itself is pain. But as Robert Nozick
pointed out via his Experience Machine thought experiment,
we in fact want *more* than experiences of pleasure. We want to
be a certain kind of person, to actually do activities in the world,
and to experience not just a waking dream but reality (Nozick
1974). To actually be an Olympic athlete, a wonderful friend, or a
world-class scientist is better than merely to have all the same
subjective experiences of an Olympic athlete, a wonderful friend,
or a world-class scientist. If we would prefer to have *both* the

subjective experiences *and* the objective reality of being a great athlete, friend, and scientist, then hedonism's claim that we *only* desire the subjective experience of pleasure is false. If hedonism is false, then utilitarianism is unjustified.

Singer continues:

> I don't think plants have interests, in the morally relevant sense, any more than, say, a car guided through traffic by a computer would have an interest in reaching its destination. Neither plants nor the car are conscious. To imagine what it is like to be a pig in a factory farm is an idea that makes sense, even if it is difficult to get it right. Imagining yourself as a plant or a computer-guided car yields only a blank.
>
> (Singer 2016, 33)

The supposition is that an individual needs to be *conscious* in order to have interests. But individuals who are not currently conscious clearly do have interests. Imagining yourself as an unconscious person in surgery only yields a blank, but if you were unconscious, you would still have interests in not getting murdered, raped, or lobotomized.

One of the other troubles with the Sentience Account is that there are some human beings who even after birth are incapable of experiencing pain. Human beings suffering from chronic insensitivity to pain syndrome feel no pain whatsoever though they are able to see and hear, think and move, like anyone else. For them, cutting off their fingers is no more painful than trimming fingernails is to normal human beings. If you had chronic insensitivity to pain syndrome, you could stick your hand in a fire, grab a burning log, and take a bite of it without the slightest discomfort. Unfortunately, persons with this condition often die young because they can fatally injure themselves, and bleed to death internally, without noticing anything is wrong.

It is evident that such human beings – exactly like us in all respects save sensitivity to pain – are also like us in terms of having a right to live. So, the capacity to feel pain is not necessary for having moral status. The fact that an adult with chronic insensitivity to pain syndrome or a prenatal human being cannot feel pain does not indicate that they do not have basic rights.

The problem of equality is also inherent in the Sentience Account. Some human beings are remarkably sensitive to pain; a vaccination at the doctor's office causes them to howl. Other human beings, as Dan Ariely shows in his books *Predictably Irrational* (2010) and *The Upside of Irrationality* (2010, chapter 6), adapt to pain and have high pain tolerance. Watergate conspirator G. Gordon Liddy entertained people at parties by holding his hand over a lit candle until others smelled his burning flesh. So, if sensitivity to pain is what gives human persons their basic value, and therefore our basic rights, and if sensitivity to pain is not equally shared by all human persons, why should we think that all persons have equal rights?

Finally, almost no one actually believes that the ability to experience pain is the characteristic that grants the right to live. Rats can experience pain, but it is hard to believe that rat exterminators are the ethical equivalent of mass murderers.

Human Appearance

Another view is that the right to life begins when the human being looks more like a "baby" than a "blob." As any *What to Expect When You're Expecting* kind of book shows, the embryonic stage of development is visually indistinguishable for human beings, pigs, chickens, dogs, and cats, at least to an untrained eye. Just before birth, of course, the human fetus looks just like a newborn. In this way of considering when the right to live begins, an individual being who looks like a blob of tissue lacks a right to live, but a prenatal human being close to birth who looks exactly like a newborn does have a right to life.

This way of establishing who has and does not have a right to live is unreasonable. Some human beings are horribly disfigured because of fires, explosions, or injuries in war. Such human beings have just as much right to live as any supermodel. On the other hand, a wax figure in Madame Tussaud's or a human hologram may look like a normal man or woman but of course has no right to live. Appearances can be deceiving, and appearances are certainly no guide to whom we may kill.

Brain Development

Some people hold that the fetal right to life begins when the fetal brain develops. Just as "brain death" marks the end of the life of a human person, so "brain life" marks the beginning of the life of a human person.

Let us assume (bypassing a much debated issue) that brain death does mark the death of a human person. Even granting this assumption, it is important to note a radical asymmetry between brain death and brain life. Brain death is considered a superior standard of determining death in comparison to the standard of death that it replaced, cardio-respiratory cessation, because cardio-respiratory cessation was reversible but brain death was not. There is no case of "brain death" reversal, where someone who is brain dead has a restoration of neurological function. By contrast, many people whose hearts have stopped can have a restoration of cardiac function, either through heart transplant or successful open-heart surgery. But in the human fetus a lack of brain function is not only possibly reversible, it is typically reversible simply through the normal course of growth. So the criterion of irreversibility gives us a reason to accept "brain death" as the end of a human person but no reason to think of "brain life" as the beginning of a human person.

Moreover, simply having a brain is irrelevant for having a right to live, unless we wish to extend an inalienable right to life also to wasps, worms, and weasels. If we hold that having a brain capable of immediate rational functioning is necessary for having a right to live, then we will exclude adult human beings in temporary comas as well as human babies, human toddlers, and young human children until they attain the age of reason.

Implantation

Dr. Bernard Nathanson cofounded an organization known as the National Abortion Rights Action League. He also was Director of the Center for Reproductive and Sexual Health, one of New York City's first abortion clinics. Dr. Nathanson personally performed and oversaw more than 60,000 abortions. He also aborted his own child. Later, this self-described "Jewish atheist" changed his mind about abortion. In his book *Aborting America*, he tells the story of how he came to his new view, in part through the development of ultrasound technology, which provided a window into the womb where he observed the humanity of the unborn. In *Aborting America*, Nathanson held that the right to life of alpha (his term for the prenatal human being) begins with implantation. At implantation, a hormone HCG is released, which allows a pregnancy to be detected. "Biochemically, this is when alpha announced its presence as part of the human community by means of its hormonal messages, which we now have the technology to receive. We also know biochemically that it is an independent organism distinct from the mother," writes Nathanson.

Later Nathanson came to reject the view that implantation is the key moment when a human being acquires a right to life. Implantation alone is not sufficient for granting personhood, since all other mammals (rats, dogs, cats, etc.) also have a moment when they first implant in the uterus of their mothers. Surely, they don't have a right to live. And if artificial wombs were developed, then a particular human being might never be implanted in the uterus of a woman. Yet surely an adult just like you whose life began in an artificial uterus would not lack a right to life simply because she was never implanted in the womb of a human being.

2.4   Is Fetal Moral Status Linked to Fetal Physiological Development?

One view, sometimes called the gradualist, developmental, or pluralistic view, holds that the moral worth of the human fetus grows over time because of the psychological and/or physical growth of the human being over time. So, at conception and in the very early development of the embryo, the embryo has almost no value, and abortion is justified for any reason. As the human fetus develops over time, so fetal moral worth increases. Various biological changes mirror increases in moral value. The heartbeat begins around 19 days after conception, at week five arms and legs grow, and at week nine toes are seen; each stage of development toward being just like us also marks a new stage of moral worth. A single thread can be easily broken, but additional threads make up a string, then twine, and finally a rope that is extremely difficult to break. So too, a human zygote of only one cell has almost no value, but as the process of maturation in utero continues, the human being becomes more and more valuable. According to the developmental view, early abortion is permissible for any reason, abortion in the second trimester is permissible for serious reasons, and abortion just before birth is permissible only for the most serious of reasons, such as to save the life of the mother. Then, after birth, the full moral worth of the human being is fully established and the newborn baby has the same right to life as you or I.

A Critique of the Developmental View

Premature birth challenges the developmental view. A baby born prematurely at 23 weeks will be less physiologically and less psychologically developed than the prenatal human being just prior to delivery. Given the developmental view, does a baby born prematurely lack the right to live, since he or she is less physiologically developed than the late-term fetus that does not have the same right to live as you and me? Or does the prematurely born baby have the same right to live as you or I, in which case, the more fully developed human being waiting to be born must also have a full right to live? Now, a person could say that birth itself marks the key transformation, but this is simply to shift the standard back to a criterion that we examined earlier. If the arguments given earlier against birth being the magic moment when the right to life kicks in are correct, then this shift does not adequately defend abortion.

Another challenge to the developmental view questions the connection between physical development and moral worth. Physical development continues after birth as the human being develops through the stages of infant, toddler, child, pre-teen, teen, young adult, and adult. We do gain certain rights as we mature, such as the right to drive, vote, and hold public office. But these rights require maturity in order to be exercised for the public good. By contrast, our basic rights – say, not to be intentionally killed or harmed – are unrelated to our physiological development. We do not think that, say, a 20-year-old has more of a right to live than a five-year-old, although a 20-year-old is much more developed. If basic moral worth is related to physiological development, why are the radical developments from infancy to adulthood irrelevant for our basic moral worth?

Moreover, why should the development of a heart beating or of brain waves be relevant for moral worth in utero? If the arguments given earlier are correct, many characteristics that some consider necessary for fetal moral worth are in fact not necessary for fetal moral worth. If these characteristics, such as sentience, viability, brain activity, and fetal movement, are not necessary for fetal moral worth, why should these same characteristics increase moral worth during the process of gestation? If these characteristics are ethically irrelevant, then they are ethically irrelevant both as necessary conditions for the right to live and as stages in increasing moral value.

Some people accept the developmental view because they believe later abortion in the second and third trimester is more ethically problematic than early abortion in the first trimester. We can account for this intuition without explaining it by linking the development of the human being in utero with increasing moral worth. A defender of the equal basic rights of all human beings, including prenatal human beings, can also hold that not all abortions are ethically equal. If the following insights are correct, then the intuition that late-term abortion is worse than early abortion can be maintained without also appealing to the increasing moral worth of the human being in the course of gestation.

In his article "Late- vs. Early-Term Abortion" (2007), Andrew Peach points to several factors that suggest that prima facie abortion closer to birth is more ethically problematic than abortion just after conception. One factor is sentience. Very late in pregnancy, everyone agrees, the prenatal human being can experience pain. Very early in pregnancy, everyone agrees, the prenatal human being cannot experience pain. Now when exactly in the course of gestation the capacity to experience pain arises remains a matter of dispute, but at either extreme there is consensus. So, one factor that differentiates very early abortion from very late abortion is that in the first case the killing can be done painlessly and in the second case the killing characteristically causes pain. To kill painfully is more ethically problematic than to kill pain-lessly. This proposition is neutral with respect to moral status of the one killed. Even if someone believes the late-term fetal human lacks all rights, nevertheless people of good will admit that killing an individual (even a being presumably without a right to life like ours, such as a pig or chicken) painfully is ethically problematic. Now this difficulty could be overcome by anesthetizing the late-term prenatal human being prior to abor-tion, but such pain-killing measures are seldom taken. So, in the normal case, late-term abortion is worse than early-term abortion.

Moreover, Peach points out that the easier it is to carry out an obligation the worse it is not to carry it out. The easier it is to help another person, the more we should help another person. I do a greater wrong when I fail to save someone from drowning when all I have to do is walk 10 feet into the water than when I have to swim one mile to save her from drowning. So, to get an abortion after having already gone through most or even almost all of a pregnancy is prima facie worse than getting an abortion earlier in gestation when months of pregnancy lie ahead.

Third, early in pregnancy the prenatal human being does not look much like a newborn baby but more like a blob of cells. As noted earlier, appearance changes nothing of the reality of a human being. Yet in terms of subjective culpability, it is much easier for the abortionist and others to treat the prenatal human being in accordance with his or her appearance as nonhuman. By contrast, shortly before birth, a prenatal human being looks exactly like a newborn, and so the rationalizations denying the humanity of the fetus are much harder to make. So, to kill a being with (in many cases) greater knowledge of the being's humanity is worse than killing a being with some question about the humanity. This prima facie difference, like the others, would not apply in every single case (since subjective culpability varies widely among agents) but in many cases.

Fourth, culpability may also differ in that, early in pregnancy, the shock, horror, and panic caused by the pregnancy may prompt someone to get an abortion under a kind of emotional duress. By contrast, as time goes on, the intense fear generated by the surprise typically subsides. People acclimate and adapt to even shocking news such as an unplanned pregnancy. So, in terms of subjective culpability, someone who chooses to get an abortion late in pregnancy would be choosing abortion without the mitigating factors of surprise and shock. This factor is not in play in cases in which pregnancy is discovered only very late in gestation, but such cases are rare.

A final factor is that women characteristically experience late-term abortion (as well as late-term miscarriage) as more traumatic than early abortion (or early miscarriage). It may be that, in general, the longer you have had a relationship with someone, the more traumatic it is for the relationship to end. So, if a mother–child relationship has existed for eight months of pregnancy, it will probably be more traumatic to have this relationship end than if it ends after three weeks. This last factor may not apply in some cases. A mother overwhelmed with her young children might not mourn a late miscarriage. A woman struggling with fertility problems might intensely mourn her early miscarriage. But in most cases, the later in gestation the pregnancy ends, the more traumatic it is for the woman. In such cases, later abortion will be more problematic than early abortion.

If any of these five differences between later and earlier abortion is correct, then we can account for the moral intuition that later abortion is more ethically problematic than early abortion without denying equal human rights to all human beings at whatever stage of development.

The Time-Relative Interest Account

Perhaps the most powerful defense of the view that the value of the prenatal human being increases in the course of pregnancy is provided by Jeff McMahan, who points out that most people, even those who oppose abortion, hold that the death of the 20-year-old is worse than the death of a human fetus. If we had to choose between saving a 20-year-old from death or saving a prenatal human being from death, almost everyone would choose to save the 20-year old. Why do we think this?

In his book *The Ethics of Killing*, McMahan explains this common intuition by what he calls the time-relative interest account (McMahan 2002). Usually, a prenatal human being has more years of a valuable future ahead than does a 20-year-old. So, if the badness of death is explained in terms of the loss of a valuable future, it would seem that the death of a prenatal human being is worse than the death of a 20-year-old. However, McMahan points out that we must discount this overall value of these future years because of the weak psychological relationship between the fetal human being now and the future human being who will enjoy these goods. The prenatal human being's present self and future self stand in weak (actually nonexistent) psychological relationship to each other. By contrast, the present self and the future self of a normal 20-year-old stand in a strong psychological relationship to each other. If a human being has strong time-relative interests, then that human being has powerful ties between current and future selves. This is the case for most adults. By contrast, if a human being has weak time-relative interests, then that human being has few or no psychological links between the current self and future self. This is the case with the human fetus and the human adult.

For a 20-year-old to die is worse than for the human fetus to die because the 20-year-old human being cares deeply about his future self, in the accomplishment of life plans. By contrast, a prenatal human being in early gestation does not know that she exists and does not care about her future. The fetal interest in a future-like-ours is radically discounted because there are no psychological links between the prenatal human and the 20-year-old human. Very late in pregnancy, a human being in utero may begin to have some psychological states, and these weak links give rise to some decline in the discounting of interests. So, the time-relative interest account can also make sense of the intuition that third-trimester abortion is more ethically problematic than first-trimester abortion.

How might a defender of equal rights for all human beings respond? First, we must distinguish two different senses of "interest." Interest could be understood objectively, namely, as a good for the individual regardless of that individual's consciousness. Or interest could be understood subjectively, as what an individual takes a conscious interest in. If interests in the time-relative interest account are understood objectively, as the future goods of a whole life regardless of whether these goods are consciously desired, then subjective considerations are irrelevant. If subjective considerations are irrelevant, then the psychological strength or weakness of links between current selves and future selves is also irrelevant. But if the time-relative differences in psychological strengths is irrelevant, then time-relative differences cannot be used to discount the value in question. Put differently, if human beings have objective interests in living, regardless of what they desire or their states of consciousness, then time-relative differences in relationship between current self and future self are irrelevant in determining who has a right to live. In other words, regardless of particular psychological states such as what the individual may subjectively be interested in, or care about, or desire, the individual has an objective interest in the matter under consideration. So, if prenatal human beings or newborn human beings have an objective interest in life (a future-like-ours), then regardless of the time-relative psychological strength or weakness of the present self to the future self, the objective interest remains unaltered.

On the other hand, if we understand interest in the subjective sense, then the "time-relative" aspect becomes relevant. No prenatal individual has any subjective interest at all, since no human being before birth is aware of his or her own existence. As we saw earlier, this view justifies not just prenatal abortion, but also postnatal infanticide. No newborn has self-awareness, so no newborn can subjectively take an interest in continuing to exist

(Giubilini and Minerva 2013). So, unless we are willing to condone infanticide, the time-relative interest account does not help us justify abortion.

Now one response to this objection, inspired by Derek Parfit's brain division cases, is to claim that identity does not matter in survival. What matters is whether or not there is a psychological continuity between me now and qualitatively the same thoughts, beliefs, and memories later in what could very well be a different person. So whether or not the individual prenatal human being will later have a good life is not ethically relevant for deciding about how to treat the individual human being now.

But when people are facing death, they do not ask, "Will there be psychological replicas of me around?" People facing death ask, "Will I, myself as a unique individual, be around?" (Baker, 2000). Likewise, when we care about other human beings, we care about these individuals, not about the (perhaps millions of) psychological replicas who would be created as copies of the original human being we love. If individual continuity does matter, both to us and to those whom we care about, then we cannot assess the loss of death for a human being simply in terms of psychological states.

Moreover, the thesis that "identity doesn't matter to survival" is another way of saying that without psychological connections between "me" now and "me" later, the survival doesn't matter to me. This is simply another way of saying that we are not subjectively interested in survival, so we are back to a subjective account.

Patrick Lee offers a third way of challenging the view that not identity but psychological continuity is what matters in survival in the following case. Suppose that I would die if I did not undergo brain surgery that would erase my memories, beliefs, and desires. In this case, there would be no psychological connections between "me" now and "me" after surgery. As Lee points out, "If someone told me that, although I will not remember who I am, I will suffer excruciating pain after the surgery, I would be very afraid" (Lee 2015, 237). But the fact that I would be afraid suggests that what I care about is not merely the psychological connectedness between present and future selves. I also deeply care about what will happen to this individual human being who exists before, during, and after the surgery. Individual continuity does matter, not just psychological connectedness. The "I" before the surgery is the same as the "I" after the surgery. I am the one who is afraid before the surgery, I undergo the surgery, then I suffer afterward. But if being numerically the same human being makes a later bad state (painful surgery recovery) important for an individual now, then it would seem a later good state (value of future life) is also important for an individual now.

The Harm of Death

What is the harm of death? In one sense, the harm varies from person to person. Someone with great friends, a loving family, meaningful work, and pleasant hobbies loses more in dying than someone with no friends, alienation from family, no satisfying work, and endless hours of boredom. In terms of all these circumstances, the loss involved in each death is utterly unique.

In thinking about why death is a harm we might distinguish two aspects of harms, the circumstantial aspects and intrinsic aspects. Let's say Ryan buys a brand new blue Prius, and Lisa buys a brand new red Prius. Each car costs exactly the same amount, and each person buys the car outright with cash. Unfortunately, each car is stolen the next day, never to be seen by its rightful owner again. Intrinsically, Lisa and Ryan have both lost exactly the same thing, a new Prius. But circumstantially, the loss is catastrophically worse for Ryan than for Lisa. Ryan is an Uber driver, and the loss of his car is also the loss of his sole source of income. Lisa, by contrast, was going to use her new car only rarely, since she tries to walk or ride her bike unless she absolutely has to drive.

With respect to the intrinsic harm of death, whoever dies loses exactly the same thing as every other person who dies – namely, their life. The harm of death is intrinsically alike for the baby, the university student, and the senior citizen. Circumstantially, however, the harm of death is different for each person. In terms of loss of future goods, the baby loses the most, since typically 70–80 years of future goods of life will never be enjoyed if death comes to the one in the crib. The university student loses circumstantially less than the baby in terms of future goods, say, 50 or 60 years of life. Death is worse in this respect for the university student than for the senior citizen who, if killed in old age, may lose only a few years of life.

In terms of currently enjoyed goods, it may be that the university student loses the most because it may be that the student currently has more friends, knowledge, vigor of body, and meaningful activity than either the baby or the elderly person. However, in a particular case, some 80-year-old may have a richer life in terms of friends, knowledge, vigor, and meaningful activity than a particular 20-year-old. Death is worse for some victims than for others in terms of these circumstantial considerations.

Circumstantially, some deaths are worse than others also in social terms. The death of a mother with small children is worse (other things being equal) than the death of someone who is not a parent. The death of a president or prime minister is worse (other things being equal) than the death of someone without responsibilities to others.

Given all these circumstantial factors, we can explain why the death of a 20-year-old is a greater loss (to the 20-year-old and to others) than the death of a prenatal human being or a newborn baby without resorting to the time-relative interest account. Although the prenatal human being and the newborn baby loses more future goods, this is not the only circumstantial factor that can be considered. The 20-year-old loses more currently enjoyed goods, typically causes greater sadness for others, and may be unable to discharge responsibilities to others. These factors are not in play in the death of the prenatal human being or newborn baby. So, although the prenatal human being or baby loses more future life, the death of the college student is worse than the death of the prenatal human being or newborn baby when all circumstantial factors are considered.

2.5   Does the Right to Live Begin Whenever a Human Being Begins to Exist?

The Elimination Argument

This chapter began with a relatively uncontroversial claim. If someone were to put a knife to your throat and kill you right now, that person would wrong you. Put in other terms, people have a prima facie duty not to kill you, you have a right to live. When did this right to live begin? You have it right now, you had it yesterday, you had it last week, and last year. But when did it begin?

The most radical justifications of abortion (both prenatal and postnatal) hold that your right to live began when you first began to be self-aware and began to desire to live. Since psychologists indicate self-awareness of this kind does not begin until around two years of age, to kill you before this time would not have wronged you, since you did not have a right to live at that time. Slightly less radical is the view that your right to live began when you were born. Moving still earlier in your life the conscious desires account holds that your right to life began at 25–32 weeks after conception. The sentience account holds that that right to live arises when someone is capable of experiencing physical pain. Or perhaps your right to live began at the point of viability, or at the point of quickening, or with fetal movement, or fetal brain waves. If the analysis given earlier of these markers is correct, none of these characteristics is necessary for having a right to live. Nor, if the arguments given earlier are correct, is it true that the right to life gradually strengthens as the prenatal human being develops physically and psychologically.

So, if our right to live did not begin at any of these markers, when did it begin? Having examined and rejected a number of rival answers, we turn now to the answer that your right to live began when you began to exist. By process of elimination of other accounts, a remaining possibility is that the right to life begins when a human being begins. When do human beings begin to exist?

Let's start with a more basic question. What differentiates a living thing, such as a black stallion, a red rose bush, a goldfish, or a blue whale, from a nonliving thing, such as a chunk of gold, a square of Astroturf, a Heineken beer, or a piece of paper? Organic living things have self-directed internal activities that nonliving things do not. Living organisms have self-directed activities including the assimilation of nutrition, proportionate growth toward maturity, and reproduction of new cells or entirely new organisms. So, if we use these three conditions in order to consider whether or not a human zygote, a human embryo, or a human fetus is alive, what would we conclude?

A human zygote, a human embryo, and a human fetus have the self-directed activities of assimilating nutrition, growing proportionately, and reproducing new cells, thereby exhibiting the characteristics of living organisms. The human zygote, the human embryo, and the human fetus are all capable of dying, which again is a characteristic of living things. A sapphire, a piece of ice, and a candlestick might be destroyed, but such things do not die, for such things were never alive. By contrast, a human being, whether at the embryonic, fetal, or postnatal state of development, can die. Various scientific texts point to the same conclusion. For example, in *Human Embryology and Developmental Biology*, Bruce M. Carlson writes, "Immediately after fertilization, the zygote undergoes a pronounced shift in metabolism, and begins several days of cleavage [cell multiplication]" (2013). The internally directed activities of both metabolism and cell replication are characteristics of living organisms. In *Life Unfolding*, Jamie Davies writes, "The fertilized egg with which human development begins is unusually large, about a tenth of a millimeter across and visible to the naked eye" (2014). From this one cell the entire full developed human being emerges by what Davis calls "adaptive self-organization." An organic being with adaptive self-organization is a living being.

Outside of debates about abortion, informed people typically acknowledge that the embryo is a living being. For example, on May 4, 2016, Sarah Knapton, the Science Editor of *The Telegraph*, reported, "Human embryos have been kept alive in a petri dish for an unprecedented 13 days, allowing scientists to finally see what happens in the mysterious days after implantation in the womb" (Knapton 2016). Of course, something cannot be "kept alive," unless it is already living. If even the human embryo prior to 13 days is living, the prenatal human being in the fetal stage of development weeks or even months later (when abortions take place) is even more obviously a living being.

Even if it is true that these organisms are alive, an objector might question, why should we think these are human? Maybe they *turn into* human beings sometime during gestation, for example, with the beginning of the heartbeat, or brain waves, or movement. Or maybe birth transforms a nonhuman organism into a human organism.

This response risks confusing a biological question (what species is this individual?) with an ethical question (does this individual have moral status?). When an organism is living, we can ask the scientific question, "To what species does this organism belong?" The answer to this question might require empirical investigation. What kind of blood does it have? What kind of cells does it have? What is the trajectory of growth of this being? What species did the parents of this organism belong to?

When these questions are posed about a human being prior to birth, the answers are evident. This creature has human blood. The individual in question is composed of human cells, actively self-developing toward human maturity. These human cells are not a disorganized mass of tissue like a tumor, but rather a unified organism exhibiting adaptive self-organization. This individual is on the human trajectory of growth toward human maturity. Both the mother and the father of the being in question are members of the species *Homo sapiens*. To what other biological species could this individual belong? If an individual has a human mother and human father, he or she cannot be a salmon, a tiger, or a bald eagle. The living organism reproduced by two human beings is always and only another human being (or more human beings, if twinning occurs). So, given you and I now have a right to live, we must have gotten that right to live at some point. If the right to live did not begin after birth, nor during birth, nor during our gestation within our mothers, then the remaining possibility is that we began to have the right to live when we began to exist, namely, as a human embryo. To violate someone's rights is to wrong him or her. Abortion, the intentional killing as a means or as an end of a human being prior to birth, violates the right to life of the human being prior to birth.

The Argument from a Future like Ours

Let's consider a second argument. Some people believe that the view that abortion is wrong depends on religious premises and is put forward only by religious believers. Against these assumptions, atheist Donald Marquis provides a powerful counterexample. In his article "Why Abortion Is Wrong," Marquis begins by considering why it is wrong to kill someone like you or me, someone with a right to live that is uncontroversial (Marquis 1989). For example, why would it be wrong to kill Jennifer Aniston? Killing her deprives her of the valuable goods of her future. If she had lived, she would have enjoyed her friends, learned new things, appreciated beautiful art, and so on. Killing Jennifer Aniston harms her by depriving her of all the goods that she would have enjoyed in her future.

We can generalize the principle at work in the example of Jennifer Aniston to include everyone reading this work and everyone else who has a "future like ours." Killing any being with a future like ours is wrong because all such killing deprives the individual who is killed of a future of value, a future like ours. But the newborn human being and the human being in utero also has a future like ours. If not killed, the baby or the prenatal human being will also enjoy her friends, learn new things, appreciate beautiful music, and so on. So, killing a newborn or human being in utero is wrong for the same reason it is wrong to kill you or me. Killing any one of us deprives us of our future of value.

Marquis notes that his argument does not show that *all* abortions involve killing a being with a future like ours. A tiny percentage of prenatal human beings, such as anencephalic infants, do not have a future like ours. But 99.99 percent of human beings in utero do have a future like ours, so killing them is wrong for the same reason killing us is wrong.

One objection to the future like ours argument is that it proves too much. If losing a future like ours is what makes abortion wrong, then killing a human fetus is worse than killing a 50-year-old, since the prenatal human being loses approximately 80 years of life (assuming an average lifespan) but the 50-year-old loses only 30 years of life. But no one thinks abortion is worse than murdering a 50-year-old.

Marquis responds that this objection rests simply on lack of imagination. If we could see all that the human being in utero lost (fun as a toddler, learning to read, senior prom, getting married, her first baby born, etc.), we would see that it is worse. Moreover, as noted earlier, one killing may be worse than another in one way (more future lost) but not as bad in another respect (say, no one else adversely affected, no actual plans thwarted). So, to kill a toddler is worse than killing the prime minister of the United Kingdom in terms of future of value lost, but killing the prime minister is worse in terms of generating global unrest and perhaps even causing world war. All thefts are wrong because all thefts deprive individuals of their property, even though we can recognize that stealing millions is worse than stealing thousands and stealing from the poor is worse than stealing from the rich. Similarly, the killings in question are wrong because all such killings deprive individuals of their futures of value, even though there are innumerable circumstantial differences in killings of beings with a future of value that make them more or less bad (degree of pain, fear, loss to others). In other words, we can say that an action is wrong without making any claim about the relative gravity of that action in comparison to other wrongful actions.

Another argument against the future of value is that it proves too much; namely, it proves that not just abortion but also contraception is wrong. Contraception also prevents the emergence of a being with a future of value. So, unless we are ready to condemn all contraception, we should reject the future of value argument.

But the future of value argument does not depend on the claim that it is always wrong to prevent a future of value from emerging. The argument is that killing an individual is wrong if that individual has a future of value. If contraception is effectively used, then sex does not result in conception. In such cases, no new individual being is brought into existence. Just as a nonexistent individual has no height, a nonexistent individual has no future like ours. If a particular individual does not exist, then the future of value of this individual also does not exist. So, in cases of successful use of contraception, there is no individual who is deprived of a future of value. Effective use of contraception simply prevents a new individual from coming into existence. Abortion, by contrast, destroys an individual (or in the case of twins, two individuals) with a future of value. So, the future of value argument does not entail that the use of contraception is immoral.

The Argument from History

Should all human beings be accorded basic rights? Are all human beings due respect and consideration as beings of moral worth? Or should we divide the human family into two camps, those human beings (invariably "those like me") who are accorded protection by law and recognition in ethical judgment and those human beings who are not?

For centuries, human beings with power have divided human beings into two classes – those who have basic rights and those who do not have basic rights, those deserving of the protections of society and those excluded from these protections. For example, some Europeans looked on the appearance of "savage natives" in the "new world" as barely more than beasts and treated them accordingly in taking their lands, stealing their riches, and destroying their culture. White slaveholders divided the human family according to race. Black human beings were viewed as tools for ownership and domination. Indeed, the US federal government denied the equal personhood of slaves, who counted as three-fifths of a person for purposes of bolstering Southern representation, but as no person at all when it came to liberty. For centuries, men regarded women as not fully their equals and not meriting the right to vote or own property. The pattern of exclusion casts some class of human beings (those not like "us," the powerful) outside those meriting basic respect and protection. As Nicholas Wolterstorff puts it:

> Deep in humanity is the impulse to regard those human beings who are members of one's in-group as having a right to be treated in certain ways that those human beings who are members of some or all out-groups lack ... There is something about Greeks, something about Athenians, something about white people, something about Aryans, something about Serbs, that sets them apart and gives them an inherent dignity that others lack.
> (Wolterstorff 2007, 297)

Every time in history when we have excluded some class of human beings from basic protection by law and cast them outside the scope of our ethical concern, we have made a catastrophically bad moral choice. We can see clearly now the errors of men excluding women, European peoples excluding native peoples, slaveowners excluding slaves, the rich excluding the poor, religious majorities excluding religious minorities, and straight people excluding gay people. The choice of abortion repeats the pattern of exclusion, the pattern of exploitation of the vulnerable, the pattern of dehumanizing those who stand in the way. If we learn anything from history about ethical judgment, it is that our past errors of exclusion were seriously wrong. We now face another moment in history in which we must choose between the ethics of inclusion and the ethics of exclusion. We can affirm that all human beings are created equal and endowed with inalienable rights. Or we can affirm that only those human beings who are like me have rights but those human beings who are not like me do not. The lessons of history point to the wisdom of the ethics of inclusion.

Note that every single time that we have divided the human family into those who have basic rights and those who do not, we have made a terrible mistake. When Germans did this to Jews, when "true believers" did this to "heretics," when Soviets did this to dissidents, in all these cases, we look back and recognize moral mistake. Now too, some propose to divide the human family, granting privileges and immunities to those like us, but denying them to the less powerful, the vulnerable "other." Whenever in the past we have chosen the "exclusive" view over the "inclusive" view, we have made a horrible moral mistake. If we are to learn from the painful lessons of history, we will choose the inclusive view that all human beings, even those who are not like us, should be included within the scope of protection. Although human beings in utero are not like us, not powerful, unable to protect themselves, and as vulnerable as a human can be, these characteristics do not change in the least the fact that they are just as human as any of us. History teaches us that we have always made a mistake in choosing the ethics of exclusion.

The Argument from Personhood as Endowment

The value of a thing is based on supply and demand. The smaller the supply, and the greater the demand, the more valuable a thing is on a sliding scale. What determines demand? One factor is how well the thing in question functions. Other things being equal, a car that functions well in terms of fuel efficiency, safety, and comfort is worth more than a car that functions badly or not at all.

Should human beings be valued according to the same functional standard? Or should we think of persons as having a kind of value that things do not have? On one view, although *things* have a value based on how they function, *persons* have intrinsic value and are therefore endowed with inalienable rights. Should we endorse an endowment account of personhood or a functional account of personhood?

Consider two different views of personhood: the functional view and the endowment account. Then we can consider which individuals count as persons according to the various accounts.

First, an endowment account of personhood provides a basis for securing the equal rights of all persons. If we have value because of who we are rather than what we are doing (or have done), then we have a basis for the equal rights of all.

By contrast, functioning (understood in terms of sensitivity to pain or in terms of rationality) exists on a sliding scale. Philippe

Rochat distinguished five stages of self-awareness, beginning with a total lack of self-awareness to "meta self-awareness" in which people are aware that others are aware of them. For example, if we say that functioning self-awareness is necessary for personhood, we discover a scalar degree of functioning self-awareness from those not having any self-awareness, such as newborns, to those with just barely any self-awareness, such as toddlers, to those with moderate self-awareness, such as the teenager, to those with maximal self-awareness, such as the sage. If self-awareness is what gives us our moral status, and self-awareness comes in various degrees, then why wouldn't our value as persons also come in degrees? If the amount of water in a glass is what makes a glass valuable, then the more water a glass has the more valuable the glass is. If self-awareness is what makes a person valuable, then the sage has more value than the teenager. If our rights are tied to our value, it is a mistake to say that the teenager and the sage have equal rights.

Second, an endowment account of personhood secures our value over the course of our lives. On the endowment account, the kind of thing we are, our nature, is what gives us our value. We are endowed with the same basic value as long as we exist. We have this value when we come into existence and we lose this value only when we die. By contrast, if our value depends on how we are functioning, then whenever we fall below the (arbitrarily chosen) threshold of functioning, our value and therefore our rights disappear. So, if a functional account chooses autonomy as the basis of our value, as our autonomy waxes and wanes, so too our basic rights wax and wane. If we lose our autonomy, we lose our rights. If our autonomy returns, our rights return.

Third, the endowment account avoids the problem of thresholds. Ethics is a practical endeavor, seeking guidance about how to live. In real life, we can easily determine whether or not a particular organism is a human being. We can inquire whether the organism in question has a human mother and a human father. We can take samples of blood or tissue or DNA from the organism to determine whether he or she has human blood, human tissue, and human DNA. By contrast, for example, how do we determine whether or not a particular organism is self-aware? The onset of self-awareness will vary from child to child just as does the onset of speech. A particular test might make manifest that the child is self-aware, but self-awareness is only revealed by such tests; self-awareness can and does exist prior to the administration of tests of self-awareness. Decisions about who shall live and who shall be killed cannot justly be made on the basis of vague and arbitrary tests.

Fourth, defenders of functionalist accounts in fact appeal to a quasi-endowment in their accounts. No one holds, for example, that one must be actually experiencing pain or actually functioning rationally in order to have moral status. It would be absurd to claim that our basic rights evaporate the moment we are put under with anesthesia for surgery and that we only regain our basic rights when we regain consciousness. Rather, it is sufficient for moral status to be *capable* of sentience or *capable* of rational functioning. An appeal is made here not to actual functioning but to the kind of thing the being is, the kind of being capable of sentience or rational functioning. We have, in other words, an appeal to nature by those who claim to reject nature as ethically irrelevant.

If we adopt the endowment view of personhood rather than a functional view, then what matters is what kind of being the individual is, the nature of that being, rather than how that individual is functioning at a particular time. What matters is what the individual is substantially and essentially, rather than the fleeting characteristics an individual may have accidentally or nonessentially. To be a human being is to be the kind of being that matters, the kind of being endowed with inalienable rights, the kind of being with rational nature.

2.6   Is the Pro-life View a Form of Speciesism?

When Aristotle defined human beings as "rational animals" or when Kant viewed human beings as having a rational natures, they were both well aware that all human beings do not always function rationally. The substance view rests on the claim that each and every human being (born and unborn) actually (not just potentially) possesses a rational nature, and therefore merits fundamental respect as a rational being.

We are familiar with the term "racism," defined as a prejudice or attitude of bias in favor of the interests of members of one's own race and against those of members of other races. Sexism, too, is familiar – a prejudice or attitude of bias in favor of the interests of members of one's own sex and against those of members of the opposite sex. Less familiar to most, however, is the term "speciesism," which Peter Singer popularized and which he describes as "a prejudice or attitude of bias in favor of the interests of members of one's own species and against those of members of other species." According to Singer, speciesism is a moral mistake akin to racism and sexism.

On Singer's view, a prenatal human being has no value simply in virtue of being a member of the human species. To be human is as ethically irrelevant as to have white skin, brown skin, or black skin. In Singer's words,

> For on any fair comparison of morally relevant characteristics, like rationality, self-consciousness, awareness, autonomy, pleasure and pain, and so on, the calf, the pig and the much derided chicken come out well ahead of the fetus at any stage of pregnancy – while if we make the comparison with a fetus of less than three months, a fish would show more signs of consciousness.
>
> My suggestion, then, is that we accord the life of a fetus no greater value than the life of a nonhuman animal at a similar level of rationality, self-consciousness, awareness, capacity to feel, etc.
>
> (Singer 1993, 151)

On this view, the fact that abortion ends the life of a *human being* in his or her prenatal stage of development is ethically irrelevant. The killing of a prenatal human being early in pregnancy is of less significance than the killing of fish.

I think Singer is mistaken. There are good philosophical grounds for thinking that human beings should be accorded a greater moral status than nonhuman animals. Suppose we are comparing two kinds of cars. One kind of car has some valuable characteristics (high safety rating, low fuel consumption), but the other kind of car has all these characteristics and more (high safety rating, low fuel consumption, and attractive design). Other things being equal, the second kind of car would be more valuable. All human beings and nonhuman animals are alike in having an orientation to existing, living, and sensing. But only humans (among all the animals of which we are aware) also have an orientation to reason and freedom as autonomous agents. This is why we only hold human beings criminally responsible, and we never charge pit bulls with murder, even though pit bulls sometimes kill people. Thus, human nature has all the characteristics of nonhuman animal nature, but it also has more, insofar as it also has an orientation to freedom and reason as autonomous agents. Since human beings have an orientation not only to living and sensing, but also to reasoning and freedom as autonomous agents, human beings as such are more valuable than, say, dogs as such. Because an orientation to living, sensing, reasoning, and freely choosing is greater than an orientation to living and sensing alone, human beings have greater moral status than nonhuman animals.

Since male and female human beings share equally in human nature, they are equally valuable. In a similar way, the various races of human beings all share in the same human nature, so they too are equally valuable. Thus, there is no inconsistency in defending speciesism but condemning sexism and racism. Equality in nature provides grounds for supporting the equal basic rights of all members of the human species, but denying such rights to dogs, fish, and cats. Equality in nature also provides grounds for condemning sexism and racism, for every man and every woman, every black human being and every white human being, share equally in human nature.

The view that basic moral dignity rests on nature rather than on exercise of capacities also secures equality among human persons. For on any fair comparison of the exercise of morally relevant characteristics, such as rationality, self-consciousness, awareness, and autonomy, the artist, the professor, and the much derided truck driver come out well ahead of the intellectually disabled adult or the normal toddler. Indeed, no two human persons, no two persons reading this book, are equal in basic moral status, for neither of them is equal in terms of the exercise of rationality, self-consciousness, awareness, and autonomy. As psychologists Paul Bloom and Dan Arieli note, even our experience of pleasure and pain is deeply wedded to our beliefs, which in turn hinge on our rationality, self-consciousness, awareness, and autonomy. The inequality of those uncontroversially considered persons in all manner of exercise of capabilities is an inescapable fact. So, our equality in basic moral worth cannot be based on our unequal exercise of capabilities.

Holding that human beings have greater basic value than nonhuman animals does not entail that we may do anything we please to them. Nonhuman animals have a nature greater in dignity than plants or nonliving things do. It is thus a moral error not to show due regard for nonhuman animals, in a manner appropriate to their particular value. As Shelly Kagan pointed out in his critique of Singer's views on speciesism (Kagan 2016), virtually no one holds that *only* the interests of human beings count and that the interests of nonrational animals count not at all. No one thinks that arbitrarily setting fire to a cat is ethically permissible. Nor does anyone think that trivial human interests outweigh any animal interests whatsoever. The human desire to find out what a cat on fire sounds like would never justify dousing Mittens with gasoline and lighting a match. Properly loving the goodness of animals – a lesser goodness than that of human beings, but a goodness nonetheless – is incompatible with inflicting pain on them without sufficient justification.

"What exactly is supposed to be *wrong* with speciesism?" asks Kagan. The answer, according to Singer, is that it violates the principle of equal consideration of interests. To give greater weight to those of one's own race, or to those of one's own sex, or to those of one's own species, is to act arbitrarily and unfairly. If we wouldn't allow a human infant or an intellectually disabled human adult to be subject to medical experimentation for the sake of others, we should not subject animals (of equal or greater cognitive capacity) to the same sorts of experiments. Pain is pain, whoever suffers it, animal or human.

Is speciesism a prejudice? Well, it could be if it were based on false empirical beliefs, such as that animals feel no pain. But an ethical prioritizing of human beings over animals could also be based on something else. Kagan writes:

> But if one's speciesism is based instead on a direct appeal to moral intuition – and that is how I envision the speciesist – and if one is then prepared to give presumptive weight to moral intuitions in other matters as well, then that, it seems to me, is not prejudice. The view in question may or may not be correct; but it is not a mere prejudice and nothing more. So Singer's argument against speciesism fails.
>
> (Kagan 2016, 9)

In 1776, the American founders held that it was a self-evident truth that all men (by which they meant I believe "all human beings") are created equal and endowed with inalienable rights. This proposition is a first premise in the Declaration of Independence. As a first principle, this premise was not justified by still prior premises. Every argument must ultimately depend on some first principles that are not themselves demonstrated on the basis of some prior suppositions. Singer, too, must also rely on intuition of first principles at various points of his argument. The ubiquitous invocation of the first principle that all human beings deserve respect and protection by law in virtually all human rights declarations suggests that this first principle is intuitively plausible.

Kagan goes on to point out that very few people are speciesist at all. Kagan writes, "Superman isn't human. He isn't a member of our biological species. But is there anyone (other than Lex Luthor!) who thinks this makes a difference? Is there anyone who thinks: Superman isn't human, so his interests should count less than they would if he were? I doubt it"(Kagan 2016, 9). Indeed, many people of faith explicitly reject the idea that human beings and human beings *alone* have moral status as persons, since they believe also in divine persons. It is not being *human* that is necessary for being a person, but being an individual substance of rational nature. So, following Kagan, many people of faith might say they are not speciesists but personists. What is necessary is not that the being share our *species* but that the being is a *person*.

How are persons to be treated? Persons are to be cared for and loved for their own sakes. A Kantian might say that persons are beings that deserve to be treated as ends in themselves rather than used simply as means. A contemporary philosopher might say that the goods of persons give us ultimate reasons for action rather than merely instrumental reasons (Girgis 2014).

These views about the treatment due to persons suggest that "person" is a binary concept rather than scalar. To be a person is to merit treatment as an end, to be worthy of love not mere use, and to be an ultimate reason for action. Instrumental reasons can come in degrees because the usefulness of things comes in degrees. Some*thing* may be a more or less effective means to some end. By contrast, some*one*, a person, is in a radically different category of an end-in-herself, a being to be loved for herself, an ultimate reason for action.

Does holding that all human beings have basic rights constitute a form of speciesism, a bias in favor of one's own species? Not at all. I believe that I am a human being, but let's say I am wrong. Suppose I merely look like I am human, but it turns out that I am actually of the same species as Superman. Clark Kent looks, sounds, and usually acts like a human being from Earth, but he is really an alien from the planet Krypton. Let's say that today I discover my superpowers and realize that I am not human, but rather a Kryptonian. If I realized I was not human, I would still hold that human beings have a higher moral status than all animals lacking rational nature. I would realize that there are also other animals having rational nature, namely, Kryptonians. The fact that human beings are (or are not) *my own* species is therefore irrelevant to defending the view that all human beings have intrinsic dignity and basic rights.

Indeed, it is a bias in favor of one's own kind that informs the denial of basic rights to prenatal human beings. This bias can be expressed in a number of ways, including the following. Unless a human being is like me (e.g., valuing her own life or born or viable), the human being has no value, or lesser value than I have. My group has full moral status and deserves full legal protection. Human beings who are not like me have lesser value or no value at all. Steven Pinker has noted "the nasty feature of human social psychology: the tendency to divide people into in-groups and out-groups, and to treat the out-groups as less than human" (Pinker 2003, 157). The use of dehumanizing words to speak about prenatal human beings, to describe them as "para-sites," and to defend the extermination of their lives reflects the bias in favor of our own in-group and a prejudice against individual human beings who are not like us.

By contrast, in his *Groundwork for the Metaphysics of Morals*, Immanuel Kant articulated this fundamental principle of ethics, "Act in such a way that you treat humanity, whether in your own person or in the person of another, always at the same time as an end and never simply as a means." Note that Kant does not say that *only* humanity, whether ourselves or other members of humanity, is to be treated as ends and never used as means. Kant's principle is open to the possibility that other species should also be treated as ends in themselves and never used simply as means. Maybe there are other species such as Kryptonians, angels, or dolphins who merit this respect, or maybe humanity is the only such species. Kant leaves these as open questions. Also left open is the possibility that some other characteristic, such as sentience, is sufficient for moral status. Kant's principle as stated is strictly neutral with respect to these possibilities. It claims only that humanity deserves respect, not that other species do not deserve respect. If someone says that all women deserve respect, that person is not (even implicitly) denying that men and children also deserve respect.

Rational Animals

The view I have been exploring presupposes that we are (rational) animals, human organisms. "But the view that we are human organisms is, I believe, refuted by counterexamples" such as cerebrum transplants, writes Jeff McMahan. If my brain were transplanted into someone else's body, I would be in my new body, which shows that I am not a human organism but rather my brain. "If, therefore, I were irreversibly to lose the capacity for consciousness, a living human organism might remain, but there would be nothing left that could plausibly be regarded as me" (McMahan 2016, 28). On McMahan's view, since each one of us is not a human organism, we are rather an embodied mind, a cerebrum.

But the imaginary case of the cerebrum transplant also undermines McMahan's view that we are minds embodied in our cerebrums. Imagine two human beings, Frank and Jane, who have had their cerebrums removed. Now imagine we transplant one-half of my cerebrum into Frank's body and the other half into Jane's body. Since I am, on McMahan's view, an embodied mind, I would be both in the body of Frank and in the body of Jane. This is impossible, since the bodies of Frank and Jane are not in the same place. Imaginary cases of brain transplants undermine the claim that we are embodied minds as much as the claim that we are human organisms. So, this imaginary case cannot be used to show that we are not human beings but rather are our cerebrums.

But we need not appeal to fantastic imaginary cases to see that we are not identical to our cerebrum. The corpus callosum connects the right and left hemispheres of our brain. In a corpus callosotomy, the connection between the right and left hemisphere is deliberately severed as a last-resort means of treating patients with epilepsy. The patient then has a "split brain" in which the hemispheres of the brain no longer communicate and each side has its own perceptions, ideas, and desires.

No one thinks that such a procedure, performed across the world since the 1940s, results in "two persons," even though it results in two spheres of consciousness via two independently functioning bits of gray matter. The spouse of a person who has had this procedure is not guilty of being married to two people at once. When a patient who has had a corpus callosotomy dies, there are not two death certificates issued. Killing a patient who has had a corpus callosotomy does not bring charges of double murder. Imagine doctors discover that they can reestablish the connection between the right and left hemispheres of the brain severed by the corpus callosotomy. The reconnection would turn the two centers of consciousness into one again. Would anyone object that the reconnection should not be made because the reconnection would destroy a person, one of the two embodied minds?

For no other species of which we are aware, other than the human species, does anyone claim that the numerical identity of the individual member depends on when an embodied mind comes into existence. We identify an individual member of every other species as a distinct, whole biological organism with no reference to when or if consciousness arises. So, if we are to treat our species as if it were ethically irrelevant, then in our ethical analysis we should be identified as individuals according to the same standard used for individuals of other species, namely, as biological organisms. It is not consistent to condemn speciesism in ethical analysis, but then use a standard of identity in ethical analysis that applies differently to different species.

Is it wrong to take species into account when considering the moral status of a being? Inasmuch as moral status has something to do with nature, and nature has something to do with species, there is nothing illegitimate in taking species into account in making moral judgments.

But what is meant by "nature" and what does it mean to have a "rational nature"? The term "nature" can refer to what characteristically happens in the statistically average course of events. So, human beings have a rational nature means that 99.9 percent of human beings exhibit rational activity at some time in their lives. However, imagine that a new disease damages most human beings as children, so that only 49.9 percent of human beings exhibit rational activity in the course of their lives. A meaning of "nature" that would remain even in such a case is that which belongs to a thing when its generation is brought to proper functioning. So, the generation of a human being is brought to its proper functioning when the human being is able to exercise rationality and thereby attain the human goods that can be attained only through the exercise of reason, such as establishing friendships, acting with personal integrity, and gaining insight. A human being who never attains the exercise of rationality has not yet achieved flourishing in the sense described. But such an individual still has a rational nature inasmuch as this human being is still the kind of individual who would be perfected by the exercise of reason.

But why should we say that a particular being has a rational nature, if in fact this being has not done any rational activities and may (in the case of serious mental handicap) lack the actual potential to perform rational activities? Rob Loving notes that if we hold that human beings prior to birth have a rational nature because most or many of them will develop to the point where they possess either proximate or immediately exercisable rational agency, then a problem arises. Due to spontaneous miscarriage of 60 percent of pregnancies, only 40 percent of prenatal human beings will ever exercise rational agency. If we hold that 40 percent or even a much lower percentage of successful development of rational agency is sufficient, then we are acting arbitrarily and moving closer to the view that rational agency is relevant (Lovering 2014, 381).

Even if we assume for the sake of argument that 60 percent of pregnancies spontaneously miscarry, this argument is problematic. Let's consider what it is to be a mammal. Part of what distinguishes mammals from nonmammals is the ability to nurse their young. So, human beings, dogs, and zebras are mammals; iguanas, tapeworms, and wasps are not mammals. Not so fast, replies the critic, do you not realize that some human beings, dogs, and zebras do not nurse their young, even cannot nurse their young? Males of all these species cannot nurse their young, females before puberty cannot nurse their young, and elderly females cannot nurse their young. There are even cases of females of reproductive age who cannot or do not nurse their young. The percentage of human beings, dogs, and zebras that capable of nursing their young is, therefore, well below 40 percent. So, are we mistaken in claiming that all human beings are mammals?

Of course not. In fact, all human beings, dogs, and zebras are mammals, not just females, and not just females of reproductive age who are nursing, because all these creatures belong to the kind of species that nurses its young. So too, there is nothing arbitrary about including prenatal human beings in the category of rational animals. Edward Feser clarifies what is at issue:

> The distinction between essence and properties makes sense of the distinction between normal and defective instances ... Given its essence, a cat has four legs, but this property might not manifest itself in a particular cat if the cat is genetically or otherwise damaged ... Its lack of four legs just makes it a defective cat, and precisely because fourleggedness is one of its properties.
>
> (Feser 2015, 233)

Feser goes on to point out that all human beings are rational animals, even if some human beings because of genetic malfunction, brain injury, or immaturity do not engage in rational activity. Why? We identify this human being as immature, or brain damaged, or genetically malformed because we have already properly categorized them as a rational animal and then seen their deficiency in light of this standard. The defect is understood only in light of the nondefective. Immaturity is understood by reference to maturity.

Now consider another objection to the substance view offered by Lovering. Imagine scientists discover a rational agency serum that can boost the intelligence of chimpanzees so they are like the apes in the movie *Planet of the Apes*. These chimps would clearly be persons with rights to live. "Now, clearly, the ultimate potential for rational moral agency in their case would be an accidental property," writes Lovering, who concludes that, therefore, "It's not the case, then, that an entity's moral standing *must* be a function of its essential properties" (Lovering 2014, 383). An entity's moral standing, as in the case of these apes, can rest on accidental properties.

This objection rests on the assertion that the apes in the sci-fi example have acquired their standing as rational agents because of an accidental quality. I disagree. That some apes got injected with the rationality serum may be accidental in some senses. For example, maybe, much like penicillin, the rational agency serum was found through an accident rather than as part of a deliberate plan to create rational agents. The property in question could also be accidental in that these particular apes rather than other apes in the lab were injected. Perhaps the scientists injected whichever apes happened to be on one side of the cage or perhaps they injected a particular ape if a flipped quarter landed heads but did not inject if the coin landed tails. The apes may have an accidental property in these senses, but in another sense the property in question cannot be accidental. The rationality serum causes not an accidental but rather a substantial change in the ape. The ape, in virtue of gaining radically new abilities, becomes a radically different kind of creature with a radically different moral status. Just as an injection that kills an ape brings about substantial change in the ape from living to deceased, so too the rational agency serum brings about a substantial change in the ape from being a nonrational agent to a rational agent.

Lovering also raises a dilemma against the substance view. Do dolphins, apes, and whales have intrinsic value or extrinsic value? He writes, "By 'intrinsic' value I mean value it's logically possible for something to have even if it were the only thing that existed" (Lovering 2014, 378). So, "extrinsic" value means a value that it's not logically possible for something to have if it were the only thing that existed. If there were only one person, that person would have intrinsic value. If there were only one toothbrush, that toothbrush would not have intrinsic value because a toothbrush gains extrinsic value only because people like to have clean teeth. Intrinsic value does not come in degree; a being either has it or does not have it. Extrinsic value, again by contrast, may come in degrees (this toothbrush is more or less useful). If intrinsic value does not come in degrees, then dolphins, apes, whales, and other intelligent animals either have moral status just like us (which advocates of the substance view reject) or must have no intrinsic value at all (which is counterintuitive, "given their similarities to beings with the ultimate potential for rational moral agency"; Lovering 2014, 383–384). On the other hand, if such creatures are to have only extrinsic value, then they have the same moral status as tools, which also seems counterintuitive because almost everyone condemns animal cruelty, but no one condemns toothbrush cruelty.

If nonrational animals do not have equal moral status with human beings, does it follow that they are mere tools with which human agents can do anything they please? This conclusion does not follow. Let's say that someone legally obtained Michelangelo's *Pieta* and decided to destroy it for no good reason. Is this action ethically problematic? Yes, you might say, because it deprives innumerable people of the chance to see this most amazing sculpture. So, let's say, the owner was the last man in the world, could he destroy it then for no good reason? The *Pieta* after all is a mere piece of marble, and so lacks intrinsic value. True, but the man who destroyed it would be acting badly inasmuch as it is against reason to destroy something of spectacular beauty without proper justification. A reasonable response to a thing of beauty is to contemplate and cherish it, not deface and destroy it. On the other hand, if he had to break apart the *Pieta* to make a barricade so that wild animals don't eat him, he would be justified in destroying the statue. In a similar way, a reasonable response to potential or actual suffering is to alleviate it. Just as beauty is something in general to be contemplated, suffering is something in general to be alleviated. Just as it is unreasonable to destroy an artistic treasure without sufficient justification, so too it is unreasonable to inflict pain on a sentient being without sufficient justification. To delight in inflicting pain is irrational. So, unless a person has a sufficient justification for inflicting pain on an animal, an agent is unjustified in doing so. Animal cruelty is therefore wrong, but we don't need to assume that animals have rights (any more than that statutes have rights) in order to come to this judgment.

Some Objections Considered

Some authors hold that an individual human being does not begin to exist until the point at which a human embryo is no longer able to split and become twins. As long as twinning is possible, we cannot say there is an individual human being. If there is no individual human being, then there is also no being who has a right to live. Twinning ceases to be possible after the development at three weeks after conception of the primitive streak (forerunner of the spine). So, until three weeks after conception, there exists no individual who has a right to live, so abortion is ethically permissible.

This objection confuses being an *individual* with being *indivisible*. One individual car is still one individual car despite the fact that it could be deconstructed and its parts used to make several other cars. The tapeworm is an individual tapeworm before it is cut and turns into two tapeworms. The possibility of twinning does not show that an embryo is not an individual, so it does not show that the prenatal human being in the embryonic stage of development does not have a right to life.

Embryo Rescue Case

In the Embryo Rescue Case, a firefighter runs into a burning hospital and must decide to save either ten embryos or one seven-year-old girl. Given the strength of the blaze, he cannot save both. Virtually everyone, even those who call themselves pro-life, think the firefighter should save the girl rather than the embryos. But if all human beings have an equal right to life, then surely, the firefighter should save the ten embryos rather than the girl, since it is better to save ten lives than just one. So, the pro-life view is not consistently believed even by people who claim to believe that every human being has inherent value.

To respond to the Embryo Rescue Case it is important to be precise about what the right to life means. The right to life is the duty of agents not to intentionally kill anyone with this right. So, whether the firefighter rescues the girl, allowing the human embryos to die, or rescues the human embryos, allowing the girl to die, assuming that the death(s) are not chosen by the fire-fighter as a means or as an end, then no one's right to life is violated. Moreover, on a pro-life view, although all human beings have an equal right to life it does not follow that all human beings have an equal right to be rescued. It may be permissible, all things considered, for a mother to rescue her own son or daughter rather than ten other children. In determining who should be saved a variety of circumstances matter in coming to an ethical decision. So, the firefighter in saving the girl rather than the ten human embryos might reasonably conclude, "This girl has plans, goals, dreams, and desires that would be thwarted. She has social relationships with her mom, dad, brothers, sisters, and friends. Her teachers have already taught her to read and invested so much in her education." By contrast, these circumstantial considerations do not bolster the case for rescuing the human embryos. Indeed, most human embryos are doomed to death, abandoned by their parents and never to be nourished to maturity. In cases of triage, a wide variety of considerations is morally relevant in making a determination about which lives are to be saved, and we need not deny the basic value of any human being in order to come to such decisions.

Bag of Marbles Analogy

Some people hold that an early human embryo is not really an organism at all, but a disorganized heap of cells that only later turns into an organism. If the early human embryo is not an organism, then the early human embryo is not a human organism. If there is no human organism present, then there is no human person with a right to live.

Empirical evidence provides a challenge to this view. Biologists recognize that even beings constituted by a single cell can be organisms. If even unicellular beings can be organisms, a multi-cellular human embryo cannot – simply on the basis of paucity of cells – be excluded from being an organism. But perhaps it is not the paucity of cells but a lack of inner organization in the cells that is the reason that a human embryo is not an organism. The challenge for this response is that the cells of an early human embryo are responsive to one another and exhibit a unified trajectory toward human maturity and an adaptive self-organization.

2.7   Is Abortion Permissible, Even If the Prenatal Human Being Has a Right to Live?

Perhaps the most famous article in philosophy is Judith Jarvis Thomson's "A Defense of Abortion" (1971). Thomson offers the violinist analogy as a way of justifying abortion even if the human fetus is a person with an equal right to life to you or to me. (Since the violinist analogy is supposed to work on supposition of fetal personhood, I won't be begging questions by speaking of the "unborn child" in this section.) Even if every human being has a right to life (including the human embryo and human fetus), abortion is still justified. Imagine that you wake up tomorrow hooked up to a world-famous violinist, such as Janine Jansen. A doctor comes into your room, and she tells you, "I'm afraid the famous violinist Ms. Jansen has a rare kidney disorder, and you've been selected to serve as her human dialysis machine. We cannot unhook you from Janine without killing her. So, since every person has a right to life, you'll have to be hooked up to her for the next nine months until she recovers from her ailment." Thomson says that surely you have a right to unhook yourself from the violinist, even though the violinist will die. So, Janine's right to life does not entail your duty not to unhook yourself. By parity of reasoning, the right to life of the child does not entail the duty of a pregnant woman not to unhook herself from the prenatal human being via an abortion.

   Philosophers have lodged many objections to Thomson's violinist analogy for abortion. We cannot, given limitations of space, explore all or even most of these objections, nor the replies to these objections, and the responses to these replies. Still, it is useful and important to get a sense of some of the major objections.

   The bodily integrity objection begins with the premise that persons have the right not to have their bodies used by others. This premise is sometimes used as another way to defend abortion. For example, no one should be forced to donate a kidney to save someone else's life, and so therefore no one should be forced to support a pregnancy until live birth.

But if we follow Thomson, holding that the unborn child is akin to a violinist, then this premise also entails that the human fetus has a right not to have her body used in order to keep someone else alive (or a fortiori for any lesser purpose). But in abortion, at least as characteristically performed, the bodily integrity of the unborn child is violated. If we have a right not to be forced to lose one kidney to keep someone else alive, we surely must also have a right not to involuntarily lose both kidneys, lungs, and our life itself in order to help someone else not to be pregnant. If the "right to control your own body" means anything, it means that no one can dismember a person without that person's consent. But this is precisely what takes place in a typical abortion. As abortion defender Jeff McMahan points out, "The standard methods for performing abortions clearly involve killing the fetus: the fetus dies by being mangled or poisoned in the process of being removed from the uterus" (2002, 378). To mangle or poison a person's body without the person's consent is to violate that person's rights.

Another challenge to the violinist argument is the consistency objection. If we have a right to detach ourselves from Janine at the cost of her life, if every person has fundamental equal rights, she surely has the right to detach herself from us at the cost of our lives. (Maybe there is someone else she'd prefer to be attached to.) But we presumably do not think that Ms. Jansen can detach herself from us at the cost of our lives. So, neither may we detach ourselves from her at the cost of her life. If correct, an agent acting on behalf of the human fetus may not detach the pregnant woman to save the unborn at the cost of the woman's life, nor may an agent acting on behalf of the pregnant woman detach her from her child at the cost of the child's life.

The intention/foresight objection is another reason to reject the violinist argument for abortion. In the case of the violinist, after Janine is unplugged, she dies of her underlying kidney disease. By contrast, the unborn child prior to viability is typically

suffering from no illness or disease. Abortion as typically performed is not a simple "detaching"of the unborn child who later
dies from an underlying disease. Rather, the goal of the abortionist is to end the life of the unborn child. That is why a "failed
abortion" refers to the case in which an abortion is attempted but
the child in fact does not die and is born alive. The goal of the
abortionist, as a means or an end, is not simply to end a pregnancy (which is also accomplished by live birth). The goal of the
abortionist is to kill, to make sure that the child in utero dies.

To make the violinist analogy more like abortion, imagine that
we "detach" ourselves from Janine by paying someone to remove
her arms and legs and then decapitate her with the goal of
making sure she is dead. Intentionally killing a person differs
ethically from foreseeing that a person will die. Hitler ordered
that German troops retreating from the Russian front be shot to
death. Eisenhower ordered that American troops storm the
beaches at Normandy. Both commanders knew that these orders
would result in death. But Hitler intends to kill his soldiers and
Eisenhower merely foresees the deaths of his soldiers. Given the
ethical import of the intention/foresight distinction, abortion is
not like the case of detaching from the violinist.

Yet another objection to the violinist analogy is that parents
have special duties to care for their own children. Even if a man
used contraception and did not want to become a father, a man
who conceives a child has special duties to support his child, to
love his own progeny, and above all not to intentionally harm his
son or daughter. Even if she used contraception and did not want
to become a mother, a woman who conceives a child has special
duties to support her child, to love her son or daughter, and
above all not to intentionally harm her child. We do not have
special duties to support famous violinists. Parents do have special
duties to support their own (minor) children.

It might be objected that no "parents" are involved in abortion, since the pregnant woman is making the choice in abortion
not to become a parent. This supposition is not consistently
embraced even by ardent defenders of abortion rights. For
example, former US President Barack Obama, who garnered

100 percent approval from the National Abortion Rights Action League, said, "We need fathers to realize that responsibility does not end at conception. We need them to realize that what makes you a man is not the ability to have a child – it's the courage to raise one" (Obama 2008). Indeed, a father's responsibility does not end at conception but begins at conception. If there is a father at conception, there is also a mother at conception. But a man is only a father, and a woman is only a mother, if the man and woman have a child. Ardent defenders of abortion, just as much as ardent critics, may ask a pregnant woman, "Who is the father?" We do not ask pregnant women who *will be* the father. We ask, "Who *is* the father?" This question presupposes that there currently is a father. But if there is a father, there is a child, and if there is a child, there is also a mother. Unless they have used in vitro fertilization with someone else's egg, pregnant women are the biological mothers, since the organism developing inside them is her own biological son or daughter. In every case, a pregnant woman is the gestational mother. Defenders and critics of abortion alike speak of "surrogate mothers" of cases in which a woman becomes pregnant with the intention of placing the child in another family after birth. If there is a mother, there is a child. And if there is a dependent, vulnerable child, both the child's father and mother have serious responsibilities to that child.

Now, these examples all might be explained away as inconsistencies of a merely verbal nature. If advocates of abortion were consistent, and spoke in accordance with what they truly believe, they would never speak of gestational mothers, or ask pregnant women, "Who is the father?" The relational terms "mother" and "father" do imply "child," but we can clear up the inconsistency *either* by speaking of a "child" or by not speaking of "mother" and "father."

But the violinist analogy is supposed to work on the supposition that the fetus is a human person, with a right to life. Human persons have parents, so the human fetus has parents. And parents have special duties to support (and above all not intentionally harm) their own dependent children. So even if the verbal inconsistency is eliminated, the objection against the violinist argument from special duties of parents to children remains.

These considerations also lead to the rejection of the intimacy argument for abortion. The reality of pregnancy – the unique, intimate relationship of the human being in utero and the pregnant woman – changes the ethics of feticide. As Dennis O'Brien notes, "The pregnant woman's womb is not just a geographic location for an independent entity that would be the same if it were located someplace else" (2011). To deny this reality, he says, is to reduce the pregnant woman to a "container."

The intimacy argument begs an important question: what reason do we have to think that independent *moral* status requires independent *physical* status? In cases of conjoined twins, one twin may depend on the other for continued life. But we don't think that the stronger twin may licitly or legally authorize a third party to kill her conjoined sister in order to terminate their intimate relationship. The moral status of conjoined twins has nothing whatsoever to do with whether one is dependent on the other. So, a relationship of intimacy and dependence is not an authorization for killing the vulnerable party.

Indeed, the intimate relationship of every pregnancy provides a powerful argument *against* abortion. Every human fetus is a mammal, and every mammal has a mother (Marquis 2010). As noted, and accepted in all other contexts outside abortion, sound ethical reasoning and just laws hold that human mothers and fathers have serious duties to care for and, above all, not harm their own dependent children. The intimate relationship that exists in every pregnancy can be further specified as the relationship of a mother to a child. Precisely because an expectant woman is a mother rather than a mere container, she has duties to her dependent unborn child.

Cases of Rape and Incest

How then does a consistent pro-life view handle cases of the rare but real instances of rape resulting in pregnancy? Cases of rape account for only about 1 percent of all abortions, but since there are millions and millions of abortions each year, the numbers of cases are far from negligible. Dennis O'Brien writes:

> A woman may have no moral or legal obligation to carry a child conceived by rape – but she may decide to do so. She has no obligation in justice to continue the pregnancy, but she may act from benevolence. Depending on circumstances, benevolence moves into the realm of moral heroism – in Christian terms, into saintliness. As Christians we are all called to saintliness, but saintliness is not a direct moral demand and it certainly is not enforceable by law.
>
> (O'Brien 2011)

On this view, abortion in the case of rape is ethically permissible.

O'Brien is correct that a woman who continues her pregnancy resulting from rape is a hero. In choosing to act heroically, she radically contradicts the act of her attacker. He imposed himself on her; she gives of herself for her child. He acted selfishly; she acts benevolently. He diminished her life for his pleasure; she nurtures a life despite the pain. The acts of such a woman contradict in a most striking manner the acts of the rapist.

Does it now follow that since such a woman is heroic, it is morally permissible to have an abortion? Unfortunately, evil people can force other, more vulnerable people into situations where the morally permissible but not heroic option is gone, and the only available choice is between moral heroism and moral evil. A torturer may force a prisoner to choose between remaining silent to protect his friends or telling secrets it would be immoral to reveal. A terrorist can force a hostage to choose between getting killed and helping the terrorist to kill. The rapist who impregnates a woman forces her to choose between enduring an unplanned pregnancy and inflicting life-ending harm on her own innocent daughter or son. It takes heroism to choose the former, but it is still wrong to choose the latter.

Pregnancy Risking the Life of the Mother

Is abortion ethically permissible if it is needed to save the mother's life? Imagine a woman named Caroline who is 10 weeks pregnant and learns that she has cancer of the uterus. The doctors tell her that if she is to have any chance of surviving the cancer, she must have her uterus removed immediately before the cancer becomes more advanced. Given current technology, no fetal person can survive outside the womb at only 10 weeks' gestation. If Caroline accepts that all human beings have basic rights, then she appears to be stuck between two ethically unacceptable alternatives. If she authorizes surgeons to remove her uterus, then her unborn son or daughter dies. If she does not authorize surgeons to remove her uterus, then the cancer will spread and she will die. Either she gets an abortion or commits suicide. It would seem that both choices are ethically unacceptable.

But this analysis of the case of a woman with a gravid cancerous uterus is mistaken. In fact, the choice she has is not between committing suicide or getting an abortion. Abortion is properly understood as any action that intentionally kills a human being prior to birth, either as a means or as an end. So, if Caroline chooses to have her uterus removed so as to remove the cancer from her body, this choice is not properly speaking abortion. She would have her uterus removed even if she were not pregnant. She would have her uterus removed if she didn't realize she was pregnant. The death of the child is not her goal, as a means or as an end. She is not, therefore, intentionally killing the child, so her action is not properly described as abortion. (Some writers call such actions "indirect" abortions as opposed to "direct" abortions in which the agent intentionally seeks the end of the child's life as a means or as an end.) Rather, the fetal death is a side effect of her decision to treat the cancer by hysterectomy.

In a similar way, a woman in this case could choose to not have her uterus removed because she seeks to give her baby a chance to live. She is not, by this choice, intending to kill herself but accepting her own death from cancer as an unfortunate side effect of not having her uterus removed. Perhaps she chooses this because she already has cancer elsewhere or because she desperately wants her child to survive. She is not killing herself as a means or as an end in order to save her child. It is not that she is intentionally killing herself (which would be suicide) in order to donate her heart to save her child who needs organ transplants.

We can generalize the principles applicable to cases in which the mother's life is endangered as follows. It is permissible to do one action with two effects, one good and one bad, so long as the action itself is ethically acceptable, the evil effect is not chosen as a means or as an end, and there is a proportionately serious reason for allowing the evil side effect. Double effect reasoning (or, less properly, the principle of double effect) is the name used to describe such general principles governing the ethical evaluation of action with more than one ethically significant effect. So, in cases in which a woman's life is endangered by pregnancy, she may undertake any otherwise licit medical treatment that would be used were she not pregnant, even if as a side effect of this treatment, the life of the human being in utero is ended. In such cases, the action done is ethically acceptable, the death of the child is neither a means nor an end of the agent, and there is a proportionally serious reason (namely, saving the mother's life) that justifies allowing the serious evil of the child's death as a side effect.

Abortion and the Law

Dennis O'Brien proposes that the law should tolerate abortion: "Grave as the moral fault may be, it [abortion] is not something that can fall under legal restraint" (2011). He is right, of course, that not all grave moral faults should also be illegal: it is seriously wrong to rudely insult your mother, hurting her feelings just for fun; it is seriously wrong to willfully and without excuse neglect development of good character; it is seriously wrong to waste all of your time and excess income merely on self-indulgent whims, like playing Star Wars video games 18 hours a day. None of these moral faults, however, should be matters of criminal law.

By contrast, many other moral faults, such as assault, theft, rape, and murder, should be against the law. One way to draw the line between these two kinds of cases is to consider whether the wrong done seriously injures the bodily or material well-being of another person. Private vices, like wasting all one's money on plastic surgery to make oneself look like Yoda, do not intentionally harm others. Insulting your mother does not seriously harm her in terms of her bodily or material well-being. By contrast, assault, theft, rape, and murder do impose serious bodily and material harms on innocent persons.

If morality and law are related in roughly this way, then abortion – understood here as the intentional killing of a human being prior to birth – is not merely a moral fault that deserves legal tolerance. Rather, fetal killing imposes a serious bodily harm on an innocent human being. The law in its role of protecting the innocent from serious harms imposed by others without due process of law should prohibit abortion just as it does other serious harms to the well-being of persons, such as assault, rape, kidnapping, and theft.

2.8   Punishing Women? First-Degree Murder?

Sometimes it is alleged that advocates of the pro-life view are inconsistent. Advocates of the pro-life view typically do not think that abortion should be punished like first-degree murder. So, they must not really believe that the life of a human being after birth and the life of a human being prior to birth have the equal value. The talk about "equal rights" is mere rhetoric.

If the pro-life view is correct, then abortion and murder of an adult are alike in that both involve the intentional killing of an innocent person. But there are important differences between an abortion and a typical case of murder. The first difference has to do with culpability in terms of knowledge and in terms of voluntariness. If I kill my auto mechanic, it is implausible in the extreme for me to try to excuse my act by claiming that I did not realize that the repairman was an innocent human being. By contrast, in many (maybe even most) cases of abortion, the woman obtaining the abortion does not believe that her authorization is terminating the life of an innocent human being. It could be that this ignorance is culpable or that this ignorance is inculpable, but ignorance of the identity of the victim is almost never involved in typical cases of murder.

Second, the voluntariness of the act is often mitigated by great fear or anxiety on the part of the woman, which lessens the voluntariness of the act. When mothers kill their own newborns, as sometimes happens, it is not unusual for the punishment due for killing an innocent person to be mitigated in light of the subjective factors, such as postpartum depression, that led to the killing. By similar reasoning, mothers who authorize an abortion are often motivated by intense fear, which reduces the voluntariness of the act. In many cases of abortion, again unlike typical cases of murder, duress is involved in which the father of the child, and sometimes others, pressures the woman into getting an abortion that she would have never gotten had the news of the pregnancy been greeted by all with joy.

Third, the victim of abortion – although fundamentally equal – is not equal in all respects to the victim in a typical murder. In a typical murder, the victim's death negatively impacts the victim's relatives and friends. The victim can no longer carry out his or her responsibilities at work or at home. The killing involved in murder may also make other people fear for their lives. The typical murder also brings a loss for all those who contributed to the life of the victim, including parents, caregivers, and teachers who helped the victim gain maturity. Finally, the typical murder thwarts the life plans of the victim whose dreams, ambitions, and plans are demolished by death. These characteristics – present in a typical case of murder – are not present in an abortion. A prenatal human being does not have friends, and relatives may not even know of his or her existence. Human beings who have been born need not fear for their own lives, if killing is confined to prenatal human beings. An unborn child does not have responsibilities at work or home on which others depend. Only one person – the pregnant woman – has contributed to the maturation of the fetus, and this one person is the one who is authorizing the abortion. Moreover, the prenatal human being does not have plans, ambitions, and dreams thwarted by getting killed. So, although the killing involved in abortion and the killing involved in a typical murder are the same in the most important fundamental sense – an innocent person's life is extinguished – in many other ways, they are not the same. It makes sense, therefore, for the law to take these many differences into account when determining the punishment appropriate for abortion and appropriate for typical murder.

By similar reasoning, assassination of the president of the United States should be treated more severely by law than the murder of a regular citizen in virtue of the president's role in society and the fact that the president's death can adversely affect not just immediate family members and friends but potentially the entire world. So too, the murder of a regular person should be treated more severely by law than the intentional killing of a human being prior to birth. Yet making such differentiations is consistent with holding that in terms of basic human dignity the president, the regular citizen, and the human fetus have equal basic rights. It is not inconsistent for a defender of prenatal human beings to embrace lesser penalties for abortion than for murder of post-natal human beings.

Moreover, prudential considerations of the enforceability of the law suggest that the penalties for the violation of laws forbidding abortion should fall upon abortionists rather than upon those getting abortions. Abortionists ending the lives of prenatal human beings typically perform their tasks as part of their regular routine without such mitigating factors. If women were subject to criminal penalty, it would make prosecution of abortions much more difficult, since women would be implicating themselves in criminal activity by testifying against the abortionists. Like laws against illegal drugs such as heroin, the law should focus on the drug dealers who profit from endangering others rather than on drug users who often suffer from their use. Similarly, laws against abortion should focus on abortionists who profit from killing, rather than women who often suffer from abortions.

2.9   The Myth of the Vampire Children

In her book, *Wandering in Darkness*, Eleanor Stump distinguishes two modes of philosophic discourse, arguing that both are needed to gain maximum insight. The first mode is impersonal and abstract, the second is personal and concrete. Up to this point, my presentation has been entirely in the first mode, but I'd like to conclude my remarks in the second mode.

As a university student in Boston, I participated in intercollegiate track and edited a campus newspaper. My professors prompted me to fall in love with learning, and I contemplated graduate school. Life was great, an ocean of potential.

A single phone call, a single sentence, changed my life forever. With just two words, Jennifer shook my world to its foundation: "I'm pregnant."

I had no income, no degree, and no set future plans. When the phone line went dead, I put on my running shoes and took off into the night. It was cold, Boston cold. I ran hard for eight, maybe ten, miles. My legs raced; my mind raced faster. I screamed at the sky.

Of course, you can't run away from your problems forever, so within days I settled into stage two of my reaction. I pouted. I pouted through my new summer job, painting houses in the hot sun. The previous summer I had taken a course in creative writing. Now I was alone on rooftop gables, taping up windows, and scraping away peeling paint.

I felt intense social isolation. No one I knew was going through anything like this. My college roommate Chad emailed me, asking about how my summer was going. I wrote I was doing a lot of painting. Imagining that I was imitating Monet, wearing a black beret, and dabbling in watercolors, he rejoined, "I'm so glad to see you are exploring your artistic side." "Yes," I replied, "I'm working with very large surfaces and exploring a bi-chromatic, domestic theme."

I even pouted through Jennifer's early labor. At one point, I actually told her to "pull herself together." (Future fathers, do not do this.) The nurses, luckily, were more sympathetic and were keeping a close eye on her. They watched the baby's internal heart monitor and noticed that it was dropping rapidly.

Suddenly it flatlined, and within seconds the entire room was filled with scrambling nurses and frantic doctors. Jennifer was prepped for an emergency C-section, and I quickly put on a sterile gown to join her.

The tiny little family that I had resented was in mortal danger. Jennifer was possibly dying. My unborn baby was surely dying. I was horrified.

Until that moment, I had bought into the myth that children are nothing more than a drain: a financial drain, an emotional drain, a dream-killing drain. I viewed children as little more than vampires, sucking the lifeblood out of their parents. I feared becoming one of those pale, shaky, duty-deadened adults. Only when I thought either Jennifer or my unborn child – or even both – could die did I realize how important they were and how destroyed my life would be if I lost them.

And then, suddenly, the baby's heartbeat returned. Minutes after the knife had been poised above her abdomen, Jennifer pushed, and our daughter, Elizabeth Anne, was born. It was the happiest day of my life. Elizabeth was perfect, gorgeous. I smiled so much that day that my cheeks were sore, and a joy surged through me that has never been equaled before or since.

On that day, I learned something vitally important. Having a child, even an unplanned child, is the most wonderful experience you will probably ever have. Children are not vampires. They are lovable, exasperating, insanely cute gifts. They don't drain parents of their life force – they enhance it. What do I mean?

One of the most important gifts that Elizabeth gave to me was a radical increase in gratitude to my own parents. I wanted to thank them right away. With Jennifer stable, I carried Elizabeth out into the waiting room. I was still in scrubs – sweaty and shaking. My parents were there. I was so happy that I just sort of fell into their arms. We were all overwhelmed with joy. Only when I had a child of my own did I truly begin to appreciate all that my parents had done for me: caring for me as a baby, raising me through turbulent teenage years, and helping me through the crisis of an unplanned pregnancy.

Gratitude and humility rise together. We do not feel grateful for what we are entitled to, but rather for what comes to us as a gift. The humble person is a grounded person, a person who realizes he or she is not master of the universe with power to define the meaning of life. Humility is often gained through humiliation, and children are inadvertent experts at humiliating their parents. When Elizabeth was getting potty-trained, we were invited to an acquaintance's house for brunch. It was a lovely morning, everyone joyous. I showed Elizabeth where the bathroom was and instructed her to make sure to make it there before any accident. In the course of the meal, she told us she had to go and wandered off. Minutes passed, and she returned. "Did you make sure to wipe?" I asked. "Yes, Daddy." Just to make sure everything was in order, the bathroom needed to be checked. Yes, indeed, Elizabeth had wiped her butt, but not with toilet paper. Apparently, she thought it would work better to use the white cashmere sweater of our host. Of course, we offered to have the sweater cleaned. Of course, the offer was declined. Of course, we never heard from the host again.

Perhaps the best gift that children bestow on their parents is the opportunity to reengage with the world, to relive life. I'm not talking about the psycho father who terrorizes his son on the football field and the creepy mother who heaps mascara on her five-year-old pageant princess in deeply misguided attempts to relive their own lives. I'm talking about the exciting, delightful ways in which parents get to teach their children, encourage their children, and play with their children. Before Elizabeth, I was passionate about running. After Elizabeth, I have continued to run, and I've competed in a mud run with her – having more fun than I ever thought running could provide. Before Elizabeth, I valued education and wanted to be successful. After Elizabeth, I still value education and success, and I've gotten to see her also adopt these values. Before Elizabeth, I loved to travel. Since Elizabeth, I still love to travel and have gotten to live with Elizabeth for two years in Europe. In other words, having a child isn't an "end" to the good things of life; it is an "and" to the good things of life.

Twenty-two years ago, I thought that having a baby was the worst thing that could have happened to me. I could not have been more wrong. Late this spring, Elizabeth graduated from college. A delightful tradition at my university is that faculty members may accompany their children on stage as their children receive their degree. While I was waiting for her name to be called, I remembered choosing that name with Jennifer. "Elizabeth Anne" is perfect, she had said. "It's sophisticated, feminine, classic, and strong. It's the perfect name." I had agreed, and so she was named. As I waited, recollections of Elizabeth's childhood overwhelmed me: teaching her to ride a bike, coaching her soccer team, taking pictures of her before prom. I started to weep quietly. But this was Elizabeth's day, and I didn't want the focus to be on some professor in tears, so I pulled myself together, made it to the front of the stage with her, and beamed with love and pride as she accepted her degree. I was not alone. The sunken gardens were full of parents all doing the same thing – glad not to have fallen for the myth of vampire children.

3   A Reply to Kaczor

Kate Greasley

There are certainly some things about which Professor Kaczor and I agree. I too think that "anyone who cares about creating a more just world should care about the issue of abortion." And, like Professor Kaczor, I believe that the central philosophical question for the abortion issue is the question about the moral status of the human fetus. In saying this, I must acknowledge again that I am not representing the full spectrum of philosophical defenses of abortion rights. Some such defenses, as we have seen, vehemently deny that the morality or legality of abortion depends on the personhood status of prenatal human beings. Arguments to this effect can be incisive and imaginative. But I believe that they ultimately fail.

Consequently, I am not going to contest Professor Kaczor's refutation of Judith Thomson's well-known violinist analogy argument, which I think is basically correct, even though there are many facets to the Good Samaritan argument that I think are worth exploring in depth. I wish my general defense of abortion to be right for the right reasons, rather than to field every potentially persuasive argument. As I say in Chapter 1, then, let us assume that opponents of abortion are right about what follows if the human fetus merits inclusion in the category of persons. If this were true, I agree with Professor Kaczor that abortion would be justified only in extremely limited circumstances.

3.1   Rules of Engagement

Professor Kaczor begins his essay with a few remarks about the terms on which abortion debate ought to be conducted. I am of course in agreement with him that men are entitled to form and express opinions on abortion, but would, perhaps, add a qualification to his comment there. I am not sure that reservations about men's standing to opine about abortion are always forms of ad hominem arguments. That is, I do not believe it necessarily ad hominem to remind a person that they are not among the main stakeholders in a disputed issue, and that this may inform how they think about it. Nor, I think, is it an ad hominem fallacy to suggest that those whose interests are the most deeply implicated in a debate have a special right to be heard in respect of it. While it is no doubt true that men do not alone possess the right to discuss their possible mandatory drafting for military service, it surely would be particularly important to hear men's views on a matter that concerns them so significantly. Questions of standing cannot feature in philosophical arguments about the morality of abortion, but they can nevertheless be worth attending to in certain contexts.

Next, we come to terminology, which Kaczor rightly notes is especially important in this topic. To be sure, some epithets such as "anti-choice" and "unborn child" are question-begging insofar as they will only be the correct terminology if the arguments propounded by those employing them are correct. Kaczor believes that the term "fetus" shares this feature of tendentiousness. He quotes the words of Professor John Finnis, who has claimed that to use that word in nonmedical contexts is "offensive, dehumanizing, prejudicial, manipulative" and "does not suggest an open heart." With respect to Professor Finnis, I would strongly contest this. The term "fetus" is in common use, not only in medical contexts, and is not morally loaded in favor of abortion rights. Using the word "fetus" does not prejudge the abortion issue, but rather refers to the subject at the center of the issue in a manner that underscores its distinctive characteristic *for* that debate: the fact that it is a nascent human being that exists inside someone else's uterus.

Neither do I believe that the term "fetus" is dehumanizing or depersonifying. People can and do regard creatures they refer to as "fetuses" with a considerable degree of reverence, and may well attribute to them full moral rights. But the term does not entail those things either, and this is a virtue here. Unfortunately, to describe such a patently morally neutral term as "prejudicial" and "manipulative," as Professor Finnis does, is itself a kind of (unwitting) manipulation. For my part, I would be satisfied to use the equally morally neutral terms "prenatal human being" or "fetal human being" of which Kaczor approves. However, since he does not stick to these terms, referring to fetal human beings at various points as a "child" or a "baby," I shall not entirely keep to them either.

There is, however, more than one way to be tendentious in moral discussions. When Kaczor defines the pro-life view as holding that "*all* human beings – regardless of race, religion, age, disability, or birth" have equal human rights, he builds into that very definition the foregone conclusion that denying equal moral status to fetuses is *just like* denying equal moral status to born humans of a certain race, religion, age, or disability. But this is not what defines the pro-life position. It is a possible implication of its being right, and that is a different thing. This may sound like pedantry, but it is not. In the abortion debate, the distinctive feature of the pro-life view is that it takes the human fetus to possess full moral status and the fundamental right to life. To say that the crux of the pro-life view is a principle of nondiscrimination on the basis of race, religion, and so on is to nudge the reader, ahead of any arguments, toward thinking that if he does not accept the pro-life view, he must embrace all such forms of discrimination, and that a general principle of nondiscrimination is the defining feature of that view, when it is not. What makes the pro-life view different from its antithesis is *only* the claim that human beings in utero have full moral rights from conception.

Last, and on a similar theme, I wish to stress the importance of accuracy when relaying facts about abortion provision and its legal availability. Sometimes, facts about abortion practice that are in one sense true can be presented in a way that distorts the reality of access and provision. Toward the beginning of his essay, Kaczor states that "in some countries, like the United States, abortion is legally permitted all the way through pregnancy to birth for any reason." This is very much a half-truth. The US Supreme Court recognized a qualified constitutional right to termination of pregnancy. The "qualified" aspect is very important. In *Planned Parenthood v. Casey* (1992), the Court held that, pre-viability (around 24 weeks), state-imposed restrictions on abortion were permitted so long as they do not place a "substantial obstacle" in the way of women seeking abortion. Post-viability, states are free to prohibit abortion under *Casey*, so long as they maintain exceptions to preserve the health and life of the pregnant woman. States have availed themselves extensively of this liberty they have to pass abortion restrictions both pre- and post-viability. Mandatory ultrasound laws, waiting requirements, state mandated counseling (some of which requires providing information about a medically rejected link between abortion and breast cancer), and parental notification requirements for minors are all numerous (Sanger 2008). Moreover, so-called targeted regulation of abortion providers (TRAP) laws, which require abortion clinics to meet emergency room facility standards, or obtain hospital admitting privileges, left the sole remaining abortion clinic in the whole of Mississippi fighting to remain open in 2014, and reduced the number of open abortion clinics in Texas from more than 40 to around seven or eight, leaving many women 300 miles away from the nearest clinic (*Whole Woman's Health v. Hellerstedt* 2016).

The Guttmacher Institute records that 46 separate abortion restrictions were enacted in state legislatures in 2016 alone, including bans on abortion for genetic fetal anomaly enacted by Indiana and Louisiana (2016). Forty-three states prohibit abortions past some point in pregnancy, and not all with the necessary health exception required by *Casey*. The law in Michigan, for example, permits post-viability abortions only where the woman's life is endangered. Several states in recent years have enacted post-20-week abortion bans, the constitutionality of which has been disputed (Guttmacher 2017). Moreover, limits on public funding for abortions means that accessing abortion even within state regulations can be difficult for many women.

All of this is a far cry away from the notion that abortion is legally permitted all the way up to birth for any reason. Kaczor's statement makes it sound as if any woman in America can simply walk into an abortion clinic at 30 weeks of pregnancy and get an abortion, just because she has changed her mind about childbirth, when this is very far from being the case. The facts about legal restrictions and abortion access are not relevant to the philosophical arguments that form the backbone of our competing views. But presenting the full picture about such things still matters in abortion discourse. It may have a considerable effect on a reader's sympathies if she is led to believe that abortion is more readily available, and at a later stage, than it really is.

At another point, Kaczor also describes abortion providers as people who "profit" from killing. This is another example of where I think we must be careful about how we state things. The word "profit" here has clear connotations of cynicism, exploitation, and capitalization on the need for abortion. I am not aware of how lucrative abortion provision is in the United States, but in the United Kingdom, abortions are provided either by the state-run National Health Service or by registered charities, sometimes working under NHS contracts. Neither kind of organization is a for-profit enterprise. Those working in abortion practice are of course paid to do their jobs, but I doubt that Professor Kaczor would describe himself as "profiting" from academia because it is how he earns a living. Far from seeking to make money out of abortion, medical practitioners who go into abortion treatment tend to do so out of a belief that they are providing a social and moral good, and often at some personal cost. They can be derided and stigmatized by their peers in the medical profession, as well as by others, and, by specializing in abortion provision, may well be passing up the opportunity to work in more prestigious and profitable areas of healthcare.

None of these issues goes to the heart of our arguments for and against abortion rights, to which I now turn.

3.2   Thresholds and "Magic Moments"

I agree with Professor Kaczor that an individual biologically human organism is present by the end of conception. With this undisputed, we both turn our attention to the question about when morally considerable human life, or personhood, begins. At what point does the immature human being come to possess the right to life? Kaczor takes the familiar approach of considering a number of putative thresholds for personhood in turn and finding them all wanting, with the exception of the conception threshold. One strand of argument, deployed against the birth threshold in particular, suggests that post-conception thresholds must be rejected because they do not identify a "magic moment" when the nature of the developing human being changes dramatically. If it is not clear why a certain threshold marks a cataclysmic change, or at what precise point that change comes about, then it ought to be rejected. Hence, of birth, he says: "The question arises why should birth be the 'magic moment' giving rise to the right to life." Equally, a problem for those who would place that threshold after birth is that they "decline to state at what moment after-birth abortion becomes ethically wrong."

It seems that, for Kaczor, the "magic moment" problem shows up, among other places, wherever a threshold for attaining full moral rights cannot be pinpointed precisely in a way that distinguishes it from its closest neighboring points. Thus, he asks supporters of the birth threshold:

> And precisely what location is it that gives us a right to live? Did we gain the right when any part of our body exited our mother's body? If half our body is outside our mother, say, past our hips, is this sufficient for the right to live? Must our whole body be outside our mother?

He continues:

> Of course, there is also no difference in the neurological development or the capacity of experiencing sensations of pain, or any other traits of personhood that emerge in the few moments that separate the partial birth of a human being and the completed birth of a human being.

As I have tried to show, someone may ask these questions about the conception threshold as well. With which microscopic development does the right to life begin? And what meaningful difference in development has occurred between, say, one moment during which the sperm and egg nuclei are fusing, and another moment? If the challenge is to find a nonarbitrarily distinguishable "moment" at which personhood begins, the defenders of the conception threshold will come up as short as everyone else, for no moments of that kind exist. I do not try to argue that birth, or anything else, is a "magic moment." Rather, I eschew the notion that there *is* a "magic moment" of this kind, such as would make the beginning of personhood a sharp borderline. The view that personhood does begin completely and instantaneously in a nonarbitrarily identifiable "moment" is what I called "punctualism." I presented some initial reasons for rejecting the punctualist view about how personhood and the right to life begins, which it may be worth briefly restating and elaborating.

What else might we be committed to saying about personhood were we to accept the punctualist thesis? I think that view would commit us to some untenable implications about the attainment or disappearance of personhood status. For instance, all discussants in the abortion debate presumably agree that dead human bodies, while being biologically human, are not persons and do not possess the right to life. The standard medical definition of death is irreversible brain death. Let us take an imaginary case, then, where a person's brain begins to die, one single cell at a time. At the beginning of the process, there is certainly a person in existence, and at the end, there is certainly not one. With which *individual* cell death did the human being's personhood and right to life extinguish? Just as punctualism posits that there is a correct answer to the question about exactly when personhood begins, so I think it must hold that there is a correct answer to the question here about exactly when it ends. Yet there is no individual cell with which it seems sensible to identify the sudden disappearance of personhood status. Certainly, whichever cell one might pick is not nonarbitrarily distinguishable from the cell deaths on either side of it.

We might also want to ask which further views about the nature of personhood would sponsor the punctualist thesis about personhood's beginning. What reason do we have for thinking that personhood begins suddenly and sharply? Perhaps some version of body–self dualism, a view that Kaczor considers, could underwrite the punctualist view. Someone who, for instance, believes that "we" are really immaterial entities separate from and further to our human bodies, such as souls or Cartesian egos, might be tempted to say that "we," persons, emerge suddenly and completely. Perhaps it makes little sense to think of such substances materializing vaguely and incrementally. But Kaczor does not accept body–self dualism, and I do not wish to accept it here either. If, instead, the properties on which we take personhood to supervene, be they physiological or psychological, fade in vaguely and gradually, this is itself compelling reason for thinking that moral status begins in the same way.

As soon as we reject punctualism, the standards that an acceptable threshold must meet immediately become different. To be sure, we will still expect a threshold to correspond with morally significant, personhood-relevant developments, but not to pick out a "magic moment" of complete transformation that is nonarbitrarily distinguishable from its closest neighboring points. This falls prey to the sorites-type fallacy of thinking that if no such moment can be identified, then no change has in fact taken place – that the nonheap has not turned into a heap at all if we cannot say with which individual grain the change occurred.

But I think Kaczor can also be understood to be arguing here that birth is simply lacking in any moral significance relevant to the right to life, regardless of it being a process comprised of innumerable points. In other words, there is nothing to suggest that the fact of having been born is in any way constitutive of personhood. As he says, plenty of creatures lacking a strong right to life have been born, including rats and aphids. He also thinks the birth threshold suggests that human beings without morally relevant differences can nevertheless have different moral standing. As he says, "It is hard to believe the right to life is episodically related to us based on our current location."

On my account, however, these complaints misconstrue what a threshold of personhood ought to be like and what counts as a virtue of one practical threshold or another. It is not my, nor, I think, anyone else's contention that the fact of being born is a sufficient condition for personhood. Rats and aphids are not persons by virtue of having been born. They are not persons at all, at any time in their biological lives, and hence we have no cause to think about when the threshold of personhood might fall in respect of them. We do not already believe that they are creatures which gradually and vaguely become persons. But we do think this about nascent human beings, which is why the threshold issue becomes pertinent. I argued that there is a moral and practical necessity driving the need to stipulate an absolute and clear threshold of personhood somewhere within the range of reasonable answers. I think that it goes strongly in favor of birth that birth does in fact correspond to a development of momentous significance socially, biologically (in the ways I described), and psychologically, in that it places the new human being in the necessary context for the development of conscious life, a sense of self, agency, and so on. Moreover, birth has the legal and practical virtues of being clear, practically usable, and universally salient and recognizable.

This is not the same as saying that birth corresponds to a magical, transformative moment; but neither does it entail that the threshold of personhood is a matter of pure stipulation. Reason still constrains where the acceptable range of thresholds lies. Nor would supporting the birth threshold require us to believe that anything's right to life is based on its current location. The suggestion, rather, is that no precise threshold – birth, 24 weeks, 30 weeks, and so on – makes all the difference between the right to life and its absence, but that it is nonetheless important to settle on one, and that there is much to recommend birth, assuming that it is within the range of acceptable answers and that there is no obvious consideration against it.

3.3   Constitutive Properties and Counterexamples

Most philosophical defenses of abortion rights take personhood or the right to life to be grounded in developmentally acquired, usually psychological, characteristics. I argue that this is basically right, even though I am drawn to the idea that a derivative moral status extends to individuals that are related to paradigm persons in the right way – say, through sharing their mode of embodiment – even if they do not bear out the constitutive properties of a person.

Kaczor argues that personhood cannot be basically constituted by developmentally acquired capacities that are not present from conception. In seeking to demonstrate this, he employs the standard reductio ad absurdum argumentative approach, showing through the use of counterexamples that any developmental property one might pick is neither necessary nor sufficient for personhood. For example, considering the conscious desires criterion, Kaczor asks how it could account for the personhood of hypothetical persons who manage to extinguish all desire for life or anything else. He also thinks it cannot account for the right to life of young infants, who do not experience conscious desire properly defined. The sentience criterion is inadequate, he argues, for the capacity to suffer and to experience pain does not appear to be a necessary condition for the right to life (what about those born with the rare condition that renders them incapable of pain experience?). It does not seem to be sufficient either – rats can also experience pain, but they are not persons. Infants and more mature human beings may not be capable of self-awareness, but surely they *are* persons. And episodic problems blight nearly all developmental criteria. If consciousness or self-awareness is necessary for the right to life, do I lose the right to life when I fall asleep, or go under anesthetic, and regain it again on waking? This does not seem right.

As we can see by now, almost any post-conception human development can be either unnecessary for personhood, insufficient, or both. After finding this to be true of the main candidates he surveys, Kaczor cites an "elimination argument" in favor of

the conception criterion of personhood. "By the process of elimination of other accounts," he writes, "a remaining possibility is
that the right to life begins when a human being begins." The
elimination argument does not exhaust Kaczor's case in favor of
the conception criterion, but it is nonetheless worth underscoring
its limitations here. Kaczor believes that the reductio ad absurdum arguments applicable to developmental criteria of personhood point in favor of the conception criterion. However, as we
have already seen, the conception criterion has its own share of
reductios to answer, and in fairness they must be treated just as
seriously.

I am not convinced this is the case when, for example, Kaczor
answers the reductio based on the relative badness of a zygote's
death as compared with the death of a fully matured human
being. The apparently absurd conclusion here, stemming from
the conception criterion, is that killing the zygote or embryo is
every bit as wrong as killing the mature human. On the "future-
like-ours" account, it is even *more* wrong, since the zygote has a
greater amount of valuable future ahead of it. Kaczor's reply to
this counterintuitive conclusion involves asserting that there are
two different metrics of the badness of death and the wrongness
of killing – the "intrinsic" and "circumstantial" aspects. On one
metric, it is equally as wrong to kill any conceived human being,
and equally as bad when one dies. On another metric, not all
deaths are as bad and all killings as wrong. The death of a
university student is "circumstantially" worse than that of a baby,
since she will have friends, investments, and meaning in her life.
And the death of a president is "circumstantially" worse than the
death of an ordinary person in virtue of its worse knock-on
effects.

Kaczor believes that by recognizing these dual aspects of the
badness of death, we can preserve the intuition that the deaths of
mature human beings are worse than the deaths of zygotes, while
accepting the thesis that the right to life begins at conception.
However, one is left wondering here what space there really is
between the things Kaczor wishes to affirm and deny: that all
conceived human beings have an equally strong right to life, and

that the death of all human beings is not equally bad. He claims that "in one sense the harm [of death] varies from person to person," since someone who has great friends, meaningful work, etc., can lose more from dying than someone who does not have those things. Likewise, his claim is that, all things considered, the death of a president is worse than the death of an ordinary person. Yet it seems to me that this is precisely what the equality thesis Kaczor supports must deny. If equal moral status among humans means anything, it must surely mean that all human deaths are equally as bad, and killings equally wrong, on the only metric that matters. I do not see how one can hold that in an important way the death of a person with friends, family, and purpose is worse than the death of someone lacking such things *and* be seriously committed to the equality thesis.

Moreover, Kaczor's theory about the dual aspect of the badness of death does little to answer the Embryo Rescue Case reductio. This is because we can amend that case to hold that the deaths of the embryos will in fact cause far more sorrow for others and many more negative side effects than the death of the baby or child. Here, the deaths of the embryos are "circumstantially" worse on Kaczor's account, and they are also "intrinsically" worse, since the embryos will lose more in the way of a valuable future than the older human beings. Consequently, in this case we still get the counterintuitive conclusion that it is better to rescue the many embryos than the one born child.

Some of Kaczor's arguments, such as his arguments against the birth criterion and the sentience criterion, attack the sufficiency of the supposed marker of personhood. As he argues, creatures that are clearly outside the category of persons can be both born and sentient, so these things alone cannot be constitutive of personhood. Of course, the same thing is true of the conception criterion. Mice have been conceived too, and so have horses. Insofar as it is a reason to reject a personhood criterion, then, the insufficiency problem applies to conception as well.

As I outlined in my original essay, however, defenders of post-conception personhood criteria do not always claim that one capacity or development is individually necessary and sufficient for full moral status. Rather, the approach I endorsed took the concept of a person to be constituted by a cluster of psychological and sentience-based capacities, no single one of which is absolutely necessary for bearing out personhood. Kaczor might reject the potential for this pluralistic approach to get around the problem that every capacity (linguistic ability, rationality, conscious desires, and so on) is subject to a counterexample. If none of these characteristics is individually necessary to constitute personhood, how are they combinedly sufficient to constitute it? Do the counterexamples not reveal each criterion to be simply irrelevant to personhood status?

However, many of our everyday concepts and categories are complex in precisely this way. We can take, as an example, the ordinary concept of friendship. There are many constitutive features of friendship: loyalty, shared interests, enjoyment of one another's company, mutual care, regular contact, and a common world view, perhaps. If we analyzed each of these features individually, we would surely conclude that some friendships can do without them, and that they are therefore inessential. But we would be making a mistake if we inferred from this that none of these traits is constitutive of friendship. The right test for conceptual salience with friendship is not to ask whether a friendship could conceivably exist without this or that feature, but whether it would be impoverished qua friendship by its absence. Friends *can* be distant, careless about each other's lives, lack common interests, and so on. But it seems clear that a deficiency in any of these respects is a deficiency relative to what it means to be someone's friend. Furthermore, it seems that even though any one trait is disposable, a sufficient number of friendship-constitutive traits must be present before a friendship can be said to exist. The developmental concept of personhood that Mary Anne Warren proposed follows the same structure. On this account, the concept of a person grasps at a certain kind of being that bears out a sufficient number of characteristics related to cognition and sentience, such as facilitate a strong attachment to what happens to her.

3.4   The Future-like-Ours Argument and the Argument from History

As well as the elimination argument, Kaczor presents two further positive arguments in favor of the claim that personhood begins at conception: Don Marquis's future-like-ours argument, and the argument from history. The first argument, which I considered briefly in my own essay, is a form of potentiality principle. Marquis argues that since the deprivation of a valuable future is what explains the wrongness of killing mature human beings, killing prenatal humans is just as wrong, since it too deprives the individual of a valuable future – indeed, an even more valuable future, for the prenatal human probably has more life ahead of it. Kaczor considers the objection that Marquis's theory proves too much by implying that the death of a prenatal human is *worse* than the death of a 20-year-old. He rehearses Marquis's own response that the objection merely demonstrates a lack of imagination, for if we could only see everything that the prenatal human has lost by being killed – an entire lifetime of human goods – we would agree that killing it is worse.

But this, to me, does not adequately answer the objection based on the counterintuitive implications of Marquis's theory. We are well aware of the sort of future that characterizes a full human life, and can easily impute this future to a zygote, even if we cannot determine specifically what that life will be like. The problem, I believe, is that even when we can imagine that future and impute it to a zygote, we are not convinced that the zygote has a strong interest in realizing it. It seems that the zygote is simply not the kind of creature that can have a stake in its own future, and that more is required than merely "having" the future of a person in order to possess all the rights of a person. In Michael Tooley's "talking cats" thought experiment, a cat that has only just been injected with the transformative, person-making serum now possesses the future of a person, even though the serum has yet to take effect. Barring any interference, it will come to have a future like ours. But the cat does not, for this reason, seem to possess any stronger rights than it did the second before it was injected.

The future-like-ours account of the wrongness of killing may also present a problem for those committed to the view that all conceived human beings are equal in respect of their right to life. As we see, Kaczor abjures capacities-based accounts of personhood for being irreconcilable with basic human equality. If those capacities are themselves scalar, as they seem to be, then how can personhood status be absolute and equal? But the future-like-ours account also propounds a basis for the wrongness of killing that is a matter of degree: the deprivation of a future of value. We do not all have the same amount of valuable future left. Some of us have a lot of it, others very little. And, of course, we never know for sure just how much of a future we really have. Kaczor cannot argue that the equality problem is salient for capacities-based accounts of personhood but not for the future-like-ours account, when it, too, ties personhood to a property that admits of gradations. If, instead, there were some way, on the future-like-ours account, to explain or justify the extension of an equal right to life to all human beings regardless of their amount of valuable future, we will need to know why the same sorts of considerations could not neutralize the equality problem in respect of developmental accounts of the right to life.

Next, the argument from history. Professor Kaczor reminds us that every time we have gone about the business of dividing human beings into full rights holders and other partial or non-rights holders, we have fallen into grave moral error. Since the argument for abortion rights depends on another division of the same sort, the mistakes of history speak strongly against it. As he writes, "History teaches us that we have always made a mistake in choosing the ethics of exclusion." Perhaps we might say that a human nonperson is a kind of "suspect classification," as constitutional lawyers would term it – a category the very existence of which should alert us to the presence of some pernicious discrimination. I must admit that I used to find the argument from history fairly persuasive, at least insofar as it places the burden of argument more squarely on defenders of abortion rights. I am far less sure about that now. One reservation I have about the argument is that it is a little too easy. By immediately placing the pertinent distinctions for abortion in the same category as, say, race, sex, and disability discrimination, it denies that the main problem at issue in abortion – when and how human beings get their right to life – is a genuine problem. Rather, it simply asserts that the very idea of human organisms without full moral rights ought to be put out of our minds because of a sound rule of thumb that holds outside the context of abortion. While it is true that the philosophical argument for abortion does make distinctions between living human beings with different moral rights, I believe that it prejudges the important questions too much to think that this counts strongly against abortion rights.

An analogy might be drawn here with the debate about animal rights. Following Kaczor's line of argument, someone might point out that almost every time a minority voice has spoken out in support of living beings whose moral rights they believed were being underestimated, the minority voice has been in the right. Is this, in itself, a strong ground for accepting the claims by animal rights protestors that we ought to cease using animals for food and other products? I do not wish to suggest there is no merit in those claims; surely there is. But the animal rights debate invites challenging questions about the basis of moral status that an "argument from history" of this kind just denies can be seriously asked.

3.5 Endowment and Substance

In the "argument from personhood as endowment," Kaczor contrasts what he terms an "endowment" account of personhood with a "functional" account. He claims that only if we are valued because of "who we are," as per the endowment account, rather than "what we have done," as per the functional account, do we have the basis of equal rights for all. This is because our functioning (meaning, for Kaczor, the capacity for rationality, self-awareness, and so on that we exhibit) exists on a sliding scale. So the functional account suggests that we should value persons in degrees.

"On the endowment account," he writes, "the kind of thing we are, our nature, is what gives us our value." However, the same thing can be true of a capacities-based account of personhood as well. Those who think that personhood supervenes on developed psychological capacities such as rationality or sensitivity can claim that these things are part of the nature of persons. So by possessing their rights in respect of such capacities, persons *do* get their rights through things that are part of their nature.

Kaczor also claims that the endowment account, when understood to support personhood-from-conception, "avoids the problem of thresholds." Which threshold problem exactly is he referring to here? He suggests that the issue is one of practical line-drawing: we can easily determine whether or not a human being exists, but not whether it is self-aware. Tests for self-awareness, he says, cannot be precise, and "decisions about who shall live and who shall be killed cannot justly be made on the basis of vague and arbitrary tests." But we can easily determine whether a human being has been born or not, or reached the point of viability. There are no serious practical issues there. If Kaczor's worry is that sorites-type arbitrariness surrounds these thresholds, then, as we have seen, this will not be a point of distinction from conception. There is, of course, a time by which it is indisputable that a human being has been conceived, but the same is true of birth or of viability. Moreover, the practical concern about avoiding any ambiguity in the relevant tests does not show the self-awareness criterion of personhood to be wrong. Practical usefulness may well be a virtue of a stipulated threshold of personhood within an acceptable range, as indeed I argue. But it cannot support one or another view about the basic concept of a person. When it comes to the constitutive features of a person, the accuracy with which certain traits can be gauged do not bear on the correctness of one conception or another.

Kaczor also claims that "what matters is what the individual is substantially and essentially, rather than the fleeting characteristics an individual may have accidentally or nonessentially." In his view, it seems, the only thing that human beings are "substantially and essentially" is human beings, in possession of a "rational nature" and "oriented" toward realizing certain goods, such as reasoning and language ability. Moreover, *all* biological human organisms share this same nature, whether they express it or not. Thus it is that human beings "as such," possessing a rational nature, are more valuable than dogs "as such." Being rational is part of a human being's "essence" in the way that having four legs is part of a cat's essence, even though there are three-legged cats. The view does not succumb to "speciesism," he argues, because it is possible that nonhuman species (Kryptonions, angels, or dolphins) share the same rational nature. Against the speciesism charge, then, Kaczor states that it is not being human that is sufficient for personhood, but being an "individual substance of rational nature."

I propose we break down Kaczor's argument here as follows, then:

1. We possess the right to life in virtue of the *kind* of being we are, not the kind of example we are of that sort of being – by dint of our essence not our attributes.
2. What we are essentially and substantially are human beings with a rational nature, ergo:
3. All human beings with a rational nature have a right to life.

Is this correct? The notion that we possess the right to life by virtue of what we are essentially, through our nature, and not what we happen to be like "accidentally" is a compelling one. However, as I have already noted, defenders of capacities-based accounts of personhood might say the same thing. That is, they might say that psychological capacities of a certain kind are the essential characteristics belonging to *persons*, without which they would not be the very thing that they are. They are just not essential characteristics of *human beings*.

Kaczor may respond by suggesting that this answer implies body–self dualism, the belief that human beings and the persons that inhabit them are separate entities, not one and the same thing. This is a belief he thinks we have much reason to reject. Yet I think it possible to reject the claim that all living human organisms are essentially and substantially persons without being committed to any such view. Let us assume that we, persons, are identical with our human bodies. We are just conscious, thinking animals, and nothing separate from or further to them. Would this make it true that all human beings are persons from conception? I think not. One remaining possibility is that personhood or the right to life is a nonessential characteristic of human beings, which they may possess at one stage and not at others, like the quality of being a philosopher, or being 25 years old. On this view, we are all identical with our human bodies, but we are simply not persons at all stages of our existence. I think that, on reflection, someone who rejects body–self dualism must accept that this is the case, since she presumably would not agree that dead human bodies are persons with full moral rights, even though they are, she must admit, numerically identical with the human being that was alive.

This answer would involve denying that personhood is an essential property of all human beings. Does that also entail that personhood is not an essential property of creatures that are persons – that it is one of their attributes, rather than part of their nature? If "nature" is taken to mean just the conditions for continued existence as the same numerical thing, there is nothing obviously problematic about this claim. It seems clearly correct to me to hold both that person-beings like mature humans are identical with their bodies and that they are not persons at all times of their existence. But this is not to deny that being a person is a fundamental part of a human being's nature in some other way. Just as a caterpillar that metamorphoses into a butterfly appears to go through a fundamental and substantial change in nature *while remaining the same thing,* so it seems true to say of human beings that they go through a fundamental change in nature as and when they become persons, while remaining the same numerical entity. As is the case with the butterfly, to hold that the creature remains the same individual being throughout the transformation in no way belittles the very substantial nature of the change. Being a butterfly is an important part of the nature of creatures that are butterflies, even though those same creatures were once caterpillars.

Kaczor considers a thought experiment–based objection to his "substance view" where a "rational agency serum" is able to transform ordinary apes into the reasoning, speaking creatures that we see in the movie *Planet of the Apes* (similar to Tooley's talking cats thought experiment). The objection is that the capacity for rational agency seems accidental in their case, not an essential part of their nature, though they are still persons. Kaczor replies that the person-making properties would not be accidental here, however, even if acquired through accident. He writes:

> The rationality serum causes not an accidental but rather a substantial change in the ape. The ape, in virtue of gaining radically new abilities, becomes a radically different kind of creature with a radically different moral status. Just as an injection that kills an ape brings about a substantial change in the ape from living to deceased, so too the rational agency serum brings about a substantial change in the ape from being a nonrational agent to a rational agent.

However, on a bodily criterion of numerical identity (which Kaczor supports), rational agency does *not* appear to be an essential feature of the ape. We know this because the ape did not possess rational agency before he was injected, but was still the same basic thing, the same ape. It appears to be plainly true of the ape both that he is now a person and that he is the same ape from before, who was not a person and did not have a rational nature. If this is correct, it shows we accept that the same individual being can be a rights-holding person at one time of its existence and not at another.

3.6   Some Objections Reconsidered

In his penultimate section, Kaczor addresses some objections to the hard-line pro-life stance based on the counterintuitiveness of its implications. In different ways, he attempts to take the sting out of some of these objections by showing how the putative implications can be softened. Answering the Embryo Rescue Case

argument, he states that the right to life is violated only when
someone is intentionally killed, not when a person is allowed to
die. But this answer evades the main thrust of the Embryo Rescue
Case, which is that in choices about whom to save when personal
attachments are not in play (when none of the imperiled parties
are related to me), the moral imperative is to save the many over
the few. Hence, if the embryos are the many and the baby the
few, we ought to save the embryos. Here, however, it seems
outright perverse to rescue the embryos over the baby. Moreover,
this intuition holds regardless of the knock-on effects of saving
one or the other. That is, even if we knew that the baby, or child,
had no social connections, no plans, dreams, desires, investment,
and that the death of the embryos would cause vast human
sadness, the original intuition still, I think, holds.

Second, Kaczor acknowledges that the pro-life view cannot
countenance exceptional abortion permissions when pregnancy
results from rape or incest. But he attempts to soften this implication, first by underscoring the "rareness" of abortions as a result
of rape, which he claims account for only 1 percent of all abortions. I do not know from where he draws this figure, but it is
widely known that rape is vastly underreported. Moreover, as
feminist scholars have pointed out, women may lack control over
their sexuality in a number of ways that do not amount to the
degree of coercion required to meet the legal standard of rape.
Kaczor also suggests that, while aborting a pregnancy brought
about by rape is morally impermissible, it is nonetheless an act of
heroism for a woman to continue a pregnancy in such circumstances. However, this does raise a question about the consistency
of saying that an act is both morally required *and* heroic. We tend
to think of heroic acts as supererogatory. *Perhaps* it is possible that
we are sometimes morally required to do a heroic thing. Usually,
though, if a person is acting heroically by making a certain choice,
this indicates that it is not morally obligatory.

Third, Kaczor argues that an abortion performed in order to
save the life of a pregnant woman by removing her cancerous
womb is still permissible on the pro-life view. This is because,
even though a fetus is a person, such a choice, which aims to save

the life of the pregnant woman and would be chosen even if the fetus were not present, is not "properly speaking abortion." He cannot mean to say, though, that homicide is permissible wherever the death of the victim is, strictly speaking, a side effect of the desired result, or where the act would be carried out regardless of the victim. If this were so, a bomber who explodes an aeroplane with the intention to collect the insurance on a valuable package, merely indifferent to the inevitable deaths of all the passengers, would not fall afoul of the prohibition on homicide.[1] Permissible killing *also* involves proportionality requirements. Conventional morality holds that killing a person, other than in self-defense, is only ever permissible when it is necessary to prevent an even greater loss of life. In abortion, when would that be?

It seems to me that the only scenario in which killing the fetus prevents an even greater loss of life is where both woman *and* fetus are doomed to die unless the fetus is killed. No other scenario could justify killing, intentionally *or* as a side effect, where two persons of equal moral value are concerned, as Kaczor believes is true in abortion. Consider, for example, a case of two conjoined twins whose bodily interdependence has the consequence that unless one of the twins is killed, the other will quickly die. If we do nothing, however, one twin will still survive. Here, killing one twin will not preserve the greater amount of life, since it will have the same result as doing nothing: one twin lives and one twin dies. Assuming that the lives of woman and fetus are of equal moral value, the implication in abortion is that performing an act that will kill the fetus is not permissible unless doing nothing will result in the death of *both*.

Suppose differently, though, that killing *either* one of the twins would save the other, in circumstances where, if we do nothing, both will die. Even here, when killing one person does prevent greater loss of life (because it is the only way to avoid *two* deaths), some might think that the choice between lives prohibits us from

---

1 This is a famous example constructed by the criminal law theorist Glanville Williams (see G. Williams (1987), Oblique Intention, *Cambridge Law Journal*, 46(3), 417.

killing either twin. If this is right, then again assuming that both pregnant woman and fetus are persons, the only scenario in which abortion will be permissible is where killing the fetus can save the woman, but killing or allowing the woman to die cannot save the fetus, and where doing nothing will result in the deaths of both individuals.

Furthermore, if Kaczor really does mean to make it a condition of a life-saving abortion that the act carried out would have been chosen even if not for the fetus's existence (as I assume he does when he underscores that in the cancerous uterus abortion, the woman "would have had her uterus removed even if she were not pregnant"), this will, on the pro-life view, limit the conditions for a permissible life-saving abortion even further, to only those in which the particular procedure that kills the fetus would have been carried out regardless of the pregnancy. A woman would not, on this reasoning, be permitted a life-saving abortion where the pregnancy itself is endangering her life, say, by causing pre-eclampsia. I think that these very extensive constraints on permissible abortion may well be what follows if we suppose that the fetus is a person from conception. Thus, the fact that most of us will find them difficult to accept is an indication that we do not accept the proposition about fetal personhood.

Fourth, Kaczor attempts to rebut the claim that if pro-life advocates really view abortion as homicide, then they should, if consistent, support punishing women who abort as murderers. One reason Kaczor argues this is not so has to do with women's reduced culpability for abortion. He argues that women who abort are not culpable to the same extent as ordinary murderers because of their genuine, if mistaken, belief that prenatal human beings are not rights-holding persons. But this is not convincing. It is not a mitigating factor in murder if a defendant falsely, even if honestly, believes that her victim was not a person in the fullest sense. Just imagine a killer pleading in court that his punishment ought to be stayed because he did not believe that the victim, being of a different race, possessed the right to life.

Returning to an earlier theme, Kaczor also argues that since killing an "unborn child" is in some ways not as bad as killing more mature human beings (a prenatal human lacks friends, ambitions, and plans; its relatives will probably be less grieved by the death; and so on) there may be reason for the law to apportion less punishment for abortion than for "typical murder." Again, though, these are not the sorts of considerations that can ever be relevant when we are discussing punishment for the murder of full rights-holding persons. We do not punish murder proportionately to the bad consequences of a victim's death, or discount sentences to account for a victim's lack of ambition, plans, relationships, and so on. These are simply not mitigating (or aggravating) factors in murder. Neither do I agree that it makes sense, on the pro-life view Kaczor espouses, to enforce abortion prohibitions only against abortion providers and not against women who avail themselves of their services. This, surely, would be akin to punishing hit-men for the murders they commit but not those who employ them as their agents.

3.7   Vampire Children and Reproductive Choices

Finally, and very briefly, Professor Kaczor closes his essay with his own personal story of an unplanned child who brought a lot of joy to his life. The story is a lovely tribute to his daughter and to everything wonderful that parenthood can bring. I feel moved to remind the reader, nevertheless, that just as he is utterly glad, in retrospect, for the life of his daughter, so too can people be glad and satisfied in respect of their decision to terminate a pregnancy. Stigma may often preclude people from being brazen about their affirmation of an abortion decision. Abortion stories are not socially acceptable or heart-warming tales to tell. It would also be strange to celebrate a termination decision the way that Kaczor celebrates the life of his daughter. Yet people *do* celebrate the many things for which a termination decision might be a sine qua non: the education it allowed them to complete; the particular friendships and relationships that might not otherwise have formed; perhaps even future children who would not otherwise have existed. Many good things in life that people are moved to affirm exuberantly, including the lives of their children, can be causally dependent on abortion decisions, even if the abortion itself is not a direct object of affirmation.

There may well be value in reminding someone uncertain about a reproductive decision that any new child they bring into the world will surely bring them enormous joy and be cherished. Of course children are not life-destroying vampires. What I am unsure about is how strongly this consideration can really figure in rational and prudential reproductive decision-making. I do not think women facing unplanned pregnancies are in much doubt that should they go on to have the child, he or she will become a much celebrated and loved part of her life. But even if a person could be certain that she would relish becoming a parent to a new child, and come to affirm the decision, this might not tell her whether becoming a parent will make her better off relative to the preferences she has *now*. Some recent philosophical work in rational decision theory has helped to illuminate why this is so. Becoming a parent is such a life-changing event that it may quite dramatically change who we are and the preferences we harbor. Along these lines, the philosopher Laurie Paul has suggested that becoming a parent is a "transformative experience" that can itself change someone into the kind of person who values and finds joy in parenthood (2014). But if this is right, then one cannot deduce from the fact that one *will* come to affirm the choice to have a child that this choice will leave one better off using the baseline of one's current preferences.

To continue here with the vampire theme, Paul actually explains the problem of transformative experience by reference to an imaginary story about vampires. Suppose, she says, that you are trying to decide whether or not to become a vampire. Some people you know have already undergone the transformation, and are extremely satisfied with their new vampiric existence. They love being nocturnal, drinking blood, and don't mind cutting garlic out of their diet since they now think it's disgusting. It is clear to you that should you become a vampire you will be just as happy with your new existence. But this is only because the dramatic transformation into a vampire turns you into the sort of creature that is happy living a vampire's life, radically altering your preferences in that direction. Should your knowledge that you will be happy *once* a vampire persuade you that becoming a vampire is a good decision for you? The problem here is that it probably would not make you better off according to the preferences you have now, yet becoming a vampire would be such a "transformative experience" that your preferences would just change.

Paul suggests that becoming a parent is a real-life example of a transformative choice that can change fundamental features of our personal identity and our preferences. This is in no way to suggest that it is bad to become a parent (as it might be objectively bad to become a vampire). It is only that when reasoning prospectively about whether parenthood will make our lives better or worse we might be confronted with the same problem as in the vampire example: that parenthood would so dramatically change us (by bringing into the world a new person whom we love and whose life we unqualifiedly affirm) that it is not straightforward to think about whether it would improve our well-being according to the preferences we now have. All we know is that we will (probably) become different people who love and value being parents and everything parenthood involves.

Unfortunately, there is no space to explore this interesting problem more thoroughly here.

4   A Reply to "In Defense of Abortion Rights"

Christopher Kaczor

I wholeheartedly concur with Kate Greasley's remarks in many respects. We both agree that the contemporary scientific evidence shows that "embryos and fetuses are human lives or human beings. This much is not in contention." We both agree with countless biologists and embryologists that "'Human being' ... is used to denote individual members of the human species. All embryos and fetuses are certainly human beings, in that they are all individual human organisms." And we also concur that, "if the fetus is a person, equivalent in value to a born human being, abortion is almost always morally wrong. Moreover, if that were true, legal abortion permissions are almost entirely unjustified." We both hold that pro-choice arguments that do not deny fetal personhood, such as Judith Jarvis Thomson's violinist argument, in the end fail to justify abortion. Finally, she assumes and I agree that "abortion does indeed involve the deliberate killing of the fetus and that, were the fetus a person, hardly any abortion scenarios would meet the moral and legal conditions for justified homicide." So, in what respects are we not yet in full agreement?

In my response, I will focus on (1) terminological issues, (2) passages in which I believe my co-author may have misinterpreted the views of others, (3) the interests of women seeking abortions, (4) human abortion and female equality, and (5) the criteria governing who has a right to live.

4.1   Clarifying Terminology

I wish to call into question some of the terminology used by my co-author, specifically the terms "reproductive rights," "termination of pregnancy," and the "sanctity of life." The term "reproductive rights" is a euphemism for abortion that begs one of the most important questions at issue. If a new human being has come into existence at conception (as Greasley holds), then successful reproduction of a new human being has already taken place. Contraception, not abortion, prevents reproduction. As Greasley noted, abortion is the intentional destruction of a prenatal human being. Those who oppose abortion are not against people reproducing or in favor of forcing people to reproduce against their will (all pro-life advocates also oppose rape). Opposition to abortion is opposition to the destruction of the individual human being who has been brought into existence by successful reproductive activity.

Likewise, the term "termination of pregnancy" is equivocal and euphemistic. The term is equivocal because live vaginal birth, stillbirth, miscarriage, cesarean section, and abortion all equally "terminate pregnancy." Everyone is in favor of some forms of terminating pregnancy, but not everyone is in favor of abortion. "Terminating pregnancy" is also a euphemistic term that conceals the reality of a procedure aimed at not just ending a pregnancy, but ending the life of a young human being. In botched abortions, like some of those performed by Kermit Gosnell, live birth sometimes results. In such cases, a pregnancy has been successfully terminated but an abortion has not been successfully carried out, hence the term "botched abortion."

The term "sanctity of life" can be misleading in this discussion. This term suggests or may easily be interpreted to mean that opposition to abortion is always or necessarily based on religious dogmas, theological suppositions, or faith commitments. It is of course true that many people of faith are pro-life. To explain religious opposition to abortion by means of various passages from the Bible is, I think, to misunderstand religious (or at least Christian) opposition to abortion. The real grounds are much,

much deeper. They have to do with the spiritual impulse to care for those who are in need, to protect the vulnerable, and to act justly toward the disadvantaged. The basic biblical injunction to love your neighbor leads to a desire to support and care for human beings who are poor, vulnerable, and in need. For example, Mother Teresa of Calcutta based her opposition to abortion on the same grounds that she based her service to the poorest of the poor in the slums of Calcutta. She viewed any human being in need as an image of Jesus. Because she sought to love and to serve Jesus, she sought to love, to protect, and to serve the hungry, the homeless, the leper, the blind, and the unwanted (including the unwanted unborn child). In her view, and in the view of countless others who aspire to love as she loved, service to human beings in need does not depend on the correct interpretation of any particular Scripture passage. Mother Teresa did not puzzle over the question, "are lepers 'made in God's image'? Rather, her mission in life arose from the fundamental message of the entire Bible as she understood it. That message is: God loves all human beings, and we are called to love all human beings.

While a call to universal love might well be distinctly religious, the proposition that all human beings are equal and endowed with inalienable rights is a creed that atheists and agnostics as well as deists and theists can and do profess. The United Nations Declaration on Human Rights (whose signatories held a wide variety of religions and nonreligious viewpoints) proclaimed a "recognition of the inherent dignity and of the equal and inalienable rights of all members of the human family." Any person of good will (regardless of their religious beliefs) can hold that all human beings deserve respect from one another and protection by law.

It would therefore be a serious mistake to believe that all opposition to abortion is theologically based. Attentive readers will note that my presentation of the pro-life view in the previous section makes no reference whatsoever to faith, the soul, the Bible, or distinctive religious beliefs. The case against abortion follows from premises that all people of good will can accept. For this reason, many atheists defend the pro-life view, for example, Don Marquis in "Why Abortion Is Wrong" and many other articles (1989, 1991, 2007), civil libertarian Nat Hentoff in his journalism for the *Village Voice*, Bernard Nathanson in his book *Aborting America*, and Kelsey Hazzard in her leadership of the group "Secular Pro-Life." The pro-life view does not depend on belief in God or the "sanctity of life" understood as a religious creed. The pro-life view rests on a scientific premise (the prenatal human being is a human being), and on an ethical premise all human beings deserve to be welcomed in life and protected by law (to use the phrase of Richard John Neuhaus). Neither premise requires religion. Both premises can and are held by people of good will of every faith and of no faith.

My co-author contrasts two senses of the "sanctity of life," namely, "nature's pure biological creation" and "all of the human creative investment that goes into human beings throughout their lifetime." It is certainly true that primarily parents (and especially mothers) but also teachers, coaches, and friends give countless blessings to growing children throughout their lifetimes. This "investment" does help explain our horror at deaths, especially at deaths of people in their early 20s. At the funeral of a young person, we can sometimes hear the remark, "How heart breaking for the parents to have raised their child and now have to bury their child." But the basic intrinsic value of an individual is not properly measured by extrinsic considerations such as how much (or how little) parents, teachers, friends, and coaches have invested in the life of a person.

In May 1972, a four-year-old boy was found among wolf cubs in an Indian forest. With dirty, matted hair, a taste for blood and chasing chickens, the boy could not speak, imitated the actions of wolf cubs, and ate raw meat. After admission to Mother Teresa's Home for the Destitute and Dying, the boy was named Pascal. A feral child such as Pascal has had only a minimum investment from parents. But Pascal nevertheless has equal basic value to Prince George of England. Human creative investment adds extrinsic value to a human being, but this value is in addition to the basic, intrinsic, and equal value that all human beings enjoy whether they are a future King of England with the Queen in

Buckingham Palace or a lost boy among wolf cubs in an Indian forest. Equal human dignity is the inheritance of all human beings, not just the pampered and the privileged, but also the unplanned and the unwanted.

4.2 Misinterpretations of Perspectives

Does the pro-life view require, as Greasley puts it, "the preservation of all biological human life, no matter how radically immature, or radically degenerated"? Defenders of human rights for all oppose intentionally killing innocent human beings, but they do not hold that it is necessary to take extraordinary measures to keep extremely sick human beings alive at all costs. If the burdens of a treatment outweigh the benefits of a treatment, the treatment may be discontinued or not begun. For example, a 90-year old woman learning she has aggressive cancer might reasonably forgo potentially life-saving radiation and chemotherapy treatments, if she judges that the burdens of the treatments outweigh the benefits of the treatment. She might think, "At my age, and given my heart condition, I don't have much time to live anyway. Radiation and chemotherapy might extend my life a bit longer, but these treatments will also make me feel incredibly sick and sap my limited energy." If she judges that the burdens of the treatment outweigh the benefits of the treatment, she may not begin a treatment or may stop a treatment. Or she might decide that the treatment is worthwhile, all things considered. At issue in this reasoning, however, is the worthwhileness of the *treatment*, not the worthwhileness of the *woman*. Not every medical intervention is instrumentally valuable, but every human being is intrinsically valuable. So, the pro-life view is simply not committed to the preservation and extension of the lives of all human beings no matter the cost (Keown 2002b).

I wish that Greasley had provided some examples of scholars who defend the following position, "Some defenders of the view that all human beings are full rights-holders from conception seek to explain and justify the moral significance of human species membership by reference to potential ... According to this view, the property of being a potential person qualifies one for the same basic rights as a fully realized person, especially the right to life. This is known as the potentiality principle." I've never encountered a single scholar who defends the view that the prenatal human being has a right to live because he or she is a potential person. This view is not held by Helen Alvaré, Elizabeth Anscombe, Mary Anne Glendon, Patrick Lee, Gabrielle Girgis, or any of the other pro-life scholars whom I've ever read. Defenders of abortion attribute this view to the pro-life scholars, but I'm still left wondering if they are not critiquing a straw man. At least as articulated by informed participants in scholarly debate, the classic pro-life view is not that the prenatal human being is a *potential person*, but rather that the prenatal human being is a *person with potential*.

Another misrepresentation is the characterization of Donald Marquis's future-like-ours argument as a version of the potentiality principle. Greasley characterizes Marquis's argument as "one particularly well-known iteration of PP [potentiality principle]." Marquis's argument is that killing is wrong because it deprives an individual of a future like ours. The typical case of killing an adult like you or me is wrong because it deprives us of our futures; all the enjoyable experiences we would have had are taken away from us when we are killed. But the human fetus (the human newborn, the human toddler, etc.) has a future like ours. So, killing a human fetus is wrong for the same reason killing you or me is wrong. If this argument is cogent, the human fetus has a right to live even if she or he is not a person (however this term is defined).

On Marquis's view, abortion is wrong because it deprives the human fetus of what she *actually* has, namely a future like ours. He points out:

> [The future-like-ours] argument does not rely on the invalid inference that, since it is wrong to kill persons, it is wrong to kill potential persons also. The category that is morally central to this analysis is the category of having a valuable future like ours; it is not the category of personhood. The argument to the conclusion that abortion is prima facie seriously morally wrong

proceeded independently of the notion of person or potential person or any equivalent.

(Marquis 1989, 192).

So, Greasley is mistaken in characterizing Marquis's "future like ours" argument as lending "more substance to a potentiality-based account of moral status." Whether the human being is a person (in Warren's or anyone else's sense of person) is irrelevant to the future-like-ours argument. And so, a fortiori, it is also irrelevant for the future-like-ours argument whether or not the human fetus is a potential person (in Warren's or anyone else's sense of potential person). More importantly, Greasley has provided no reason whatsoever to call into question, let alone reject the substance of Marquis's argument or his replies to objections (1989, 1991, 2007).

Greasley also misinterprets the views of David Boonin in his book *A Defense of Abortion* (2013). His view is not that "basic conscious desires suffice for full moral status." Boonin does not hold that the poodle's desire to drink water from his bowl makes the little white ball of fluff into a person. Boonin builds his understanding of what gives a creature the right to life (not full moral status) on an alteration of Don Marquis's future-like-ours argument. According to Marquis, an individual who has a future like ours has a right to live. According to Boonin, an individual who desires to have a future like ours has a right to live. A fetal human being prior to 25–32 weeks of gestation does not have any desires, so these human beings cannot have a desire to live. Somewhere between 25 and 32 weeks, on Boonin's view, the brain is sufficiently developed to begin to have some desires such as the primitive desire for comfort, a preference for the mother's voice, or aversion to pain. Once any desire arises, the human being in utero also has an implicit desire for a future like ours. An implicit desire is for the conditions that are necessary in order to have what an individual explicitly desires. Right now, perhaps we have explicit desires for a swig of beer, a bowl of strawberry ice cream, or a nap in the sun. But whatever it is that we consciously or explicitly desire, we also have an implicit desire that the temperature remain within a certain range because if the temperature were to suddenly become as hot as the sun or as cold as absolute zero (−459.67 degrees Fahrenheit/−273.15 degrees Celsius), we would die and then we would (presumably) be unable to realize our explicit desires. If a human being has any actual desire, then the human being also has an implicit desire to continue to exist, to have a future like ours.

So, according to Boonin's work *A Defense of Abortion*, the right to life begins when the human being has an at least implicit desire for a future like ours, and this desire begins sometime around 25–32 weeks following conception. Boonin leaves it as an open question which other individuals have an (implicit) desire to have a future like ours. Depending on how the future-like-ours concept is understood, perhaps dolphins and great apes have a right to life. But although the dog, the cat, and the goldfish desire to feel pleasure and to avoid pain, they do not have an implicit desire for a future like ours, so they do not have a right to life. For reasons I've given earlier in this work, I think Boonin's view is mistaken. But Boonin's view is simply not that basic conscious desires suffice for the right to life, let alone full moral status.

One final misunderstanding concerns my own work. Greasley writes:

> Kaczor's flourishing-like-ours argument is just one particular iteration of a broad way of thinking about moral status that has been termed the "nature of the kind" (NOTK) theory. The defining feature of such theories is that the moral status of any particular creature is determined not by its individual capacities, but by the moral significance of characteristics that are typically or generally true of the members of its kind.

Without denying that belonging to a kind may be ethically relevant, my position is more accurately described as holding it is sufficient for moral status that an individual's flourishing involve goods like knowledge, compassion, personal integrity, and appreciation of beauty, whether or not that individual belongs to a group of similar individuals. Even if there were only just one human being ever on Earth, that individual would be someone whose flourishing would be found in goods such as knowledge, kindness, compassion, personal integrity, and appreciation of beauty. These basic goods would be the basic goods for this individual whether or not there were any other members of our humankind in existence. In other words, it is the nature of the individual's flourishing that is sufficient for moral worth, so his or her membership in a group of such beings is not necessary. So, on my view, it is not the case that "every creature's moral status derives from its group membership."

In theory, there could be creatures (like those who might result from transgenic spectrum experiments) who are "one of a kind," the only member of their own species. If such an individual's flourishing is found in goods of knowledge, kindness, compassion, personal integrity, and appreciation of beauty, then this individual, even if sui generis in species, has a right to life, meriting protection by law and respect in the community. The transgenic individual whose flourishing is like ours has basic rights that do not depend on membership in some species group, since this individual belongs to no such group.

4.3   Interests in Getting Abortions

Greasley holds that if the prenatal human being doesn't have a right to live, then the interests of women in getting abortion trump other considerations that might be brought forward against abortion. Abortion, on this view, would be similar to the use of contraception in that it would be an act that prevents a person from coming into existence, rather than an act that eliminates a person from existence.

Greasley describes one interest women have in getting abortion as follows:

> Everyone has a significant and very personal interest in determining if and when he or she will become a parent. Undeniably, procreation is one of the most profound and meaningful (and, of course, irreversible) aspects of human life. Becoming a parent, with everything that entails, goes right to the heart of

one's personal identity and life story – it changes who one is in potentially transformative ways.

How would someone who defends the human rights of all human beings respond?

The pro-life claim is that as soon as a new human being has come into existence, the man has become a biological father and the woman has become a biological mother. This view is reflected in the questions in the present tense sometimes asked to pregnant women, "Who is the father?" The view that parenthood begins before birth is also reflected in the hiring of a "surrogate mother" to nurture a human embryo created through in vitro fertilization. If a surrogate mother implanted with somebody else's embryo is a mother, a woman carrying a child made from her own egg is no less a mother. If we agree with Greasley that the human fetus is a human being, then the progenitors of this human being are already parents. All human beings arising from the union of sperm and egg have a mother and a father, so the human being in utero has a mother and a father. And if the human being in utero has a mother and a father, then the adults who gave rise to her have already become parents.

Once a new human being comes into existence in utero, the question of whether the man and woman will become parents has been answered. There is, at this point, no question of a "reproductive interest" in not being a parent because reproduction of a new human being has already taken place. Procreative interests are no longer relevant because procreation has been accomplished. Whether or not the mother and the father will be good parents is a question answered by their actions toward their son or daughter, but they have already become parents. Good parents protect, nurture, and support their son or daughter. Bad parents do not protect, do not nurture, or even intentionally harm their son or daughter. Needless to say, there is no legitimate moral or legal interest in being a bad parent.

Suppose we posit for the sake of argument that some human beings brought about by the sexual intercourse of a man and a woman (namely, the human being in utero and perhaps too the human newborn) do not yet have biological parents. On this view, a new human being arises at one time, but then at some later time the man and woman who gave rise to this human being become the biological parents. If everyone has an interest in determining if and when he or she will become a biological parent, then both men and women have this interest. So, suppose a man and a woman choose to have sex and she becomes pregnant. He urges her to get an abortion, but she chooses not to get an abortion. In such a case, his interest not to become a biological parent has been violated. Indeed, the list of deplorable consequences of unwanted motherhood appealed to by Justice Blackmun in *Roe v. Wade* could be rewritten to apply to unwanted fatherhood:

> Paternity, or additional offspring, may force upon the man a distressful life and future. Psychological harm may be imminent. Mental and physical health may be taxed by childcare. There is also the distress, for all concerned, associated with the unwanted child, and there is the problem of bringing a child into a family already unable, psychologically and otherwise, to care for it.

Some men coerce women they have gotten pregnant into getting abortions the women don't want. Other men abandon these expectant mothers because of their pregnancy. Still other men attempt to cause a miscarriage without their partner's consent. Some men even kill the women they have gotten pregnant in order to prevent live birth. These men view fatherhood as distressful, taxing, and unwanted on account of its financial, physical, social, or emotional burdens.

If both men and women have equal rights not to be parents, his right not to be a parent should count just as much as her right not to become a parent. But suppose we say, "Well, he chose to have sex and in choosing to have sex, he gave up his right not to become a parent. He could have known and should have known that in choosing to have sex that he was risking becoming a father. He has, in so choosing, waived his right not to become a parent." If this analysis is correct for men, the interest of sex equality suggests that women also waive their right not to become parents once they have chosen to have sex. (The case of rape is an exception to the waiver, since in these cases the woman did not choose to have sex. However, since 99 percent of abortions do not result from rape, the right not to become a parent would have been waived in the vast majority of cases.)

The fact that the man's interest in not becoming a father is trumped by the woman's decision to continue a pregnancy suggests that the interest in determining if and when someone becomes a parent is not absolute, but gives way to other interests. But equality demands that this same consideration applies to men. If men and women are to equally have procreative control, then either men should have the right to unilaterally end the life of the human being that they have pro-created or both men and women equally lack the right to intentionally kill the human being that they have pro-created.

Greasley rightly distinguishes two different senses of parenthood: the biological and the social. The biological parents are the people whose egg and whose sperm gave rise to the new human being. The social parent or parents are those who care for the new human being after birth.

Does the interest in avoiding unwanted parenthood apply simply to social parenthood or does it apply also to biological parenthood? If the interest in question is simply about social parenthood, then adoption rather than abortion would be sufficient to meet this need. "[S]uch an argument would have to claim that it is only *social* parenthood, and not biological parenthood, that constitutes the important interest in procreative liberty," writes Greasley, "and I am not convinced this is correct. Becoming the biological parent to a child from whom one is then separated, even through choice, is not without its emotional costs and, indeed, its ramifications for one's personal identity and self-conception." If men and women have equal rights not to be biological parents, then not just women but also men should have a legal right to end the life of their son or daughter. If a woman refuses to have an abortion, then the only way left for a man to exercise his right not to be a biological parent is to kill his son or daughter after birth. And what if the man finds out he is a biological father only when his daughter is 10 years old, 20 years old, or even older? Unless parents have an ongoing right to kill even their adult children, there is no right not to be a biological parent.

We can have a right to "procreative liberty" in the sense of a right not to be a biological parent prior to the emergence of the new human being. But after a new human being exists, then the man and the woman have already become biological parents. The only way to cease being a biological parent is for the child to die. Someone becomes a gestational parent when the new human being is within her body. This comes to an end whenever pregnancy is over. Social parenthood is also flexible in that one can cease for a variety of reasons to be the social parent, for example, via adoption.

Adoption is an extremely difficult choice to make. Greasley is entirely correct when she writes, "It is clear that through choosing abortion, what women seek to avoid is either of two seriously burdensome eventualities: becoming a social parent against her wishes, or being estranged from a biological child whom she knows to exist." In his article, "A Failure to Communicate," Paul Swope made a similar observation a number of decades ago (1998). Let me state clearly that I believe a woman with a crisis pregnancy is in a terribly difficult situation. Raising a child or placing a child with an adopted family both can be incredibly arduous decisions for women to make, and I believe the same is true of abortion. For this reason, I think that compassion rather than condemnation is the correct attitude to express toward all women in these situations. Greasley is also correct that serious physical harm can result from pregnancy and from birth. However, it is also true that serious physical harm can result from abortion, including death, sterility, disease, and adverse mental health outcomes. Abortion involves nonnegligible physical risks and burdens.

4.4   Human Abortion and Female Equality

The pro-life view is that abortion does not secure but radically undermines female equality. Nothing indicates the inequality of a human being like the right to intentionally kill that human being. Abortion destroys the lives of female human beings in utero. Post-birth abortion disproportionately targets the lives of baby girls, as does sex-selection abortion. As the President of Feminists for Life Serrin M. Foster notes, "The foundation of feminism is built on the basic tenets of nonviolence, nondiscrimination, and justice for all. Abortion is discrimination based on age, size, location, and sometimes gender, disability, or parentage. And it is often the result of a more insidious form of discrimination: the lack of resources and support that pregnant women need and deserve" (Foster 2017).

Is it true that "abortion prohibitions harm women as a class"? Abortion prohibitions do not harm women as a class because abortion is not even a possible choice for women as a class. Women in their late fifties, sixties, seventies, eighties, and beyond cannot get pregnant. The vast majority of women in their years of fertility are not pregnant. Only a small subset of women, pregnant women, can get abortions, and only a subset of pregnant women want to get abortions. Women who want abortions are not equivalent to "women as a class."

If we assume that transgender identity makes it possible for men to get pregnant and have abortions, then both men and women can get abortions. Let's assume, however, that only women can get abortions, so abortion restrictions uniquely impinge on pregnant women who want abortions but never impinge on men. Similarly, only men are forced to pay child support in paternity suits, but it does not follow that paternity suits harm men as a class. Only parents can have parental responsibilities for their own children, but it is not problematic discrimination to enforce parental responsibilities despite the resulting "inequality" between those who are parents and those who are not parents. The ethical and legal norms that parents should take care of their own children disproportionately burden people of child-bearing age and burdens no one prior to this age, but such norms are not unjust discrimination against people based on age.

Do women in countries lacking legalized abortion fall notably behind their sisters in countries with legalized abortion? This question has many dimensions, one of which is health. Consider overall life expectancy. Do women in countries with legalized abortion live longer lives on average than women in countries without legal abortion? The life expectancy of women in Ireland (where abortion is almost entirely illegal) is 83.4 years. The life expectancy of women in the United States (where abortion is almost entirely legal) is 81.6. The case of Ireland makes clear that legalized abortion in a country is not necessary for the women of that country to have a long life expectancy (indeed, longer than some industrialized nations with legalized abortion).

Is my co-author correct in claiming that a link between abortion and breast cancer has now been "entirely discredited"? Some experts in the field disagree. A 2014 meta-analysis of 36 studies points to a 44 percent increase in the likelihood of breast cancer in those who have had abortions (Huang et al. 2014; see too Jabeen 2013; Roy 2014). In the words of one researcher, "there was a statistically significant increase in the risk of BC [breast cancer] for induced abortions (P trend = 0.02), but not for miscarriages. The maximum risk was observed among women who had at least three induced terminations" (Lecarpentier 2012, 5). In fact, the abortion–breast cancer link remains a subject of ongoing research by investigators rather than a matter considered entirely settled by experts in the field.

Another aspect to consider in comparing the health of women in countries with legalized abortion with the health of women in countries without abortion is maternal health. B. C. Calhoon compared maternal health of women in Great Britain in which abortion is legalized with the maternal health of women in the Republic of Ireland in which abortion is not legalized. Calhoon found that:

> The Republic of Ireland has a maternal mortality rate over the last decade of 3/100,000 compared with about 6/100,000 in England and Wales; a stillbirth rate in 2010 of 3.8/1,000 live births compared with 5.1/1,000 live births in Great Britain; and a preterm (<37 weeks) birth rate in 2010 of 42.7/1,000 live births compared with 48/1,000 in England and Wales and 72/1,000 in Scotland. Legal elective abortion is associated with

higher rates of maternal mortality rates, stillbirth rates, and preterm birth.

(Calhoon 2013, 42)

In terms of maternal deaths, rate of babies born dead, and premature birth, women in Ireland, a country without legalized abortion, had fewer problems than women in Great Britain, a region with legalized abortion. Many factors are relevant in the comparison, but what the data make clear is that legalized abortion is not necessary for women's health rates to be as good or better than countries with legalized abortion.

One of the physical risks to maternal health posed by abortion is an increased likelihood of future ectopic pregnancy (Debnath 2013; Lawani, Anozie, and Ezeonu 2013). In ectopic pregnancy, the prenatal human being develops outside the uterus, typically in the fallopian tube. Ectopic pregnancy is the leading cause of maternal deaths (Cecchino 2014). At least some women who die of ectopic pregnancy would not have had an ectopic pregnancy had they not had an abortion. However, the deaths of these women are not included in the normal tally of abortion-related fatalities. (On the ethics of treating ectopic pregnancies with double effect reasoning, see Kaczor 2009.)

And what about women who would die from illegal abortions? Dr. Bernard Nathanson helped found the National Abortion Rights Action League (NARAL), a group that pushed for abortion legalization. He later admitted lying about the numbers of women who died from illegal abortion in order to justify legalizing abortion:

> In N.A.R.A.L. we generally emphasized the drama of the individual case, not the mass statistics, but when we spoke of the latter it was always "5,000 to 10,000 deaths a year." I confess that I knew the figures were totally false, and I suppose the others did too if they stopped to think of it. But in the "morality" of our revolution, it was a useful figure, widely accepted, so why go out of our way to correct it with honest statistics?
>
> (Nathanson 1979, 193)

Whatever their number, some women die from illegal abortion, and each death is a tragedy. Whatever their number, some women die from legal abortion, and each death is a tragedy. Consistent defenders of the pro-life position oppose not only legal abortion but also illegal abortion. Such people work to prevent all abortion, and their work helps prevent women from dying from abortion, both legal and illegal.

Do women in countries without legalized abortion fare worse than women in countries with legalized abortion? Ross Douthat pointed out:

> Meanwhile, international rankings offer few indications that Ireland's abortion laws are holding Irish women back. The country ranks first for gender parity in health care in a recent European Union index. It was in the middle of the pack in The Economist's recent "glass-ceiling index" for working women. It came in fifth out of 135 countries in the World Economic Forum's "Global Gender Gap" report.
>
> (Douthat 2013, 12)

Douthat went on to note that the United States was twenty-second on the list, despite having some of the most liberal abortion laws in the world, much more liberal than most of Europe.

Is legalized abortion necessary for women to have political power? Again, the answer is no. Ireland shattered the glass ceiling in having its first female president before the United States. Bolivia has abortion laws similar to Ireland's, but Bolivian women hold 53 percent of the seats in parliament. In the United States, women make up only 19.4 percent of Congress. Legalized abortion is neither necessary nor sufficient for women to have political power, including the most powerful positions of all.

Catharine MacKinnon, as cited by my co-author, wildly exaggerates the negative consequences of reproduction in claiming: "Although reproduction has a major impact on both sexes, men are not generally fired from their jobs, excluded from public life, beaten, patronized, confined, or made into pornography for making babies." In the United States and the European Union (and every civilized country), it is a crime to fire a woman because of pregnancy or childbirth. When the moral and legal crime of pregnancy discrimination occurs, the answer is not abortion but enforcement of existing laws and punishment of wrongdoers. In no Western country of which I am aware are women excluded from public life, beaten, or confined because of pregnancy. Likewise, forcing pregnant women (or anyone) to make pornography is grossly immoral and is (or should be) legally forbidden. Women face real problems from sexism in society. But the rhetorical exaggerations of MacKinnon make the situation worse by focusing our attention on imaginary problems (e.g., pregnant women banned from public life), leaving less time and energy for tackling actual problems (e.g., domestic abuse of women).

Moreover, MacKinnon is also mistaken in her claim that abortion allows women to engage in sexual intercourse on the same terms as men. Men never worry about getting pregnant. Men never get pregnant. Men never debate whether to get an abortion for themselves. Men never undergo an abortion. And men never have to live with the physical, mental, emotional, and other consequences of having gotten an abortion. Abortion does nothing to erase these asymmetries (and other asymmetries such as the human papilloma virus causing cervical cancer) that occur when men and women have sexual intercourse.

MacKinnon also sees abortion as needed in virtue of the fact that many women are forced to have sex without their consent. Isn't the proper response to forced sexual intercourse to punish the rapist with imprisonment so he cannot attack again? Abortion is not an answer to rape, but punishes an innocent third party with death for an action that she did not do. Indeed, abortion facilitates rape in some cases. For example, in cases of statutory rape, a man may pressure a girl to get an abortion so as to hide his crime.

Despite these disagreements, I heartily concur with Greasley when she writes:

> The class-based interest in sex equality will still not be enough to justify abortion morally if we are assuming that abortion is tantamount to homicide, because the enhancement of sex equality is not ordinarily accepted as a justification for homicide. This, I believe, is something with which we all would

agree on reflection. One can construct all manner of imaginary scenarios in which killing one or more innocent persons will have a tangible positive impact for the empowerment of women, but which we would not, for that reason, deem permissible. This goes to show that the sex equality defense of abortion rights cannot withstand a finding that the fetus is the moral equivalent of a born human child.

I think Greasley is also right that if the human being in utero has no value, then abortion should not be legally prohibited. Abortion would just be a form of contraception that prevents (but does not destroy) the coming to be of a valuable person. Since in our disagreement the central question is "who has a right to live?," let us focus on this issue.

4.5   Who Has a Right to Live?

First, let us consider some challenges raised for the pro-life view. The intelligent alien hypothetical proposed by Greasley demonstrates that a creature does not need to be a human being in order to be a person. To be a human being is not a necessary condition for personhood. But this hypothetical is irrelevant to the claim that all human beings are persons. The intelligent Irishman demonstrates that a creature does not need to be an Englishman to be a person, but an Irishman's existence does nothing at all to call into question the claim that all Englishmen are persons.

Some people reject the ethics of inclusion because of the Embryo Rescue Case, which both Greasley and I have discussed. Steven Pinker poses a different version of the Rescue Case:

> Moral philosophers play with a hypothetical dilemma in which people can run through the left door of a burning building to save some number of children or through the right door to save their own child. If you are a parent, ponder this question. Is there any number of children that would lead you to pick the left door? Indeed, all of us reveal our preferences with our pocketbooks when we spend money on trifles for our own children (a bicycle, orthodontics, an education at a private

school or university) instead of saving the lives of unrelated children in the developing world by donating the money to charity.

(Pinker 2003, 245)

When parents choose the right door to save their own child, they are not even implicitly denying the dignity of the greater number of children behind the left door. A mother taking her daughter to see a Star Wars movie rather than donating the money to famine relief efforts like Oxfam is not even implicitly denying the humanity of the hungry she could have helped. Likewise, in the Embryo Rescue Case, to rescue a particular human being rather than other human beings is to deny the basic rights of no one. Every person has the right not to be intentionally killed in every circumstance; every person does not have the right to be rescued in every circumstance. The ethical norms governing whom we may or should rescue are not the same as the ethical norms governing whom we may intentionally kill.

Although it may have been asked only rhetorically, Greasley poses an important question:

Could it really be correct that the difference between a sperm approaching an ovum and the single-celled human organism made up of 46 human chromosomes that comes into being moments later is the difference between two human cells of no more moral importance than skin cells, and a creature that possesses all the moral importance of a fully grown human being, and whose death is as lamentable from the impersonal point of view?

Let us recall the title of this volume, *Abortion Rights: For and Against*. Abortion is not at issue immediately following conception since (1) no one knows right after conception in utero that conception has taken place and (2) even if we could know, there is no technique for aborting immediately following conception. In most cases of abortion, we are talking about a human being in utero weeks or even months more developed than the single-celled human organism. In her famous article, "A Defense of Abortion," Judith Jarvis Thomson pointed out, "By the tenth week," the fetal human being "already has a face, arms and legs, fingers, and toes; it has internal organs, and brain activity is detectable" (Thomson 1971, 47–48). At the time abortions typically take place, the human being in utero has a beating heart, two eyes with eyelids, ears, and either a penis or a vagina.

Second, we should distinguish scientific questions from ethical questions. Is it scientifically accurate that a new human being comes into existence with the union of egg and sperm? Is it true, as a matter of science, that there is a radical difference between reproductive gametes, on the one hand, and a reproduced human being on the other hand? The answer to these questions is yes. O'Rahilly and Muller's *Human Embryology and Teratology* states that fertilization is "a critical landmark because, under ordinary circumstances, a new, genetically distinct human organism is thereby formed when the chromosomes of the male and the female pronuclei blend in the oocyte" (O'Rahilly and Muller 2001, 8). In *Patten's Foundations of Embryology*, we read, "Almost all higher animals start their lives from a single cell, the fertilized ovum (zygote) ... The time of fertilization represents the starting point in the life history, or ontogeny, of the individual" (Carlson 1996, 3). There is, biologically speaking, a radical difference between egg and sperm, on the one hand, and a new human being, on the other.

A remaining aspect of the original question is ethical. Do we accept an ethics of inclusion in which all human beings have basic rights? Or do we advocate an ethics of exclusion in which human beings who are like us have basic rights but human beings who are not like us (e.g., the unwanted or weak or vulnerable or whatever) do not have basic rights?

The pro-life view does not claim that the human zygote or the human fetus "possesses *all* the moral importance of a fully grown human being." It is, for reasons stated earlier in this work, worse to kill a fully grown human being, like a college student, than to kill a human being in utero. College students have many rights (such as a right to drive, to vote, and to marry) that younger human beings do not enjoy. College students have friends, responsibilities, and future plans that death demolishes. None of these factors, all of which are ethically relevant for assessing how bad a death is circumstantially, is present in the case of abortion or infanticide. Indeed, as mentioned earlier, even cases of pre-birth abortion itself are not all circumstantially alike, but can be more or less serious depending on various circumstances. But an ethics of inclusivity holds that all human beings regardless of race, birth, class, health, religion, development, or sex have basic human rights. The most basic of these rights is the right to life, the right not to be intentionally killed, since without this right we can do nothing, enjoy nothing, and achieve nothing. In this respect, all human beings are owed basic respect, even if in other respects killing one human being is worse (or even much worse) than killing another.

Let us now consider some challenges to Greasley's view of personhood. She adopts a multicriterial and fluid conception of person that is similar to the conception proposed by Mary Anne Warren (1998). A person is a being with (1) consciousness (especially the capacity to feel pain), (2) reasoning ability, (3) self-motivated activity, (4) the capacity to communicate, and (5) a concept of the self.

No one disputes that Warren's conditions (like Locke's considered earlier) are *sufficient* for being a person, but why should we think that all or some of these conditions are *necessary* for the right to live? Thus far in this work, my co-author has provided no answer for this question.

Moreover, these five conditions admit of many degrees. We have been given (so far) no detailed analysis of exactly what degree of each is required to have a right to live. Does semi-consciousness count? Does using tools count as reasoning ability? Where exactly is the border between self-motivated activity and non-self-motivated activity? Precisely how well must one communicate and how self-aware must one be?

It is certainly true that a late-term fetal human being is not capable of reasoning, communication, and awareness of herself as a conscious subject of experiences. Warren herself acknowledged that the newborn baby fails to meet her standard of personhood, and the same could be said of the intellectually disabled teenager and the demented adult. So, unless we are willing to exclude the infant in arms, the teenager with brain damage, and the old woman with Alzheimer's from the basic rights enjoyed by all other human beings, we cannot consistently hold that reasoning, self-motivated activity, communication, and self-awareness are necessary for personhood.

Greasley argues for a moral distinction between pre-birth and post-birth abortion in ways similar to Engelhardt's and Warren's. But Greasley has not yet answered the objection that the reasons not to grant personhood prior to birth may also be present after birth.

More importantly, why should the desires of adults (including of potential adoptive parents) be relevant to an infant's right to life? In fact, basic moral status is an intrinsic property, a property an individual enjoys whether she is desired or detested, wanted or discarded, loved or loathed. To speak of an "unwanted child" says nothing whatsoever about the child herself. To be an unwanted child is not like having green eyes, or being right handed, or liking to laugh. The term "unwanted child" says something about the parents. They do not want to love and care for their own son or daughter. But the attitude of the parents, positive or negative or neutral, does not change the value of the child in question, though it says a lot about the values of the parents in question.

If Greasley is right that treating infants as expendable has a potentially morally deadening effect, why would treating pre-natal human beings as expendable not have a morally deadening effect? What if an empirical analysis of infanticide shows that killing babies after they are born does not in fact have a morally deadening effect? If an empirical analysis showed that pre-birth abortion had a morally deadening effect, would pre-birth abortion be wrong? In fact, post-birth abortion and pre-birth abortion are alike as two forms of intentionally killing vulnerable human beings. If post-birth abortion is wrong, it is primarily wrong because it violates an individual's basic rights, whether or not the action in addition has a deadening effect on the agent or on the society.

Greasley holds that a newborn human being is close to becoming a fully realized person in Warren's sense of a person. But some prenatal human beings are *even more close* to becoming a Warren-type person than some newborns. For example, a full-term human being in utero (40 weeks' gestation) is closer to becoming a person (according to Warren's criteria) than is a newborn baby prematurely born at 25 weeks. So, if "closeness" to consciousness, reasoning, self-motivated activity, communication, and self-awareness saves the newborn baby who is prematurely born, why would an even greater closeness to such activity not save a more developed human being in utero?

In reality, the newborn baby and the human fetus are not close but both are years away from achieving Warren's sense of personhood. So, even if the typical newborn is a few months closer than the typical prenatal human being, it is hard to see why these few months mark a decisive difference between who can be killed and who deserves protection. Moreover, a newborn with mental retardation may be further away from achieving Warren's sense of personhood than a healthy human being in utero. Proximity to Warren's personhood simply cannot distinguish pre-birth and post-birth abortion.

Greasley may be correct when she notes that "it is practically impossible for a populace to deny the rights of neonates while relating to one-year-olds as full rights-holders." But neither the neonate nor the one-year-old is a full rights holder on the standard of personhood articulated by Warren. A baby at 12 months cannot reason so as to solve new and complex problems. A one-year-old cannot do self-motivated activity in which she sets goals for herself independent of external stimuli and genetics. A child of 12 months cannot communicate an indefinite variety of messages about an indefinite variety of topics. And a baby at a year doesn't have self-awareness as an individual of a particular race or sex. The one criterion of Warren's that both a newborn and a one-year-old can satisfy is having consciousness of external objects and experience of pain, but prenatal human beings can also satisfy this criterion later in pregnancy. So the criterion of sentience does not help to distinguish infanticide from abortion.

The pragmatic reasons offered by Greasley for including intellectually disabled human beings within the category of persons are not compelling. She holds that we should include intellectually disabled human beings in the category of persons because of their "striking resemblance to fully realized persons." If we understand "a striking resemblance to fully realized persons" as a matter of appearance, then this justification is overinclusive. There are many beings that have a striking resemblance in terms of appearance to fully realized persons who entirely lack moral status. An android robot, the wax figure of Michael Jackson in Madam Tussaud's museum, and a hologram of Winston Churchill bear a striking resemblance to fully realized persons but lack any moral status whatsoever. On the other hand, if resemblance to a fully realized person is understood in terms of functioning like persons in Warren's sense, then human beings with radical cognitive deficiencies do not in fact resemble fully realized persons at all. Precisely in virtue of their radical cognitive deficiencies, human beings with severe intellectual disabilities function more like nonhuman animals than like typically functioning adults.

While it is true, as Greasley points out, that some human beings with radical cognitive limitations do possess a concept of themselves as individuals, can reason and communicate to some degree, and do express some agency, not all intellectually disabled human beings are so lucky. Warren's concept of personhood makes these underprivileged human beings even more unlucky as they also lack (on Warren's standards) ethical and presumably legal protections from abuse, forced organ donation, or even murder.

Consider a 19-year-old woman named Holly whose neck is snapped in a gymnastics accident and now is in a persistent vegetative state. Her injuries are so extensive that Holly does not experience pleasure and pain and entirely lacks self-awareness. She cannot reason, communicate, or act purposefully. Yet, hopefully all of us would agree to condemn the action of a man who sneaks into her hospital room and has sex with Holly.

He wrongs her in having sex with her without her consent. But this judgment presupposes that Holly is someone who can be wronged, she is someone with basic moral status. And if Holly has basic moral status, then sentience is not necessary for basic moral status.

Nevertheless, I do think Greasley is right that, "In all but the most extreme cases, then, individuals with cognitive limitations will still exemplify the kinds of characteristics constitutive of persons, even if in a compromised form." The trouble is that the most extreme cases do exist (like our example of the 19-year-old gymnast Holly). Are such human beings excluded from basic protections? Is it wrong to have sexual intercourse with Holly without her consent or is it not wrong since she is no longer a "person" on Warren's standard? On the other hand, if we reduce the standard of Warren's personhood low enough to admit individuals with severe cognitive disabilities like Holly's, then dogs and parrots who can speak or obey commands (showing intellectual functioning at a higher level than many cognitively disabled human beings) would also have a right to life equal to ours. This is hard to believe. Almost no one thinks that Polly the Parrot has a right to life equal to Hillary Clinton.

A multicriterial and fluid concept of personhood can deflect the reductio challenges to the ethics of exclusion *only* if it is clear that human beings with radical cognitive deficiencies, or newborn babies, or elderly Alzheimer's patients *would* qualify for protection. But the murky and muddled multicriterial and fluid standard (as currently articulated) cannot show that human beings with radical cognitive deficiencies, or newborn babies, or elderly Alzheimer's patients would qualify for protection or why they should. *Why* does a human being with a normal level of self-awareness typical of humans and the ability to communicate but who lacks reasoning ability qualify for personhood? What *precisely* is the sufficient number (two, three, four?) of person-making characteristics required for personhood? What exactly is the sufficient degree to which self-awareness (or communication, or self-motivated activity, etc.) must be displayed? Why this degree and not more or less? Until such questions are answered, we cannot know whether human beings with radical cognitive disabilities, or newborn babies, or elderly Alzheimer's patients qualify for moral and legal protection or are excluded.

A multicriterial conception of personhood can avoid the problem of infanticide (which Greasley seems keen to avoid), if it lowers the thresholds far enough down. But then numerous nonhuman animals would have a right to life equal to our own. A squid, a crow, and a squirrel are all demonstrably more intelligent in activity than a newborn baby. So, if we lower the multicriterial and fluid threshold standards low enough to secure the right to life of baby Tyler, these low standards also secure the right to life of Porky the pig.

Greasley writes with an admirable clarity. But when considering what we both agree is the central question in the abortion debate, namely, what standards determine who has a right to life, this clarity gives way to a nebulous cloud of imprecision, vagueness, and obscurity. My co-author proposes a multicriterial and fluid conception in order to determine who has a right to live. This proposal could be made lucid. But in the early section of this book, it is never made clear exactly which of the proposed criteria are necessary and sufficient in which circumstances. Nor is the "multicriterial and fluid" conception of personhood examined in a range of cases.

Fuzzy and nebulous standards are unacceptable when it comes to matters of basic justice. Imagine at issue a different question, "Who gets the right to vote?" Someone proposes a multicriterial and fluid standard of these criteria: (1) citizenship, (2) mature age, (3) voter ID, (4) residency, and (5) no felony conviction. However, he doesn't specify in detail whether these are necessary or sufficient conditions or some combination. He doesn't specify how these conditions apply in a range of cases. Rather, when someone requests a ballot, he intuits, on a fluid case-by-case basis, whether or not the individual in question has the right to vote. Suppose a society adopts his proposed standard of voting rights for purposes of personal morality and public law.

This vague and ambiguous standard for deciding who gets to vote lends itself to personal bias, prejudicial application, and radical injustice. An official at one voting station denies ballots to anyone who does not produce a valid passport (he has high standards for voter ID). A library card suffices elsewhere. At one polling place, 15-year-olds are considered mature enough to vote; at another polling place, a voter must be 35 or older. Here, only citizens can vote. Across town both citizens and resident aliens can vote. Just a bit further down the road, everyone (even tourists) can vote if they have passports for voter ID, boast no felony convictions, and are 18 years of age.

We would not accept a standard for voting rights so lacking clarity, precision, and transparency. But the right to life is a much more important right than the right to vote. If given a choice, no one would choose to lose her life rather than lose her vote, if only because in losing her life she also loses her right to vote. Justice and sound law require all the transparency, clarity, and lucidity we can muster. It is often the case that clear standards, such as we rightly require for our law and in ethics, are hard to apply in concrete cases. But here the standards themselves (at least as articulated thus far by Greasley) are too vague and unspecified to be helpful in determining who has a right to live when it comes to immature human beings and intellectually disabled human beings. Hence, they fail to be proper standards at all, leaving open the door to rationalizations and the abuse of the powerless by the powerful. Just laws and sound ethical judgments block, to the extent possible, such rationalization and secure, to the extent possible, the common good of all, especially those who are vulnerable, disempowered, and dehumanized.

5 A Short Reply to the Reply

Kate Greasley

5.1 Abortion and Religion

Contrary to the view that Kaczor attributes to me, I do not think nor do I suggest that all or even most opposition to abortion is formally grounded in religious doctrine. I am well aware that the best arguments about the immorality of abortion, and the preponderance of anti-abortion arguments in the academic arena, are not religious ones. My comment about religion in abortion was a different one, having to do with psychological barriers to open thinking about abortion ethics. However the academic arguments are actually framed, my concern was that many opponents of abortion believe that, in any event, their religious commitments dictate an answer to the abortion question, and that where this is the case it can prejudice their appraisal of the nonreligious arguments. That is why I started my essay by pointing out the various ways in which certain scriptural passages that could be taken to imply the impermissibility of abortion do not, in actual fact, pronounce on the philosophical questions at the heart of the issue. Biblical authority in particular does not obviously dictate an answer to the abortion question in the way that some assume it does.

Kaczor's reply to this was to say that the Christian faith in fact *does* dictate an answer on abortion (thus substantiating my worries), but not in the way I imagined its participants think that it does. It is the Christian value of loving all human beings that explains why abortion is immoral according to that faith, not any view it takes about what constitutes personhood. If this more accurately describes why many Christians think that abortion is wrong (and we should remember that many do *not* think that), it would still only solidify my concerns about open-mindedness when approaching the moral arguments.

Regardless, if I am right – and I thought that Kaczor agreed – that the morality of abortion turns on the moral status of the fetus, then what Christian doctrine *does* hold about abortion will depend on what is has to say about that question. A general exhortation to love one's neighbor (and I am quite sure that the Bible does not specifically refer to the to-be-loved group as human beings "*defined as* any living human organism from conception") does not answer the crucial question about the margins of moral personhood. We must ask, with Jesus's interlocutor, "Who counts as my neighbor?" Kaczor cannot here substitute the word "neighbor" for the words "human being" (specifically to mean: all human life from conception) and expect the sleight of hand to go unnoticed.

In short, even these different supposed grounds of religious opposition are not decisive for the abortion dispute. I did not imagine, however, that these are the most convincing grounds of abortion opposition.

5.2   On Pro-Life Arguments

Kaczor thinks I am wrong to attribute to any philosophical opponent of abortion rights the view that fetuses qualify for rights in virtue of being potential persons. In what sense, he asks, is any pro-life argument, such as Marquis's future-like-ours argument, a potentiality principle of moral status? Well, in the sense that according to a theory such as Marquis's it is the value of what the fetus can or will become, and the goods that it can or will realize, that warrants its inclusion in the category of morally protected beings. On Marquis's theory, the feature of having a future of value, a future "like ours," explains why abortion is immoral: it deprives the fetus of that valuable future, and this is the essential wrong-making factor in killing anyone. The criterion of moral inclusion is thus the possession of a future of value.

This potential is a feature that we can say fetuses in one way *currently* possess, as do we. It is an *actual* property of mine that I have a future of value. But this does not diminish the significance of what the fetus and I can and will be – the value of the futures themselves – for the future-like-ours argument. It is the value for both creatures of what is yet to come that is distinctively important on a theory such as this. And this is so whether fetuses are described as "potential persons" or "persons with potential." If they are not persons, but killing them is still considered as wrong as any person being killed because this means depriving them of the same valuable future, the value of their future is still doing the important moral work.

Whatever labels we apply to it, the important question is whether Marquis's argument goes through. Kaczor claims that I have yet to explain why it does not, or even to call its correctness into question. I am happy to reiterate my main reservations here.

I grant that the pro-life view on abortion does not entail that we are required to make efforts to preserve the lives of all human beings regardless of their state and quality of life and regardless of the futility of medical treatment. However, the boundaries of moral status that fall out of Marquis's argument do entail that killing any living human organism, even newly conceived, is impermissible in exactly the same circumstances in which killing a fully developed human being would be. This includes where refraining from that killing comes at a great cost to one or more mature human beings – serious cost to physical or mental health, risk to life, and even, as I have explained earlier, at the cost of certain death to the mature human, since one may not ordinarily kill one person to preserve the life of another, unless both are certain to die otherwise (and even then, many think that there are further constraints on how and in what circumstances one is permitted to kill). This, I believe, is a reductio ad absurdum of that view.

Moreover, efforts to neutralize that reductio by distinguishing different metrics of the wrongness of killing or badness of death ("intrinsic" and "extrinsic" or "circumstantial" senses) are unconvincing and go too far toward pulling the rug out from under the more inclusive theory of moral status. How can it be that zygotes and embryos are at one and the same time equal to us in moral status but that killing them is, in some very meaningful respects, less wrong? If the pro-life view that pre-born human beings are persons means anything, it must surely mean that killing them is as wrong and their death as bad in every way that matters. These sorts of unsatisfying answers indicate to me the failure by philosophical opponents of abortion to treat their own reductios with the same level of rigor that they apply to those of their adversaries.

Second, and relatedly, Marquis's view implies not only that killing a zygote is every bit as bad as killing a fully developed human being, but that it is the worst kind of killing there is. On his account, the deprivation of future life is the very thing that makes killing wrong and the loss of life a harm, and the pre-born human, assuming it will live a normal life span, is deprived of more life through dying than are older humans. This strikes me as deeply counterintuitive. The reasons why it seems so counterintuitive tie in to my third objection, which is that merely *having* a future of value does not appear sufficient for full moral status unless a creature can be said to have an interest in realizing that future. Recall Michael Tooley's thought experiment about the cats that, if injected with a special serum, will develop into persons. Let us suppose that once the cats are injected they will naturally turn into thinking, speaking persons, but that this will not happen immediately but rather gradually over time. It follows from the future-like-ours theory that the second after the cats are injected, they have the same moral value as persons – it is, as of right then, *as* wrong to kill them as to kill you or me. This is because the second they are injected they have a future like ours. But many will think this cannot be right. They are, one second after injection, exactly the same as they were before. It is hard to believe that their moral status could have changed so dramatically when they are still the same in every way, except for what lies ahead of them.

Moving on from the future-like-ours theory, Kaczor also claims that I misunderstand the basis of his own view of moral status. He writes:

> Without denying that belonging to a kind may be ethically relevant, my position is more accurately described as holding it is sufficient for moral status that an individual's flourishing involve goods like knowledge, compassion, personal integrity, and appreciation of beauty, whether or not that individual belongs to a group of similar individuals.

It is not made explicit, but where I take it he thinks I go wrong is in believing that group memberships – in particular, species membership – is salient to his view of moral status. But I do not see how his remarks here show this isn't so. Kaczor says that there might in theory be creatures that are the only members of their species, but whose flourishing consists in the basic kinds of goods specified above. He suggests this goes to show that group memberships are not relevant to moral status on his theory. But it does not. Kaczor says that "it is the nature of the individual's flourishing that is sufficient for moral worth." But how is that nature to be determined? It seems quite clear to me that Kaczor views the nature of an individual's flourishing as that which constitutes flourishing for a typical member of the individual's species. If not this, then what? How else does Kaczor mean to determine what the flourishing of any individual creature consists in, even when they do not instantiate it, other than by thinking about that which is typical for the species? It is for this reason that I say Kaczor's theory makes moral status depend on group membership, specifically on species membership. It makes no difference to this just how many members of a creature's species there are in existence, or if it is the only one left.

The most important question here is whether Kaczor's theory is correct. He claims that fetuses have a moral status equal to that of mature human beings because the nature of their flourishing is the same. I argued that even if there is a good case to be made that some human beings lacking all constitutive features of personhood nevertheless possess a derivative moral status based on the nature of their flourishing (meaning, what it is to flourish qua the kind of creature it is), it is not at all clear to me that this basis for moral status extends to pre-born human beings, whose flourishing really *does not* consist in rationality, agency, language, or any of the other capacities associated with personhood.

5.3   Abortion and Women's Interests

It is difficult to know where to begin in replying to Kaczor's rebuttal of the claim that women can have serious interests in obtaining abortion. As a general matter, the insistence by some pro-life quarters that abortion harms women, or certainly does not help them, has served, I think, more than anything else, to cast doubt on the intellectual rigor of their theorizing as a whole. Not only is abortion the unjustified killing of rights-holding persons, which would be enough; it is also bad for women, bad for society, medically dangerous, confers no good on anyone (perhaps it is also responsible for the two world wars), and so on. But when a person is willing to believe that abortion causes breast cancer, or that sex equality is not implicated in abortion rights, we will find ourselves wondering what levels of scrutiny or open-mindedness he can possibly be bringing to the question of fetal moral status. This, I think, has been the most self-destructive aspect of the women-protective argumentative trend.

I am not clear what moral argument Kaczor wishes to make when he claims that male and female progenitors "have already become parents" by the time conception takes place. Let alone the fact that nothing in the moral debate is determined by how people speak (in terms of "father," "mother," or otherwise), I cannot see how the interests that people have in not bearing or raising children depends on whether one thinks they are, in any sense, already "parents" to embryos. Kaczor also makes the point that if procreative control is in women's interests, it is also in men's interests. I think it is plainly true that men can have very important interests in not becoming biological parents against their will. But the leap from this to the claim that an abortion right based on the interest in procreative control would have to be mirrored by a right for men to *force* abortion in order to protect their procreative interests is entirely unwarranted. What would be required so as to afford men the right to control their own procreation *once* they have impregnated someone is no less than the right to inflict a nonconsensual surgical or medical procedure on a woman. This is a very significant asymmetry. There are powerful reasons to abstain from enacting any laws that would allow some people to assert their interests over others by means of coercive bodily interventions. This in no way entails that the interests do not exist. Men's interests in avoiding unwanted biological parenthood are surely real. But what would be required to turn that into a right is very different, and arguably unacceptable.

Kaczor is right to say that the interest in procreative control is not absolute (if he means by this that it does not ground an absolute right to protection), and I have never known anyone who defends abortion rights to claim that it is. But when he says that "equality demands this same consideration applies to men," he purports to be blind to the fact that all things are *not* equal between men and women in this arena. For one, as I have said, what is required by way of exercising the right to procreative control is not the same. For women, it is liberty to do as they wish with their own bodies. For men, it is the right to do as they wish with someone *else's* body. Nor are men and women equally positioned in terms of the nature of the interest in procreative control. For women, the interest is in avoiding months of pregnancy and significant bodily burdens, followed by childbirth, and, where adoption is too emotionally painful, the unequal burdens of childrearing, which still fall disproportionately on women. For men, the interest is, more often, in avoiding paying alimony and becoming the biological father to a child he did not want. These are still meaningful interests, but they are not equal.

Kaczor also claims that "unless parents have an ongoing right to kill even their adult children, there is no right not to be a biological parent." This seriously confuses what is involved in having an interest in something and what is involved in having a legally enforceable right to a thing. I never suggested for a moment that the interest in procreative liberty could ground a legal right to abortion if abortion amounts to unjustified homicide. Surely the only interest that could ever justify homicide is the interest in preserving an even greater amount of life. But does Kaczor believe that interests in things do not exist unless we can justify securing them through homicide if necessary? Does he believe that property rights or employment rights do not exist unless we are entitled to kill to protect them? Presumably not. If Kaczor only means to point out that the interest in procreative control cannot justify homicide, if that is what abortion is, then I can only repeat that I have all along been in total agreement on that point.

Kaczor agrees that pregnancy and childbirth can be physically damaging and risky. "However," he responds, abortion can also cause serious harm and death, even if only rarely. Yet this response to claims about the relative dangerousness of pregnancy and childbirth completely neglects the main point of comparison between the two, which is that one (childbirth) is appreciably riskier than the other (abortion), as evidenced by its far higher mortality rate. It cannot possibly be a consideration against having an abortion that abortion brings with it some physical risks if it is *less* risky than the only alternative, which it is. This is the fundamental illogicality of trying to persuade anyone against having an abortion by reference to the health risks.

Kaczor also goes to some trouble to make the point that standards of maternal health and general health are not worse for women in countries with very restrictive abortion laws than in countries with liberal abortion permissions. It is worth mentioning that the particular use of Ireland to evidence such a claim is quite inapt, given the vast swathes of Irish women who travel to Britain every year in order to circumvent their country's restrictive abortion laws. Irish women do in fact procure abortion in quite significant numbers, only not in the open and predominantly not in Ireland. But what is the consideration Kaczor deems important here? He concedes that "many factors are relevant" to comparative maternal health outcomes between two countries, but "what the data make clear," he says, "is that legalized abortion is not necessary for women's health rates to be as good or better than countries with legalized abortion." As a further demonstration of this, Kaczor cites evidence that gender parity in health care is better in Ireland than in the United States, a country with more liberal abortion laws. Never minding the fact that abortion access in many parts of the United States is in fact extremely restricted, *Roe v. Wade* notwithstanding, we must ask ourselves what sort of consideration this is against legal abortion access. Such is the importance of all the other variables in general comparisons of health outcomes between countries, that the words "legalized abortion" in the quoted sentence could be substituted for almost anything, including "polio inoculation," "breast cancer screening," and "gun control laws," and still easily be true.

The fact that legal abortion is not an essential condition for women's overall health outcomes in one country to be better than that of another country with more restrictive abortion laws therefore tells us nothing of consequence. Neither is it how anyone would assess the contributions of a medical practice. For instance, it could easily be true that women's general level of health is better in Japan than in Germany, even in a scenario where Germany had routine breast cancer screening and Japan did not. This would be no basis for asserting that breast cancer screening does not contribute to women's health. Finally, in any event, contribution to overall better health outcomes has never been the main justification for legal abortion access. That justification is rather the need to afford women control over their bodies and their reproductive destinies, although women's health does of course suffer when state abortion prohibitions encourage unregulated and secretive abortion practice.

Unfortunately, space precludes any further examination of the claims Kaczor makes relating to women's interests in abortion and the impact of abortion prohibitions on sex equality (though it is worth at least saying that there is a very good reason why no one has ever tried to argue that racial segregation did not disadvantage black people as a class because some black people, living remotely enough, were not directly affected by it).

5.4   What I Do and Do Not Claim

Intelligent Aliens and Imperiled Embryos

Kaczor considers and rejects two of the challenges I pose to the pro-life view by means of a hypothetical about intelligent aliens and the "Embryo Rescue Case" thought experiment. The intelligent alien hypothetical, Kaczor recounts, is supposed to tell us that biological humanity is not a necessary condition for personhood, since the alien is not human, but it is, most would agree, a person. Kaczor retorts that this hypothetical is "irrelevant to the claim that all human beings are persons" for the simple reason that all human beings might *nevertheless* be persons, even if their humanity is not a necessary condition for personhood, just as, say, all ballerinas might be coordinated movers, but one does not need to be a ballerina to be coordinated.

That is true. But I did not take the hypothetical to refute the possibility that all human beings are persons. If they were, this need not contradict our intuition about the personhood of the alien. Perhaps all human beings are persons, and intelligent aliens are as well. If that were true, we would still have to ask what is common to both groups that makes them both persons, since it is not humanity. In order to know that all humans are persons, we must know in virtue of what. The intelligent alien hypothetical suggests that the basis for personhood is not biological humanity but something else, since it is the alien's cognitive capacities, not its species membership, that move us to identify it as a person. But not all human beings share this characteristic. Thus, while it is conceivable that all human beings are persons and intelligent aliens are too, the criteria for full moral rights that the alien thought experiment supports suggest that *not* all human beings are necessarily persons in the philosophical sense.

Next, in response to the Embryo Rescue Case, Kaczor replies that choosing to rescue the embryos over the child does not deny the basic rights of anyone, since "every person does not have the right to be rescued in every circumstance," although every person *does* have the right "not to be intentionally killed in every circumstance." As I have explained already, this typical response wholly misses the point of the thought experiment, which is supposed to cast light on our deep-seated beliefs about the relative value of embryos and children – on the question of *who is a person*. It does not matter that not everyone has the right to be rescued in every scenario. Of course they don't. But the hypothetical merely asks you to imagine that you can easily rescue one or the other – one child or five embryos – and then asks you to reflect on what your choice tells you about the relative value you assign to children versus embryos. If you really believed that embryos and babies are equal lives, then you would rescue the many over the few, as you would do were the choice between saving one baby and saving five. Questions about the constraints on intentionally killing persons do not even come up here. The hypothetical targets the prior question concerning who is and is not a person.

Birth and Boundaries

Reading Kaczor's reply, it seems at points that he takes me to be embarking on an enterprise that I am not. He challenges in various places that my conception of personhood does not elaborate sharp and precise boundaries of the concept. But I am not searching for a precise threshold of moral personhood, or, indeed, a precise formula for personhood's constitutive properties, since, on my account, such sharp borderlines do not exist. So, when Kaczor asks where "exactly" the border lies between self-motivated activity and its absence, my answer is that there *is* no exact border between the two. But this would be a strange reason to deny that something is a constitutive property of something else. I think that mutual sympathy is a clear constitutive property of friendship, although where the precise boundary lies between mutual sympathy and its absence I could not possibly say. Kaczor throughout his reply appears to fall prey to the fallacy that no sharp boundary means no real difference. But the one has never entailed the other. There is no sharp boundary between daytime and night time, but there is a real difference.

Indeed, any attempt to identify an absolutely *precise* moment when new persons come into existence is futile, and for reasons that Kaczor would be among the first to point out. But one of my main observations was that exactly the same is true for anyone who believes that such a "moment" occurs sometime during conception. Kaczor claims that the apparent absence of a morally transformative moment during the conception process is irrelevant for the pro-life view, since abortion is only ever at issue when conception is known to have taken place. But this answer does not engage with the point of the observation. Pro-life philosophers impugn developmental accounts of personhood for failing to identify an absolutely sharp threshold of personhood. But they themselves do not identify a threshold of that kind. It may be replied that on the strong pro-life view, conception is the core sufficient condition for personhood, is a "radical" development (although, pace Kaczor, what is and is not a "radical" difference is not a scientific matter but moral through and through), and that once a woman is pregnant, there is no doubt that conception has taken place. But if this is an acceptable response to the problem of precision, then it is equally available to the defender of any developmental threshold. Birth is not a precise moment, but we will not struggle with the clear cases on either side. In any event, because I reject the "punctualist" thesis, I do not believe that there is a serious problem of precision.

Legal thresholds, of course, cannot be vague. Kaczor writes: "my co-author proposes a multicriterial and fluid conception in order to determine who has the right to live." But if he believes I am suggesting a "fuzzy and nebulous" standard for the beginning of legally recognized personhood, or the determination of moral status on a "case-by-case basis," he must think me quite mad. For such an approach to the assignation of personhood would be insanity. Indeed, it is partly in virtue of the fact that law requires "transparency, clarity, and lucidity" that I suggested birth to be a particularly appropriate threshold for the assignation of full personhood status. As I argued, there is a moral as well as practical necessity for stipulating personhood status as complete and equal above a certain baseline threshold. Given that is the case, the question then turns to reasons in support of placing the threshold in one place rather than another, cognizant of the fact that no threshold will be utterly nonarbitrary (especially not in the sorites sense), and of the fact that no metaphysically cataclysmic "moment" exists in any case.

Thus, Kaczor will misunderstand the nature of my support for the birth threshold if he takes me to be claiming that somewhere in the passage through the vaginal canal, something magical and mysterious happens to transform the young human into an entirely different sort of being. (Such is the depth of the "punctualist" assumption among pro-life advocates, I think, that they cannot resist interpreting all of their opponents' arguments as attempts to locate a sharp beginning of personhood at birth, even when explicitly stated that this is not the enterprise – although, when asked to meet their own standards, the conversation topic is quickly changed).

Nor is it entirely correct that my reasons for supporting the birth threshold merely echo Warren's concerns about the potentially "morally deadening" effects of permitting infanticide. Birth is, in the various ways I outlined, a hugely momentous event in the life of a new human. Moreover, the many significant developments that birth occasions (emergence into the world of other humans, exposure to the content of mental activity, etc.) do not depend on the gestational age of the newborn. I argued that these features of birth, along with its practical workability and high visibility, go in favor of stipulating birth as the entry point for full personhood status, given the moral and practical necessity of such a stipulation. I think it may well be true that the callous or flippant treatment of late fetuses could also threaten moral desensitization to some degree, especially if human embodiment itself is thought to be worthy of some respect. This could be a consideration in favor of somehow signposting the gravity of late-term abortion choices, even if personhood status is not legally recognized until birth (although I think it hardly likely that such a choice is ever undertaken lightly). But a concern about the potentially morally desensitizing effects of permitting infanticide was not the sole basis on which I defended birth as an appropriate threshold for the recognition of full moral status.

Radical Cognitive Deficiency

Lack of space puts paid to many further remarks about the genuinely taxing problem of persons with radical cognitive disabilities. I will clarify, however, that I do not favor extending personhood status to the intellectually disabled for pragmatic reasons alone. Rather, I expressed doubt that there are many (or any) intellectually disabled mature humans who do not meet the basic conditions for personhood on a standard developmental account such as Warren's. The permanently unconscious, such as Kaczor's Holly (if her state of vegetation is indeed permanent) raise, I believe, some distinct issues. It may be more difficult to accommodate the personhood of such insensate beings on a developmental account of what it is to be a person. But then I think most people would have less trouble accepting this conclusion than in the case of conscious human beings with intellectual disabilities. However, even in extreme cases such as Holly's, we may find, on reflection, that there are moral considerations not having to do with the rights and interests of persons for refraining from treating their bodies in particular, disrespectful ways.

6   A Short Reply to Greasley

Christopher Kaczor

I'm grateful to Kate Greasley for engaging in this dialogue with me, and I hope that she feels the same way. (Until drafting my previous reply in chapter four, I did not have a chance to see sections of Greasley's initial essay, namely, "Stipulation and Law" and "The Virtues of Birth," so I'll reply to them now.)

Greasley writes, "As we can see by now, almost any post-conception human development can be either unnecessary for personhood, insufficient, or both." I agree. Despite about 50 years of attempts, the Criteria Failure Problem still plagues legal and moral defenses of abortion that deny basic rights to human beings in utero.

Greasley responds to the Criteria Failure Problem by saying that the view that all human beings have human rights also faces challenges of reduction to the absurd, such as the Embryo Rescue Case.

Even if it were true that the reduction to the absurd challenges against the pro-life view were unanswerable, this use of the tu quoque fallacy is irrelevant to critiques leveled against denials of basic rights for human beings in utero. It does nothing to clear yourself of the charge of theft to say that your accuser has also stolen.

Another response to the Criteria Failure Problem is that, some-how, the conjunction of the failed criteria in a mix of unspecified proportion constitutes personhood as a legal or moral matter.

> Norwood Russell Hanson used to tell the story about a preacher who was finally persuaded that none of the arguments for the existence of God is valid. The preacher cheerfully concluded that the conjunction of those arguments must be valid because there are so many of them. Short of adopting the stance of Hanson's preacher, I see no basis for holding that although each of [the personhood criteria] constitutes no basis for the neonatal right to life, their conjunction is a sufficient basis for a right to life.
>
> (Marquis 1998, 384)

Arbitrary stipulations with no ethical foundation cannot be just ways of drawing the line between human beings who may be killed and human beings with legal protection against getting killed.

In another response to the Criteria Failure Problem, Greasley suggests that the concept of personhood is like the concept of friendship, without necessary and sufficient conditions for existence. We know what friendship is without these criteria, so too we can know what personhood is without these criteria.

I'm skeptical of the claim that friendship does not have necessary conditions. If two people have shared interests, regular contact, and a common worldview, but one person is torturing the other to death for the fun of it, the two people are not friends. Aristotle was right that mutual good will is necessary for friendship.

Moreover, the friendship is not like personhood in terms of its role in moral and legal reasoning. Imagine our society permitted the choice to intentionally kill any human being who didn't have a sufficient number of friends. Anyone who cares about securing justice would ask important critical questions of such legal killing. What is a "sufficient number" of friends? Who exactly counts as a friend? Why should having an indeterminate number of undefined friends be necessary for legal protection against getting killed? Inasmuch as abortion is a legal and ethical issue, the vagueness that might be fine for friendship will not do for defining who does and who does not deserve the protection of our laws and the respect due to every person. Greasley recognizes the need to avoid ambiguity: "there is a moral and practical necessity driving the need to stipulate an absolute and clear threshold of personhood somewhere within the reasonable range of answers." Greasley's threshold is birth, but I believe she does not adequately respond to the critiques lodged against birth as a legal or a moral beginning to basic rights.

6.1   Late-Term Abortion and the Law

Greasley questions the claim that "abortion is legally permitted all the way up to birth for any reason." She continues, "Kaczor's statement makes it sound as if any woman in America can simply walk into an abortion clinic at 30 weeks of pregnancy and get an abortion, just because she has changed her mind, when this is very far from being the case." Greasley is correct that, "Post-viability, states are free to prohibit abortion under *Casey*, so long as they maintain exceptions to preserve the health and life of the pregnant woman."

States *may* prohibit but are not *required* to prohibit late-term abortion. Many states have no such prohibitions. States that do attempt to protect prenatal human beings in the second or third trimester are hamstrung by the "health" exception. In the companion case to *Roe v. Wade*, the Supreme Court in *Doe v. Bolton* defined "health" as "all factors – physical, emotional, psychological, familial, and the woman's age – relevant to the wellbeing of the patient" (1973). This definition of "health" is so broad that emotional distress in not being able to get an abortion could count as a "health" justification for late-term abortion. *Doe v. Bolton*'s "health" exception is like a rule allowing states to forbid drunk driving, save *only* on two occasions: day and night. The exception destroys the rule.

Nor is the gigantic legal "health" loophole only a theoretical matter. The total number of abortions in the United States (1,006,000 in 2011) combined with the percentage of abortions that take place 21 weeks or later in pregnancy (Centers for Disease Control 2011, table 8) indicates that more than 12,000 legal abortions take place each year in the second or third trimester of pregnancy. (By way of comparison, in 2011 there were 9,878 deaths from drunk driving in the United States).

I agree with Greasley that "The point here is not that late-term abortion merely looks distasteful, but that our knee-jerk aversion to it is part and parcel of demonstrating appropriate moral respect for the human form as such." But this insight can lead to a condemnation of not just infanticide or late-term abortion but also earlier abortion. Surgical abortions, even in the first trimester, leave a bloody mess of readily identifiable human faces, legs, feet, and hands.

Like the US Supreme Court in *Roe*, Greasley holds that pre-birth abortion is permissible but post-birth abortion is not. This view faces the Pre-Birth/Post-Birth Consistency Problem described here by abortion defender Jeff McMahan:

> Those who believe that abortion can sometimes be justified after the point of fetal viability but that infanticide is never permissible face a problem of consistency, for there is no intrinsic difference between a premature infant and a viable fetus of the same age and level of development. The only difference is extrinsic, a matter of location. If, as virtually all moral theorists agree, moral status is a function of intrinsic properties only, there can be no difference in moral status between a viable fetus and a premature infant of the same age. If all infants have a status that brings them within the scope of stringent moral constraints, the same must be true of all viable fetuses. For any viable fetus could be an infant with a slight change of location that involves swapping a natural for an artificial system of life support.
>
> (McMahan 2013, 273)

McMahan notes that the US Supreme Court held that "killing a viable fetus during the second trimester was constitutionally protected, yet if the pregnant woman carrying it suddenly went into labour, killing that same individual after it had emerged from her body would have been murder. This was arbitrary and irrational" (McMahan 2013, 273). If McMahan is right, birth does not satisfy the standard Greasley herself proposes of "an absolute and clear threshold of personhood somewhere within the reasonable range of answers." An arbitrary, irrational, and inconsistent answer is not reasonable.

Does the pro-life view also have a consistency problem? The pro-life view holds that sentience, the ability to experience pleasure and pain, cannot be sufficient for personhood because rats, worms, and wasps experience pain but these creatures do not have a right to live. Greasley responds, "Of course, the same thing is true of the conception criterion. Mice have been conceived too, and so have horses. Insofar as it is a reason to reject a personhood criterion, then, the insufficiency problem applies to conception as well."

This response, another example of the tu quoque fallacy, also misrepresents my view. The premise of my argument is not that every individual who is conceived has basic rights, but that *all human beings* have human rights. So the fact that mice or horses are conceived is irrelevant to the argument, since the premise of the pro-life argument is not that being conceived is necessary or sufficient for the right to live.

6.2   Brain Death, Integrative Functions, and Human Rights

Another challenge raised to the ethics of inclusivity is that just as the death of no particular brain cell marks the end of personhood in brain death, so too the life of no particular cell marks the beginning of personhood. As my co-author puts it, if "there is a correct answer to the question about exactly when personhood begins, ... I think it [the pro-life view] must hold that there is a correct answer to the question here about exactly when it ends. Yet there is no individual cell with which it seems sensible to identify the sudden disappearance of personhood status." So too, there is no individual cell with which it seems sensible to identify the sudden appearance of personhood status.

How could a defender of the ethics of inclusivity reply? The standard distinguishing life from death is alike for all organisms: integrated biological functioning. In an adult human being with more than 37 trillion cells, it can be more difficult to determine than in a single-celled organism at exactly which point integrated function of the whole body is lost. On the basis of biology, there is no inconsistency in holding that an individual human life begins at completed fertilization (as Greasley concedes) and holding that the death of a human being can sometimes be much more difficult to determine in the case of an adult with 37 trillion cells in her body. So, there is no inconsistency in holding that there is a more easily discernible correct answer to the question about exactly when personhood begins (whenever a human being begins) and holding that it is much more difficult to determine the correct answer to the question when exactly personhood ends (whenever a human being as a living organism ceases to exist). Integrated functioning is more easily verified in a growing prenatal human being than in an adult tottering on the brink of death.

6.3   Equality of Persons

Rather than reply to the equality of persons thesis as I articulated it, Greasley misconstrues my view to be "that all human deaths are equally as bad, and killings equally wrong, on the only metric that matters."

The equality thesis is the proposition that all human beings are equal in basic worth, with the same fundamental dignity, and the same basic rights. But this view is fully compatible with other kinds of inequalities among persons and inequalities in violations of equal basic rights aggravating the severity of a crime. Intrinsically, the death of every human being is alike, the loss of integrative biological functioning. Circumstantially, the death of each human being is distinctive. Indeed, the law in the United States and Great Britain distinguishes first-degree murder of a plain person from aggravated first-degree murder of a presiding judge, a child, or an on-duty law enforcement officer. Greasley provides no reasons for rejecting these legal distinctions nor for viewing them as violations of the equality of all persons under the law. Greasley does not, therefore, respond to my version of the equality thesis but rather critiques a straw man version of it.

Should we agree with Greasley that permissibility is "the *only* metric that matters"? I believe a nuanced ethical judgment of the entire situation is more complex than a binary right or wrong. For example, all acts of theft are impermissible, violations of the right to private property, but surely there is an ethical and legal difference between stealing $10 million and stealing $10. It matters whether money is stolen from Bill Gates or from a poor widow barely able to heat her house. It matters whether the theft is done electronically or whether it is done under threat of violence at gunpoint.

6.4   The Equality Problem and the Future-like-Ours Argument

Greasley writes, "Kaczor cannot argue that the equality problem is salient for capacities-based accounts of personhood but not for the future-like-ours account, when it, too, ties personhood to a property that admits of gradations." If the future-like-ours account comes in degrees of more or less, it cannot be used to justify the equality of all persons.

However, as Marquis points out, "The [future-like-ours] argument to the conclusion that abortion is prima facie seriously morally wrong proceeded independently of the notion of person or potential person or any equivalent" (Marquis 1989, 192). The future-like-ours argument sidesteps entirely the question of personhood. So, embracing the future-like-ours argument involves no commitment to any particular position on the necessary and the sufficient conditions for personhood. Since the future-like-ours argument is not about personhood at all, the future-like-ours argument is perfectly compatible with the equality thesis, which is a thesis about persons: whatever it is that makes us to be persons is to be had equally with all persons in order to secure the equality of all persons.

Moreover, the future-like-ours argument is also compatible with the equality of the right to live (Marquis 1998, 379–380). A rich man has more money than a poor man, but they have equal rights not to have their property stolen. Everyone with a future like ours has an equal right to live, that is, all agents have an equally perfect duty not to intentionally kill individuals with a future like ours.

6.5   The Argument from History and Animal Rights

Greasley responds to the argument from history in part by invoking animal rights. In the case of animal rights, we have a similar structure of the stronger imposing their will on the weaker. Are pro-life scholars who do not embrace animal rights inconsistent? Must such scholars give up the argument from history?

The question of animal rights is an important ethical issue. Some pro-life scholars endorse animal rights (Camosy 2013; Camosy 2015). If all animals have rights, then the pro-life claim is secured, for the prenatal human being is a living animal organism. Other pro-life scholars do not endorse animal rights (Finnis 2011). Are such scholars inconsistent in making the argument from history?

There is a consensus about human rights that does not exist about animal rights. Virtually everyone condemns times in history during which we have excluded entire classes of human beings from social and legal rights (e.g., people of color). This pattern of mistaken exclusion should serve as both a presumption and a default in the case of uncertainty. If virtually everyone agreed that every single time we've excluded animals in the past, we have made a very serious mistake, that would provide good reason for being cautious now in excluding a particular class of animals from basic rights. There is a consensus about past exclusions of human beings but there is no such consensus about past exclusions of animals, so the case of human rights and the case of animal rights are not analogous.

Indeed, it is Greasley who may not be consistent in her views about abortion and animal rights. Greasley holds that birth should be the legal threshold granting the right to life. Transitioning from in utero to ex utero is an equally complex and biologically significant transition for dogs, cats, and mice. Should dogs, cats, and mice be accorded a legal right to live equal to our own?

Of course, we could appeal to the *humanity* of the babies born, but this brings us (according to many defenders of abortion and advocates for animal rights) to an unacceptable speciesism. On the other hand, if the humanity of the newborn baby is relevant, why should the humanity of the human being in utero be irrelevant?

At birth, Greasley writes, "A surge of hormones is released to regulate temperature outside the womb, new enzymes are activated, and the digestive system undergoes considerable changes." I find it hard to believe that any of these changes should have the slightest legal or moral significance. If the surge of hormones didn't happen, would the neonate not have a legal right to life? Why should new enzymes be relevant for legal protection against getting killed? Why do new digestive juices (which very well may be in dogs) secure equality before the law? The list of biological changes that differentiate a newborn human being from a human being in utero immediately before birth is a list of changes without any moral or legal importance. Indeed, such changes are undergone by all mammals in birth, but I doubt Greasley would push for legal status to all mammals who are born. Yes, birth triggers behavioral changes in the human being such as crying aloud, but none of these changes has the slightest moral or legal significance, as either necessary or sufficient for moral or legal status.

Following Jose Bermudez, Greasley suggests that the capacity for facial imitation requires at least a primitive understanding of the difference between self and other. She offers no reply to my objections to this criterion, such as the case of blind newborns who cannot imitate faces, since they see nothing. Moreover, it is not the case that this rudimentary form of self-consciousness is something that no full-term human being in utero possesses. As noted earlier, the exercised capacity to imitate account is false in part because twins in utero do exhibit a kind of social interaction that suggests a rudimentary form of differentiation of self and other.

Moreover, it is obvious that such interaction is not sufficient for social worth or relevant for legal status. Dogs socially interact, smiling at some people and snarling at other people, to a much greater extent than human newborns. Yes, it is true that babies have short-term memories, but the same is true of a late-term human being in utero. The proverbial pig has a memory that bests them both. If a newborn's mental state changes immediately on birth, the question arises, why are these changes so significant that they should mark the beginning of their legal right to life? Why do similar changes in nonhuman animals who are born not mark the beginning of their legal right to life?

Moreover, what is the *ethical* basis for the law treating humans who are virtually identical just prior to birth and just after birth in such radically different ways? If we hold with Greasley that constraints will inform the margins within which it is reasonable to stipulate the minimum threshold of the legal right to life, why should a newborn fall within the basic threshold of qualification for the legal right to live? My little white dog Lulu is much closer to satisfying the psychological criteria of personhood than any newborn baby. My dog can communicate a range of desires (e.g., for a walk or for food) that are more sophisticated than the cries of a baby. My dog knows her own name and can obey simple commands. If the minimum threshold for the legal right to life is satisfied by the rationality of a baby, it is even more easily satisfied by my dog. But defenders of birth as the magic moment of the legal and/or moral right to life do not typically defend the right to life of my dog. So, unless we believe my dog Lulu should be granted a legal right to live, or unless we invoke humanity as morally relevant, we should reject Greasley's legal standard for the right to life as contrary to justice. Justice treats like cases alike.

6.6 Body–Self Dualism and Nonhuman Persons

Let us assume with Greasley that "we, persons, are identical with our human bodies." Two things are identical if they share all their properties. Given the assumption that persons are identical with their bodies, is it also consistent "to reject the claim that all living human organisms are essentially and substantially persons"?

Personhood could be a phase sortal, like being a teenager. We exist before being a teenager, and we can exist after being a teenager. But if personhood is a phase sortal, then we, as persons, are not identical with our human bodies, because our human body can exist (in our gestation and infancy) without our personhood existing. So, if I understand Greasley's view properly, she embraces three propositions that are not compatible in conjunction:

1. We, as persons, are identical with our human living bodies.
2. The human living body is in existence following completed fertilization.
3. The human living body is not a person.

It is not consistent to hold that persons, such as mature healthy human beings, are identical with their bodies and that human beings are not persons at all times of their existence. A defense of abortion could rest on a denial of the second premise, if it were claimed that a living human body arises weeks, months, or years after conception. But Greasley accepts the premise that the human newborn, the human in utero, and the human embryo all are living human bodies.

Greasley writes that "someone who rejects body–self dualism must accept that this is the case [personhood or the right to life is a nonessential characteristic of human beings], since she presumably would not agree that dead human bodies are persons with full moral rights, even though they are, she must agree, numerically identical with the human being that was alive." I do not agree that the living human being is numerically identical with a corpse. For an individual person to change in accidental ways (e.g., to improve at shooting arrows) is compatible with remaining the same individual person. But a substantial change is the ceasing to be of one kind of thing (say, a living animal organism) and the origination of a different kind of thing (the heap of disorganized molecules known as a corpse). For this reason, dead human bodies are not persons with full moral rights because a corpse is not (pace Greasley) numerically identical with the human being who was alive. Death is a substantial change in which the human being (and therefore the human person) ceases to exist. The view that death is a substantial change is reflected in our moral and legal practices that allow us to dissect, burn, and bury lifeless corpses but not to dissect, burn, and bury living human beings. Moreover, as Eric Olson notes, "living organisms and lifeless corpses appear to be so different as to have different and incompatible persistence conditions" (Olson 2004, 272). But things with different and incompatible persistence conditions are not numerically identical. So, the living human body and the lifeless corpse are not numerically identical.

If our identity is determined by means of bodily criteria (rather than psychological characteristics), what can be said about the imaginary transformation of apes from nonrational to rational through a series of injections that gradually increase intelligence? Gradual steps can bring about a substantial change. Consider a case of someone injected with one dose of poison a day. Each dose is, considered in itself, nonfatal. But if 100 doses of the poison are given for 100 straight days, the upshot is a fatal heart attack. In such a case, the ninety-ninth dose would bring the victim to the edge of death but not over the edge. Once the hundredth dose has its effect, the person is killed, and the radical and substantial change from life to death takes place. The same could be true of the injections given to increase intelligence. Once the ape is injected with the fateful final dose the ape undergoes a substantial change from nonrational to rational, and so gains the rights that are due to every rational creature. Is the ape numerically the same ape before and after the change? If our identity is determined by means of bodily criteria, would the ape have the same body? Not necessarily. Just as the final dose of poison produces a bodily change in the heart leading to the substantial change of death, so the final dose of the rationality serum produces a bodily change in the brain leading to the substantial change of gaining a rational nature. The first substantial change is the destruction of an individual; the second substantial change is the creation of a new individual.

6.7   Abortion to Save the Life of the Mother

In treating the case of abortion to save the life of the mother, Greasley does not present my view accurately in saying, "killing one person is only ever permissible when it is necessary to prevent an even greater loss of life." I know of no pro-life scholar who claims that *two* lives must be saved in order for there to be a proportionately serious reason justifying allowing one person to die as a side effect. To save one person's life is a sufficient reason for allowing another person to die. I also do not hold that it is "a condition of a life-saving abortion that the act carried out would have been chosen even if not for the fetus's existence." If the act carried out would have been chosen even if there were no pregnancy, then this fact is sufficient for showing that the death of the human being is not chosen as a means or as an end, but this fact is not necessary for the death to be neither a means nor an end.

Moreover, I am aware of no case in which the *death* of the prenatal human being is itself necessary, as a means or as an end, in order to save the life of the mother. Take, for example, some case in which a procedure that will bring about fetal demise is medically indicated in order to save the life of the mother. Imagine, moments before the procedure, it happens by chance that the human fetus dies. Is there any medical procedure that would be called off, now that the human fetus is dead? I have explored cases of abortion to save the life of the mother in greater detail elsewhere, but have found no situation in which the child's *death* is in itself the means needed to secure the life of the mother (Kaczor 2009; Kaczor 2013, 69–95).

6.8   Abortion and Legal Punishment

Is it inconsistent to advocate for the rights of prenatal human beings and also to hold that abortion should not be punished like first-degree murder? As Robert P. George and Ramesh Ponnuru point out, the profound disagreement on abortion in our culture suggests that punishment for abortion should be no more harsh than necessary to deter the crime. The law has taught people for decades that abortion is permissible, so "the law should avoid harshly punishing those who have learned this false lesson all too well" (George and Ponnuru, 1996, 11). Moreover, a just punishment is proportionate in part to the social consequences of a crime. For this reason, killing a judge is not just first-degree murder but *aggravated* first-degree murder, for such killings not only take away an individual's life but undermine the judicial system. The typical social consequences of ordinary murder are much more dire than the social consequences of abortion. In addition, "lower penalties could increase the effectiveness of anti-abortion laws by making juries more likely to convict. Women seeking abortions could be (and historically often were) exempted from penalties altogether, due both to mitigating circumstances – a great many women are really secondary victims of the abortion industry – and to the need to get testimony to help convict the abortionist" (George and Ponnuru 1996, 11). The penalties that are just for violations of law must take into account a variety of factors taking us beyond the simplistic assumption that if abortion is wrong, it deserves punishment equivalent to first-degree murder of an adult.

6.9   All Things Considered

At the conclusion of this interchange, it is clear that Greasley and I are not yet in full agreement. But we are in full agreement that the issue of abortion is a matter of deep public and private importance. I hope that she and other pro-choice readers have a better understanding of at least one version of the pro-life perspective. And I hope that my dialogue about this matter with her, and other people of good will, can continue.

Let me conclude with a true story. In a hot southern California summer, a red-headed Irish-American girl met an African immigrant guy. She was focused on her studies; he was focused on her.

Her pregnancy hit her like a Mack truck. She had been taught that abortion was wrong because it shed innocent blood, that getting an abortion would make her like a vampire.

But now her continued existence, her identity as she knew it, was under threat. She wanted to finish her education. She wanted her freedom. She didn't want her life as she knew it to end. So, she made the most important, the most difficult, and the most gut-wrenching choice of her life.

Twenty-seven years after her decision, on a dock in Seattle, I got to thank this woman, my birth mother, for her heroic sacrifice. We embraced in tears of joy and gratitude.

Abortion is about women in crisis; it is about transformative choices. But it is also about "unwanted" children like myself, and millions of other human "surprises." To ignore human beings like me, to pretend that I do not exist, or that I never existed, or that I do not matter, does not change the reality. If sound ethical judgment involves taking into account the entire situation, then unwanted and unplanned human beings like me should also be taken into consideration. The struggle for peace and the struggle for justice cannot ignore the most defenseless and voiceless human beings. As Richard John Neuhaus said, "Nobody is a nobody." And so everybody deserves what I received, a chance at life.

Bibliography

Adler, N., David, H., Major, B., Roth, S., Russo, N., and Wyatt, G. (1990). Psychological Responses after Abortion. *Science*, *248*(4951), 41–44.

Adler, N. E. (2000). Abortion and the Null Hypothesis. *Archives of General Psychiatry*, *57*(8), 785–786.

Ariely, D. (2010a). *Predictably Irrational: The Hidden Forces That Shape Our Decisions*. Revised and expanded edition. New York: Harper.

(2010b). *The Upside of Irrationality: The Unexpected Benefits of Defying Logic*. New York: Harper Perennial.

Armsworth, M. W. (1991). Psychological Response to Abortion. *Journal of Counseling & Development*, *69*(4), 377–379.

Baker, L. R. (2000). *Persons and Bodies: A Constitution View*. Cambridge: Cambridge University Press.

Benn, S. (1984). Abortion, Infanticide, and Respect for Persons. In J. Feinberg (ed.), *The Problem of Abortion*, 2nd ed. Belmont, CA: Wadsworth.

Bermudez, J. L. (1996). The Moral Significance of Birth. *Ethics*, *106*(2), 378–403.

Boonin, D. (2003). *A Defense of Abortion*. Cambridge, UK, and New York: Cambridge University Press.

Burin, A. K. (2014). Beyond Pragmatism: Defending the Bright-Line of Birth. *Medical Law Review*, *22*(4), 494–525.

Calhoun, B. C., Thorp, J. M., and Carroll, P. S. (2013). Maternal and Neonatal Health and Abortion: 40-Year Trends in Great Britain and Ireland. *Journal of American Physicians and Surgeons*, *18*(2), 42–46.

Camosy, C. C. (2013). *For Love of Animals: Christian Ethics, Consistent Action*. Cincinnati, OH: Franciscan Media.

(2015). *Beyond the Abortion Wars: A Way Forward for a New Generation*. Grand Rapids, MI: Eerdmans.

Carlson, B. (2004). *Human Embryology and Developmental Biology*. St. Louis: C. V. Mosby.

Carlson, B. M. (1996). *Patten's Foundations of Embryology*, 6th ed. New York: McGraw-Hill.

Carter, I. (2011). Respect and the Basis of Equality. *Ethics*, *121*(3), 538–571.

Cecchino, G. N., Araujo, E. Jr., and Elito, J. Jr. (2014). Methotrexate for Ectopic Pregnancy: When and How. *Archives of Gynecology and Obstetrics*, *290*(2), 417–423.

Centers for Disease Control. (2011). *Abortion Surveillance – United States, 2008*. Retrieved from www.cdc.gov/mmwr/preview/mmwrhtml/ss6015a1.htm.

Clark, R. M., and Chua, T. (1989). Breast Cancer and Pregnancy: The Ultimate Challenge. *Clinical Oncology*, *1*(1), 11–18.

Condic, M. L. (2003). Life: Defining the Beginning by the End. *First Things*, May (133), 50–54.

Davies, J. A. (2014). *Life Unfolding: How the Human Body Creates Itself*. Oxford: Oxford University Press.

Debnath, J., Gulati, S. K., Mathur, A., Gupta, R., Kumar, N., Arora, S., and Krishna, R. B. (2013). Ectopic Pregnancy in the Era of Medical Abortion: Are We Ready for It? Spectrum of Sonographic Findings and Our Experience in a Tertiary Care Service Hospital of India. *Journal of Obstetrics and Gynaecology of India*, *63*(6), 388–393.

Dellapenna, J. (2006). *Dispelling the Myths of Abortion History*. Durham, NC: Carolina Academic Press.

Department of Health. (2013). *Abortion Statistics, England and Wales: 2012*. Retrieved from www.gov.uk/government/uploads/system/uploads/attachment_data/file/211790/2012_Abortion_Statistics.pdf.

  (2015). Report on Abortion Statistics in England and Wales for 2014. Retrieved from www.gov.uk/government/statistics/report-on-abortion-statistics-in-england-and-wales-for-2014.

Derbyshire, S. W. G. (2006). Can Fetuses Feel Pain? *BMJ*, *332*(7546), 909–912.

Douthat, R. (2013). The Texas Abortion Experiment. *New York Times*. Retrieved from www.nytimes.com/2013/07/21/opinion/sunday/douthat-the-texas-abortion-experiment.html.

Dworkin, R. (1994). *Life's Dominion: An Argument about Abortion, Euthanasia, and Individual Freedom*. New York: Vintage.

Engelhardt, H. T. (1999). The Sanctity of Life and the Concept of a Person. In L. P. Pojman (ed.), *Life and Death: A Reader in Moral Problems* (pp. 77–83). Belmont, CA: Wadsworth.

English, J. (1975). Abortion and the Concept of a Person. *Canadian Journal of Philosophy*, *5*(2), 233–243.

  (1996). Abortion and the Concept of a Person. In L. M. Schwartz (ed.), *Arguing about Abortion*. Belmont, CA: Wadsworth.

Fergusson, D. M., Horwood, L. J., and Boden, J. M. (2009). Reactions to Abortion and Subsequent Mental Health. *British Journal of Psychiatry*, *195*(5), 420–426.

Feser, E. (2014). *Scholastic Metaphysics: A Contemporary Introduction*. Neunkirchen-Seelscheid, Germany: Editiones Scholasticae.

Finnis, J. (2010). The Other F-Word. *Public Discourse*. Retrieved from www .thepublicdiscourse.com/2010/10/1849/.

(2011). *Natural Law and Natural Rights*, 2nd ed. Oxford: Oxford University Press.

Forsythe, C. D. (2013). *Abuse of Discretion: The Inside Story of Roe v. Wade*. New York City: Encounter Books.

Foster, S. M. (2017). Isn't Feminism about a Woman Having Rights Equal to Those of a Man? Retrieved from www.feministsforlife.org/isnt-femi nism-about-a-woman-having-rights-equal-to-those-of-a-man/.

Friberg-Fernros, H. (2015). A Critique of Rob Lovering's Criticism of the Substance View. *Bioethics*, *29*(3), 211–216.

George, R. P., and Ponnuru, R. (1996). The New Abortion Debate. *First Things* (62), 10–12.

George, R. P., and Tollefsen, C. (2008). *Embryo: A Defense of Human Life*. New York: Doubleday.

Girgis, S. (2014). Equality and Moral Worth in Natural Law Ethics and Beyond. *American Journal of Jurisprudence*, *59*(2), 143–162.

Giubilini, A., and Minerva, F. (2013). After-Birth Abortion: Why Should the Baby Live? *Journal of Medical Ethics*, *39*(5), 261–263.

Goila, A. K., and Pawar, M. (2009). The Diagnosis of Brain Death. *Indian Journal of Critical Care Medicine*, *13*(1), 7–11.

Gomez-Lobo, A. (2007). Individuality and Human Beginnings: A Reply to David DeGrazia. *Journal of Law, Medicine & Ethics*, *35* (3), 457–462.

Greasley, K. (2012). Abortion and Regret. *Journal of Medical Ethics*, *38*(12), 705–711.

(2017). *Arguments about Abortion: Personhood, Morality, and Law*. Oxford: Oxford University Press.

Greenhouse, L., and Siegel, R. B. (2016). Casey and the Clinic Closings: When "Protecting Health" Obstructs Choice. *Yale Law Journal*, *125*(5), 1428–1480.

The Guttmacher Institute. (2016). Laws Affecting Reproductive Health and Rights: State Trends at Midyear, 2016. Retrieved from www .guttmacher.org/article/2016/07/laws-affecting-reproductive-health-and-rights-state-trends-midyear-2016.

(2017a). Policy Trends in the States: 2016. Retrieved from www .guttmacher.org/article/2017/01/policy-trends-states-2016.

(2017b). State Policies on Later Abortion. Retrieved from www .guttmacher.org/state-policy/explore/state-policies-later-abortions.

Haidt, J. (2012). *The Righteous Mind: Why Good People Are Divided by Politics and Religion*. New York: Random House.

Hawking, M. (2015). The Viable Violinist. *Bioethics*, *30*(5), 312–316.

Hershenov, D. B., and Hershenov, R. J. (2015). Morally Relevant Potential. *Journal of Medical Ethics*, *41*(3), 268–271.

Hillman, N., Kallapur, S. G., and Jobe, A. (2012). Physiology of Transition from Intrauterine to Extrauterine Life. *Clinics in Perinatology*, *39*(4), 769–783.

Huang, Y., Zhang, X., Li, W., Song, F., Dai, H., Wang, J., . . . Chen, K. (2014). A Meta-Analysis of the Association between Induced Abortion and Breast Cancer Risk among Chinese Females. *Cancer Causes & Control*, *25*(2), 227–236.

Jabeen S., et al. (2013). Breast Cancer and Some Epidemiological Risk Factors: A Hospital Based Study. *Journal of Dhaka Medical College*, *22* (1), 61–66.

Joffe, C. E. (1995). *Doctors of Conscience: The Struggle to Provide Abortion before and after Roe v. Wade*. Boston: Beacon Press.

Kaczor, C. (2009). The Ethics of Ectopic Pregnancy: A Critical Reconsideration of Salpingostomy and Methotrexate. *Linacre Quarterly: A Journal of the Philosophy and Ethics of Medical Practice*, *76*(3), 265–282.

(2013). *A Defense of Dignity: Creating Life, Destroying Life, and Protecting the Rights of Conscience*. Notre Dame, IN: University of Notre Dame Press.

(2015). *The Ethics of Abortion: Women's Rights, Human Life, and the Question of Justice*, 2nd ed. New York: Routledge.

Kagan, S. (2016). What's Wrong with Speciesism? (Society for Applied Philosophy Annual Lecture 2015). *Journal of Applied Philosophy*, *33*(1), 1–21.

Kamm, F. (1992). *Creation and Abortion: A Study in Moral and Legal Philosophy*. Oxford: Oxford University Press.

Keown, J. (2002a). *Abortion, Doctors and the Law: Some Aspects of the Legal Regulation of Abortion in England from 1803 to 1982*. Cambridge: Cambridge University Press.

(2002b). *Euthanasia, Ethics and Public Policy: An Argument against Legalisation*. Cambridge: Cambridge University Press.

Kittay, E. F. (2009). The Personal Is Philosophical Is Political: A Philosopher and Mother of a Cognitively Disabled Person Sends Notes from the Battlefield. *Metaphilosophy*, *40*(3–4), 606–627.

Knapton, S. (2016, May 4, 2016). Human Embryos Kept Alive in Lab for Unprecedented 13 Days So Scientists Can Watch Development. *The*

Telegraph. Retrieved from www.telegraph.co.uk/science/2016/05/04/human-embryos-kept-alive-in-lab-for-unprecedented-13-days-so-sci/.

Kreeft, P. (2005). *Socratic Logic*, 2nd ed. South Bend, IN: St. Augustine's Press.

Lawani, O. L., Anozie, O. B., and Ezeonu, P. O. (2013). Ectopic Pregnancy: A Life-Threatening Gynecological Emergency. *International Journal of Women's Health*, 5, 515–521.

Lecarpentier J., et al. (2012). Variation in Breast Cancer Risk Associated with Factors Related to Pregnancies according to Truncating Mutation Location in the French National BRCA1 and BRCA2 Mutations Carrier Cohort (GENEPSO). *Breast Cancer Research*, 14(4), R99.

Lee, P. (2013). The Basis for Being a Subject of Rights: The Natural Law Position. In J. Keown and R. P. George (eds.), *Reason, Morality, and Law: The Philosophy of John Finnis* (pp. 236–248). Oxford: Oxford University Press.

Lee, P., and George, R. P. (2007). *Body–Self Dualism in Contemporary Ethics and Politics*. Cambridge: Cambridge University Press.

Liao, S. M. (2007). Time-Relative Interests and Abortion. *Journal of Moral Philosophy*, 4(2), 242–256.

Little, M. O. (1999). Abortion, Intimacy, and the Duty to Gestate. *Ethical Theory and Moral Practice*, 2(3), 295–312.

Littleton, L., and Engebretson, J. (2005). *Maternity Nursing Care*. New York: Thomson.

Lovering, R. (2014). The Substance View: A Critique (Part 2). *Bioethics*, 28 (7), 378–386.

MacKinnon, C. A. (1991). Reflections on Sex Equality under Law. *Yale Law Journal*, 100(5), 1281–1328.

Major, B., Cozzarelli, C., Cooper, M., et al. (2000). Psychological Responses of Women after First-Trimester Abortion. *Archives of General Psychiatry*, 57(8), 777–784.

Manninen, B. A. (2010). Rethinking *Roe v. Wade*: Defending the Abortion Right in the Face of Contemporary Opposition. *American Journal of Bioethics*, 10(12), 33–46.

(2014). *Pro-Life, Pro-Choice: Shared Values in the Abortion Debate*. Nashville, TN: Vanderbilt University Press.

Marquis, D. (1989). Why Abortion Is Immoral. *Journal of Philosophy*, 86(4), 183–202.

(1991). Four Versions of Double Effect. *Journal of Medicine and Philosophy*, 16(5), 515–544.

(1998). A Future like Ours and the Concept of Person: A Reply to McInerney and Paske. In L. P. Pojman and F. J. Beckwith (eds.), *The Abortion Controversy: A Reader*, 2nd ed. (pp. 372–385). Belmont, CA: Wadsworth.

Marquis, D. (2007). Abortion Revisited. In B. Steinbock (ed.), *The Oxford Handbook of Bioethics* (pp. 395–415). New York: Oxford.

(2010). Manninen's Defense of Abortion Rights Is Unsuccessful. *American Journal of Bioethics, 10*(12), 56–57.

McMahan, J. (2002). *The Ethics of Killing: Problems at the Margins of Life.* Oxford: Oxford University Press.

(2005). Our Fellow Creatures. *Journal of Ethics, 9*(3–4), 353–380.

(2007). Infanticide. *Utilitas, 19*(2), 131–159.

(2013). Infanticide and Moral Consistency. *Journal of Medical Ethics, 39*(5), 273–280.

(2016). On "Modal Personism." *Journal of Applied Philosophy, 33*(1), 26–30.

Meltzoff, A. N., and Moore, M. K. (1977). Imitation of Facial and Manual Gestures by Human Neonates. *Science, 198*(4312), 75–78.

Morowitz, H. J., and Terfil, J. S. (1992). *The Facts of Life: Science and the Abortion Controversy.* Oxford: Oxford University Press.

Mulhall, S. (2002). Fearful Thoughts. *London Review of Books, 24*(16), 16–18.

Nathanson, B. N., and Ostline, R. N. (1979). *Aborting America.* Toronto: Life Cycle Books.

Nichols, P. (2012). Abortion, Time-Relative Interests, and Futures like Ours. *Ethical Theory and Moral Practice, 15*(4), 493–506.

Nozick, R. (1974). *Anarchy, State, and Utopia.* New York: Basic Books.

O'Brien, D. (2011). Can We Talk about Abortion? *Commonweal Magazine,.* 138(16), 12–19.

O'Rahilly, R. R., and Müller, F. (2001). *Human Embryology and Teratology.* New York: Wiley-Liss.

Obama, B. (2008, June 8). Obama's Father's Day Remarks. *New York Times.* Retrieved from www.nytimes.com/2008/06/15/us/politics/15text-obama.html.

(2009, May 17, 2009). Transcript: Obama's Notre Dame Speech. *Chicago Tribune.* Retrieved from www.chicagotribune.com/chi-barack-obama-notre-dame-speech-story.html.

Olson, E. T. (2004). Animalism and the Corpse Problem. *Australasian Journal of Philosophy, 82*(2), 265–274.

Ord, T. (2008). The Scourge: Moral Implications of Natural Embryo Loss. *American Journal of Bioethics, 8*(7), 12–19.

Pakuluk, M. (1991). *Other Selves: Philosophers on Friendship.* Indianapolis, IN: Hackett.

Paul, L. A. (2014). *Transformative Experience.* Oxford: Oxford University Press.

Peach, A. (2007). Late- vs. Early Term Abortion: A Thomistic Analysis. *The Thomist, 71*(1), 113–141.

Pinker, S. (2002). *The Blank Slate: The Modern Denial of Human Nature.* New York: Penguin.

Raymond, E. G., and Grimes, D. A. (2012). The Comparative Safety of Legal Induced Abortion and Childbirth in the United States. *Obstetrics and Gynecology, 119*(2 Pt. 1), 215–219.

Reardon, D. (1987). *Aborted Women: Silent No More.* Chicago: Loyola University Press.

(1996). *Making Abortion Rare: A Healing Strategy for a Divided Nation.* Springfield, IL: Acorn Books.

Rochat, P. (2003). Five Levels of Self-Awareness as They Unfold early in Life. *Conscious and Cognition, 12*(4), 717–731.

Roy A., et al. (2014). Association of Lifestyle Variables with the Novel Mutation of BRCA1 Gene in Breast Cancer. *World Journal of Pharmacy and Pharmaceutical Sciences, 3*(6), 1213–1226.

Royal College of Gynaecologists. (2008). Briefing Note: Scientific Information on Abortion. Retrieved from www.rcog.org.uk/en/news/campaigns-and-opinions/human-fertilisation-and-embryology-bill/briefing-note-scientific-information-on-abortion/.

(2015). Best Practice in Comprehensive Abortion Care. Retrieved from www.rcog.org.uk/globalassets/documents/guidelines/best-practice-papers/best-practice-paper-2.pdf.

Sanger, C. (2008). Seeing and Believing: Mandatory Ultrasound and the Path to a Protected Choice. *UCLA Law Review, 56,* 351–408.

Savulescu, J. (2002). Abortion, Embryo Destruction and the Future of Value Argumen. *Journal of Medical Ethics, 25*(3), 133–135.

Sherwin, S. (1991). Abortion through a Feminist Ethics Lens. *Dialogue, 30* (3), 327–342.

Siegel, R. B. (2008). The Right's Reasons: Constitutional Conflict and the Spread of Woman-Protective Anti-Abortion Argument. *Duke Law Journal, 57,* 1641–1692.

Singer, P. (1975). *Animal Liberation.* New York: HarperCollins.

(1993). *Practical Ethics,* 2nd ed. Cambridge: Cambridge University Press.

(1994). *Rethinking Life and Death: The Collapse of Our Traditional Ethics.* New York: St. Martin's Press.

(2000). *Writings on an Ethical Life.* New York: Ecco Press.

(2016). Why Speciesism Is Wrong: A Response to Kagan. *Journal of Applied Philosophy, 33*(1), 31–35.

Stone, J. (1987). Why Potentiality Matters. *Canadian Journal of Philosophy, 17*(4), 815–829.

Stretton, D. (2008). Critical Notice – Defending Life: A Moral and Legal Case against Abortion Choice by Francis J. Beckwith. *Journal of Medical Ethics, 34*(11), 793–797.

Susan R., Estrich, S. R., and Sullivan, K. M. (1989). Abortion Politics: Writing for an Audience of One. *University of Pennsylvania Law Review, 138,* 119–155

Swope, P. (1998). Abortion: A Failure to Communicate. *First Things* (82), 31–35.

Thomson, J. J. (1971). A Defense of Abortion. *Philosophy and Public Affairs, 1*(1), 47–66.

Tooley, M. (1972). Abortion and Infanticide. *Philosophy and Public Affairs, 2*(1), 37–65.

(1999). Abortion and Infanticide. In R. H. Kuhse and P. Singer (eds.), *Bioethics: An Anthology*. Oxford: Blackwell.

Tooley, M., Wolf-Devine, C., Devine, P. E., and Jaggar, A. M. (2009). *Abortion: Three Perspectives*. New York: Oxford University Press.

Tribe, L. H. (1997). Constitutional Analysis of "Partial Birth Abortion" Ban. Retrieved from www.now.org/issues/abortion/dxanalysis.html.

UK Department of Health. (2016). Abortion Statistics, England and Wales, 2015. Retrieved from www.gov.uk/government/uploads/system/uploads/attachment_data/file/570040/Updated_Abortion_Statistics_2015.pdf.

Velleman, J. D. (2005). Family History. *Philosophical Papers, 34*(3), 357–378.

Waldron, J. (1981). A Right to Do Wrong. *Ethics, 92*(1), 21–39.

(2002). *God, Locke and Equality: Christian Foundations of Locke's Political Thought*. Cambridge: Cambridge University Press.

Wallace, R. J. (2013). *The View from Here: On Affirmation, Attachment, and the Limits of Regret*. New York: Oxford University Press.

Warren, M. A. (1973). On the Moral and Legal Status of Abortion. *The Monist, 57*(1), 43–61.

(1989). The Moral Significance of Birth. *Hypatia, 4*(3), 46–65.

(1998). Abortion. In H. Kuhse and P. Singer (eds.), *A Companion to Bioethics*. Oxford: Blackwell.

Weaver, J. (2011). Social before Birth: Twins First Interact with Each Other as Fetuses: Twins Interact Purposefully in the Womb. *Scientific American Mind, 21*(6), 13.

Wolterstorff, N. (2007). *Justice: Rights and Wrongs*. Princeton: Princeton University Press.

Index